JAZZ MASTERS OF THE FORTIES

JAZZ
MASTERS
OF THE '40s

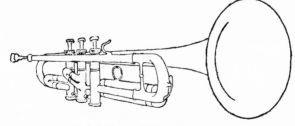

by Ira Gitler

New introduction and discography
by the author

A DA CAPO PAPERBACK

Library of Congress Cataloging in Publication Data

Gitler, Ira.
  Jazz masters of the '40s.

  (A Da Capo paperback)
  Reprint. Originally published: Jazz masters of the forties. New York:
Macmillan, 1966. (The Macmillan jazz masters series).
  Bibliography: p.
  Includes discographies and index.
  1. Jazz musicians — Biography. I. Title. II. Title: Jazz mastersof the forties.
[ML395.G58   1984]   785.42′092′2 [B]   84-11402
ISBN 0-306-80224-4 (pbk.)

*Acknowledgment is gratefully made to the following copyright holders for
permission to reprint from previously published materials:*
The Citadel Press, for permission to use excerpts from *The Legend of
Charlie Parker,* by Robert George Reisner, copyright © 1962 The Citadel
Press.
Consolidated Music Publishers, Inc., for permission to use excerpts from
Inside Jazz, by Leonard Feather, copyright 1949 Consolidated Music Publishers, Inc. Used by permission.
Down Beat magazine, for permission to use excerpts from the following
articles: "Pettiford Is Sent Home from Korea After Brawl on Plane," by
Ralph J. Gleason, February 22, 1952; "Pettiford at Fault in Brawl, Drank
too Much: McGhee," by Ralph J. Gleason, March 7, 1952; "Lennie Tristano: Multitaping Doesn't Make Me a Phony," by Nat Hentoff, May 16,
1956; "An Oscar," by Nat Hentoff, March 21, 1957; "Lennie Tristano: Return of the Native," October 30, 1958; "Dizzy Gillespie: Problems of Life on
a Pedestal," June 23, 1960; "The Years with Yard," by Dizzy Gillespie, with
Gene Lees, May 25, 1961; "In Walked Ray," by Gene Lees, August 31, 1961.

This Da Capo Press paperback edition of *Jazz Masters of the '40s* is an
unabridged republication of the edition published in New York in 1966, here
supplemented with a new introduction and discography by the author.
It is reprinted by arrangement with Macmillan Publishing Co., Inc.

Published by Da Capo Press, Inc.
A Subsidiary of Plenum Publishing Corporation
233 Spring Street, New York, N.Y. 10013

INTRODUCTION TO THE
DA CAPO EDITION

With the appearance of this Da Capo edition, I can now update my material to cover some of the changes and correct some errors in the book that have come to my attention. Production procedures will not allow me to alter the body of the text, but at the end of each chapter I include a new discography that takes into account the enormous number of reissues and bootlegs of rare "live" recordings, a phenomenon that has made the genius of Charlie Parker more firmly established than at any time since his death, twenty-six years ago.

What of the other jazz masters?

Dizzy Gillespie, still a potent force, has become an elder statesman; one who is highly visible at clubs, concerts, international festivals, and on television. Max Roach has continually grown both as an artist in public performances and a scholar in academia; and Kenny Clarke, still working mostly in Europe, finally returned on several occasions to visit and play in the United States. J. J. Johnson performed less and less during the Seventies, preferring to concentrate on writing for television. In 1979 he went into the studio with a small group for Milestone, his first record in many years, and in 1980 he followed with an LP for Pablo.

The story of bebop's resurgence is by now familiar and no one was more instrumental than Dexter Gordon. At the time of the book's first publication, he was living in Copenhagen and infrequently visiting the U.S. to no great acclaim beyond the inner circles of jazz. Rock was then at its zenith and jazz at its nadir: the vanguard of the music contained many noise-element players, which did not attract many new listeners. But with Dexter Gordon's trip to the U.S. in 1976 jazz made a comeback, and the young audience came with it, embracing the diverse styles under the music's wide umbrella. Many young musicians have made bebop part of the modern mainstream. In fact, short of the "freedom" players, most contemporary jazz players are using the contours and articulation of the language Parker and Gillespie invented in the Forties. Among the veterans, Lee Konitz, never a Parker imitator but certainly informed by him, continues to use essences of Bird as one of the resources for a rich individuality.

All has not been growth, however. The brilliant and much troubled Bud Powell died in August of 1966; Lennie Tristano, mentor to Konitz and many others, died in November of 1978 after a decade in which his main energies were devoted to teaching and performing for friends. Others who succumbed to illness or accident were Kenny Dorham, Don Byas, and Brew Moore.

One of the mistakes I would like to rectify is the credit-line to Freddie Webster on Earl Hines's recordings of *Yellow Fire* and *Windy City Jive*. Instead of trusting my usually reliable ears which found these solos atypical, I relied on research in the *Jazz Review*. The release of *The Father Jumps* (RCA AXM2-5508) proves that the trumpeter on *Yellow Fire* is Pee Wee Jackson; he and Tommy Enoch split the honors on *Windy City Jive*.

Record companies, particularly European and Japanese labels, have also fueled the bebop revival. The Jay McShann-Charlie Parker recordings at a Wichita radio station, mentioned in my chapter on Bird, are available with other rare material on *First Recordings* (Onyx). Other records mentioned as unavailable have since been issued: Fontana has re-released the Swingtime sides by Dexter Gordon and Wardell Gray as *The Master Swingers*. Many of the LPs listed at the end of each chapter in the original edition are only available as imports; others appear in altered form on their original or on new labels. Check the new listings in this edition and your local record store for the many anthologies such as *Bebop Revisited*, Volumes 1-3 (Xanadu) and *Black California*, Volumes 1 and 2 (Savoy).

The new musicians who have revitalized jazz have brought with them new listeners. At one end of the spectrum you have Dexter Gordon, a classic player with an audience that never heard him in the Forties; at the other end, country fiddlers are recording *Moose the Mooche;* and a Montana band, called the Big Sky Mud-flaps, includes in its repertoire *Groovin' High* and *Yardbird Suite*—with original lyrics!

May the music flourish and grow! As my friend David Himmel-stein says: "Bebop is the music of the future."

—IRA GITLER
around the corner from the Stanhope,
New York City, 1982

To the memory of my parents—
and to my brother, who introduced me to jazz

CONTENTS

ACKNOWLEDGMENTS

Jazz Masters of the Forties comes out of my own experience, the knowledge of my fellow writers, and interviews with musicians and other people closely connected with jazz. These interviews, given by the late Tadd Dameron, Dede Emerson, Dizzy Gillespie, Dexter Gordon, Roy Haynes, J.J. Johnson, Monte Kay, Dick Katz, Lee Konitz, Jackie McLean, Sal Mosca, Max Roach, Lennie Tristano, and Dave Usher, enriched my research as only personal revelation can.

Special thanks are due Mr. Katz. I don't agree with the point of view that says musicians necessarily make the best critics, but when it is applied to Dick, I endorse it wholeheartedly.

I should also like to mention, in appreciation, the girls of my informal typing pool: Eleanor Frischling, Marjorie Hopp, Mary Gay Heckman, Lucille Butterman, and Beverly DeLieto.

And to Martin Williams—thank you for asking me to write the book.

I. G.

INTRODUCTION

SINCE THE TIME that modern jazz, or bebop, emerged as the fully formed musical statement of an era, it has been referred to as a musical revolution. Revolution it was, to be sure, but, significantly, the music was the product of evolution. When Charlie Parker and Dizzy Gillespie recorded *Groovin' High* in 1945, a musical manifesto had been issued, but it hadn't just burst into being; several musicians—men like Lester Young and Charlie Christian—contributed to it directly, and they in turn had their forerunners. On the other hand, if the Parker-Gillespie quintet wasn't the first group to play bebop, it surely displayed the ideas and personality of the movement. And one of the great events of jazz history had occurred.

Benny Harris' comments in a 1961 interview reveal some of the thinking that went into the development of the new music. "We listened to Artie Shaw instead of Benny Goodman," said the trumpeter. "Goodman swung, but Shaw was more modern. We jumped on a record like Bobby Hackett's *Embraceable You* [the 1939 Vocalion version] because it was full of beautiful extended harmonies and unusual changes. Bobby was a guitarist and knew his chords, just as Dizzy and Kenny Clarke knew keyboard harmony. And I think one of the big early influences was Teddy Wilson. We admired very much the way he made the changes, always picking the best harmony and putting new chords in all the right places. Teddy would do all that while playing fast and clean. Art Tatum was another musician we liked very much. Benny Carter, like Teddy, played long lines, and that appealed to some of us."

One of the reasons people looked on the advent of bebop as a revolution was the lack of communication with the public at a crucial time in the development of the music. The American Federation of Musicians declared a ban on recordings on August 1, 1942. There were no instrumental records made again until the fall of 1943, when Decca signed with the union and many new, independent labels sprang into being on the same terms. It was more than a year later when Columbia and Victor stepped

11

into line. As a result of the ban, no mass audience heard Earl Hines's band, in which people like Gillespie, Parker, and Harris were playing the new music, encouraged by tenor saxophonist–arranger Budd Johnson and singer-trumpeter Billy Eckstine.

At the same time, a war was being fought—another "war to end all wars"—and while it affected the emotional climate and character of the entire period, it also kept a good portion of our young male population away from the United States. Those who returned were completely unaware of the transformation that jazz had gone through.

The early 1940's was a time of experimentation in jazz, not in the form of analytic laboratory study, but in the field—in the free musical exchanges of the jam session. The modernist pioneers were injecting their fresh ideas into the formal contexts of the big bands, but that was not enough. The need to escape the strictures of large ensembles led to a great deal of after-hours jamming. "Sitting in" was, of course, a common practice, but the real developments were made when a coterie of musicians who were thinking along similar lines came together in jam sessions in order to try out their new ideas. It was a musically rich period, and soon New York's jazz clubs could boast that the leaders of a previous generation, such as Coleman Hawkins, were working alongside the modernists, helping to advance the new musical expression.

By 1945, the new music—first known as bebop and rebop, then finally as bop—was firmly entrenched despite the protestations of some older musicians and numerous critics. Even *Metronome*, a magazine that supported the new music, gave poor ratings to some of Charlie Parker's most important records. But the proof of a new musical form's power is the degree to which musicians begin to use it. By 1946, the influence of bop could be heard in the most commercial dance bands. The music had reached a peak of creativity and popularity in 1947–1949. Most of the greats had by this time established themselves with their fellow musicians and the jazz public.

Of course, there was fine jazz of several styles being played in the forties, but most of these were established in earlier decades. The music and players that came to light in the forties, typifying the period, are the subject of this book. The discussion not only encompasses what the major figures accomplished in the forties, but follows their careers into the sixties—or, in some cases, to their premature ends.

Miles Davis, Thelonious Monk, Art Blakey, Milt Jackson, and John Lewis did not reach their greatest level of achievement and/or acclaim until the fifties, and they are treated in Joe Goldberg's *Jazz Masters of the Fifties*.

In writing a book of this kind, decisions must be made as to inclusions and omissions, decisions that do not always coincide with personal taste but revolve around historical perspective. For instance, Tony Scott and, certainly, Buddy De Franco deserve more attention than some of the secondary tenor saxophonists who are discussed in brief. But while these clarinetists contributed to the music of the forties, their instrument went into a general decline in this period. For all his brilliance, De Franco was never a great influence, one reason being that there were not many clarinetists to influence. Both men were shaped by Charlie Parker—Scott less so than is sometimes assumed, despite his great admiration for Bird. Perhaps the man who would have really brought the clarinet to the fore was Stan Hasselgard. This Swedish musician was the only clarinetist that Benny Goodman ever featured alongside himself. That was in the spring of 1948; in November of that year, Hasselgard was killed in an automobile accident at the age of 26.

The war and postwar period was a turbulent one. The jazz world, never the picture of calm, had a new intruder in the form of heroin. This narcotic had a direct influence on many of the musicians of this time. Because of its powerful grip, it could not help but affect, tangentially, even the players who did not use it. It ruined numerous careers, but in spite (or because?) of it a great music was made. What follows is a story of the masters of this music and, in less detail, of their disciples, some mavericks, and several transitional figures.

Although as a young jazz fan, I had been listening to records and seeing big bands in theater stage shows for some seven years, it was not until 1945 that I began to go to jam sessions on Sunday afternoons and to Fifty-second Street at night. In April, 1946, I wrote a review of Dizzy Gillespie's quintet at the Spotlite club for my high-school newspaper. Like many others, I had disliked Gillespie's music the first time I heard it—a 1944 "live" performance on disc jockey Alan Courtney's jazz record show. I don't remember the others in the group, but Dizzy's playing seemed to me to be laced with sour notes. In 1945 I heard him and Parker on their Guild recordings. This time I was ready for Gillespie and immediately taken with Parker. From that time on, I was totally immersed in their music.

I hope that in this book I have managed to convey to those of you who were not there the excitement inherent in the making of this music. For all of us, there are still the records with which we have been able to document jazz almost from its inception. Today, the attitude of the record companies is such that, while the course of the music can still be followed, too many dates will not be remembered in a week, much less twenty years from now. Of course, the LP, among its positive aspects, has been a valuable medium for reissuing older material in comprehensive collections.

I have not necessarily named all the recordings made by the performers who are discussed at length. However, in the LP listings at the end of each chapter, I have tried to include the particular musician's best and/or most important records.

1

CHARLIE PARKER AND THE ALTO
AND BARITONE SAXOPHONISTS

ALTHOUGH A MAN and his music are inseparable, often in writing about Charlie "Yardbird" Parker, more attention is given to the wild, lurid aspects of his life than to his music. The emphasis should be placed on his playing and composing, for he rose above the sordid to produce great and beautiful art. His friend and musical partner Dizzy Gillespie summed it up in an interview some six years after Parker's death. "You hear so much about him that I don't like to hear," Dizzy said, "about his addiction and all sorts of irrelevant nonsense. What kind of man was Beethoven? Perhaps he wasn't a very admirable individual, but what has that got to do with listening to his music?

"Not that I didn't think Bird was admirable. He was. But people talk too much about the man—people who don't know—when the important thing is his music.

"The Negro people should put up a statue to him, to remind their grandchildren. This man contributed joy to the world, and it will last a thousand years."

Others have expressed the feeling that there should be a statue of Parker. On his first visit here in the early fifties, French jazz pianist Henri Renaud was surprised when he found none standing on Fifth Avenue. But America's only native art form isn't taken seriously in its birthplace, and this was just one of the hardships Parker endured as a creative artist in a hostile environment.

Bird was a warm person, sensitive to public reaction. I remember talking to him one night at the Three Deuces in the summer of 1947, just after he returned from a seven-month confinement at Camarillo State Hospital in California, where he had recuperated from a nervous collapse. He stressed the fact that "the young people are getting with the music." It seemed very important to him to communicate the spirit of jazz to the next generation. For his music came from the very roots of jazz and always possessed its basic elements, no matter how oblique his flights may have seemed. His awareness of the entire jazz literature can be heard in his quote from Louis Armstrong's *West End Blues* in his own *Visa* solo from *Bird at St. Nick's.*

Parker was a giant figure who influenced countless lives, musically and otherwise. He affected jazz as totally as had Armstrong a generation before him, and he brought the alto saxophone to prominence the way Coleman Hawkins and Lester Young had with the tenor saxophone. Because of him, young musicians turned to the alto and tried to play like him. Later, many escaped to the tenor to avoid direct comparison.

His fans were legion; they would devour his every recording, and some were not content to stop there. One, Dean Benedetti, an alto player from California, followed Parker around the country, most often by Greyhound bus, just to capture his every note on a wire recorder. (Benedetti died of pneumonia several years ago, and the recordings were never brought to light.)

In the late forties I met a group of young Chicagoans who would listen to no other music but his. Some of the most extreme would rerecord his solos from the Dial and Savoy records on tape or wire and immerse themselves for hours in uninterrupted Parker. Among them were the hippies who would boast, through half-closed, watery eyes, "I got high with Bird."

Parker disapproved of both attitudes. He listened to all kinds of music and could find something of value in the worst surroundings. Saxophonist Gigi Gryce tells of a time when he and Bird were passing a rock 'n' roll joint. "He would stop to listen, and maybe it would be something the piano player was doing which he liked. He'd say, 'Man, do you hear that? It would be a gas to play with that guy.'"

That people emulated his narcotics addiction distressed him. During a 1947 interview with Leonard Feather, Parker said that a musician professing to play better when he was high on anything was a liar. It was true that many people copied everything he did, from his music to the drugs and kicks, but the entry of heroin into the jazz world had begun before Parker reached idolatry. There was an obscure sideman who, according to musicians, was active in "turning on" others, but I never heard of Charlie Parker recommending the drug to neophytes.

He started using heroin as a youngster, before he had a chance to know better. Parker was 34 when he died, but he looked a lot older. He had crammed at least twice that number of years of living into the thirty-four. He once was quoted as saying, "I began dissipating as early as 1932, when I was only twelve years old; three years later a *friend* of the family introduced me to heroin. I woke up one morning very soon after that, feeling terribly sick and not knowing why. The panic was on."

Before the panic, Parker had become interested in music. Born in Kansas City, Kansas, on August 29, 1920, he moved across the river to Kansas City, Missouri, when he was 7. His father, Charles Parker, Sr., was a vaudevillian who played piano and sang. He left home when Charlie was 9, and was fatally stabbed by a woman in a quarrel eight years later. Charlie's mother, Addie Parker, a nurse, raised him and encouraged him to play. Although Bird is reported to have played baritone horn in the Lincoln High band, according to his mother it was the larger tuba. "I didn't go for that," she said, "—was so funny coiled around him with just his head sticking out, so I got him another instrument."

That was an alto saxophone, the instrument through which Parker was to tell his story to the world. No doubt he had more than average talent for music, but it was not evident at first. After a year of study he began to play with the band of Lawrence Keyes, who because he played piano was saddled with the nickname 88. The band was made up of other high-school kids and was called the Deans of Swing. (Some of the members, like tenor saxophonist Freddie Culliver and singer Walter Brown, later graduated to Jay McShann's band along with Parker.) Bird was really a fledgling in 1934. Bassist Gene Ramey, who also worked with him in the McShann band, first heard him then and describes him as "the saddest thing in the [Keyes] band."

Since Parker himself told Leonard Feather that he "spent three years in high school and wound up a freshman" and since Keyes has said of him, "If he had been as conscientious about his school work as he was about his music, he would have become a professor, but he was a terrible truant," we are led to wonder why he didn't develop at a faster pace on his saxophone. Ramey, however, remembers him as seeming to be "just like a happy-go-lucky kid."

Humiliation at the jam sessions so prevalent in the Kansas City of the thirties soon made him serious about his music. Parker told of the first time he ventured into a jamming situation. "I knew a little of *Lazy River* and *Honeysuckle Rose* and played what I could," he said. "I was doing all right until I tried doing double tempo on *Body and Soul.* Everybody fell out laughing. I went home and cried and didn't play again for three months."

This was the reaction of a youth whom Ramey describes as "an only child, sheltered and coddled, and . . . not used to getting along with people."

Another time, Parker was jamming with members of Count Basie's band. Drummer Jo Jones waited until Bird started to play and then rendered his opinion of Parker's blowing by sailing his cymbal all the way across the dance floor. Jones's self-styled Major Bowes gesture caused Bird to pack up his horn and leave, his spirit dragging. This time, however, he didn't stop playing. In the summer of 1937, he joined the band of George E. Lee, the brother of singer Julia Lee, and went off to nearby Ozark Mountain resorts. With him Parker took all Count Basie's records, from which he learned Lester Young's solos inside out. (Years later, in the fifties, Lee Konitz walked into Bird's dressing room during the course of a tour and heard him play Young's solo from *Shoe Shine Boy* at twice the tempo of the original.)

When Parker returned to Kansas City a few months later, he was a changed musician. The band's guitarist, Efferge Ware, had taught him about chord progressions, and he had begun to practice assiduously. Soon he was commanding attention and respect from his cohorts. In those days, musicians used to go out into the middle of the city's Paseo Park and play all night without police interference. Some say Bird instituted this practice. Whether or not he did, he was a regular member of the fresh-air jamming group. Kansas City musicians were still doing it in the late forties, with the aid of a portable organ.

In 1937, Parker was in the band of Buster Smith, the alto saxophonist who was an early influence on his playing. Smith had known him for about five years before he joined the band. "Charlie would come in where we were playing," Smith has said, "and hang around the stand, with his alto under his arm. He had his horn in a paper sack—always carried it in that paper sack. He used to carry his horn home and put it under his pillow and sleep on it."

Professor, as Buster is called, was Bird's mentor during the latter's stay with the band. They divided the amount of solos equally. "He always wanted me to take the first solo," said Buster. "I guess he thought he'd learn something that way. He did play like me quite a bit, I guess. But after awhile, anything I could make on my horn, he could make too—and make something better out of it."

Smith, who still leads a blues band in Dallas, Texas, has told how he left for New York to find work, intending to send for the rest of the band when he had. Meanwhile, Parker started to play with McShann. This was 1938. After three months, Bird hit the rails and hoboed his way to Chicago. He showed up, right off a freight train, at the Club 65's breakfast dance. Both Budd Johnson and Billy Eckstine were present, and they have both related the story of how this raggedy man asked King Kolax's alto man, Goon Gardner, whether he could blow Goon's horn and then proceeded to "upset everybody in the joint." Gardner then got Bird some clothes, a few gigs, and a clarinet with which to play them. Soon thereafter, Gardner looked for Parker, but he had left town, clarinet and all.

Parker's next step is somewhat in doubt. Buster Smith remembers Bird showing up at his New York apartment in a bedraggled state. His legs were swollen because he had been wearing his shoes for so long. According to Smith and McShann, this was still 1938. Jay's recollection is that Parker "washed dishes in Jimmy's Chicken Shack in Harlem for a few months, while out front, Art Tatum was gassing everybody. Several months later he got a job with a group at Monroe's Uptown House [Clark Monroe's club on 138th Street]."

In Leonard Feather's *New Encyclopedia of Jazz* (1960), Parker is said to have first come to New York in 1939 and "for almost a year worked intermittently" at Monroe's.

Smith says that Bird went to Baltimore for three weeks, and then McShann sent for him. McShann states that Parker came back to Kansas City to play with Harlan Leonard's Rockets in the latter part of 1938 and that Tadd Dameron was writing for Leonard at the time.

Which is the accurate account is not clear, but before he died, Dameron said that he did not join Leonard until 1940. Considering that Parker rejoined McShann in late 1939 or early 1940 and

stayed until 1942, Dameron's version of his first meeting with
Bird raises some questions. "Bird was cleaning up the club," said
Tadd. "I never knew he played horn until one jam session he
pulls out this raggedy alto with this pipe tone he had then. I
couldn't hear anyone but him because I could hear his message.
So we got together and we were playing *Lady Be Good* and
there's some changes I played in the middle where he just
stopped playing and ran over and kissed me on the cheek. He
said, 'That's what I've been hearing all my life, but nobody plays
those changes.' So we got to be very good friends—he used to
come over to my house every day and blow. This was in 1941.
This was when war was declared—I remember it definitely. And
my wife would cook. And the people used to knock on the door,
and I'd say, 'Oh, I'm sorry we're making so much noise.' 'No,'
they'd say, 'we want you to leave the door open,' because he was
playing *so* pretty."

Dameron's reference to Bird's appreciation of the way he
played those particular chord changes has a parallel story. In
New York, Parker had jammed with a guitarist named Biddy
Fleet in a variety of places, including the back of a chili house in
Harlem. "Biddy would run new chords," said Parker. "For instance, we'd find you could play a relative major, using the right
inversions, against a seventh chord, and we played around with
flatted fifths."

In a 1949 *Down Beat* interview, Parker spoke of a particularly
stimulating session with Fleet. Bird had been getting tired of the
stereotyped changes in general use. "I kept thinking there's
bound to be something else," he said. "I could hear it sometimes,
but I couldn't play it." While playing *Cherokee* with Fleet, he
found that by utilizing the higher intervals of a chord as a melody
line and using suitably connected changes with it, he could make
the thing he had been hearing an actuality. As Bird put it, "I
came alive."

Whenever the exact moment was that Parker "came alive," the
period of wandering just prior to 1940 and the time he spent with
McShann gave his talent the nourishment necessary for him to
develop as a fully mature artist in the mid-forties.

There were other McShann men who were also working with
new ideas, like trumpeter Buddy Anderson, alto saxophonist John
Jackson, and tenor saxophonist Jimmy Forrest. Dizzy Gillespie, in

talking about his first meeting with Parker in a Kansas City hotel room—an occasion on which they spent the whole day playing the piano and discussing their ideas—also mentions Anderson. "Good trumpet player," he says. "Got tuberculosis—had to stop playing. Started playing bass—haven't seen him in years."

McShann has talked of Anderson and claims that he had an influence on Gillespie. "He played in the same style as Bird—only, on the trumpet," said Jay, who reported that Anderson was playing piano in Oklahoma City in the early sixties.

In 1941, McShann's Decca record of *Confessin' the Blues* sold eighty-one thousand copies. Mike Morales (calling himself the Vine Street Vulture) wrote in *Down Beat:* ". . . some of Jay's boys, Walt Brown, Gene Ramey, Gussie Johnson, Charles Parker and others, deserve a mention. They've helped Jay in his climb."

Parker's allegiance to the blues tradition, in evidence throughout his career, was no doubt strongly influenced by his experience with this band, although the blues had become part of his musical makeup long before. But the band's basically blues-oriented framework was obviously conducive to the early experiments of certain members.

Parker was in charge of the reeds, under McShann's system of separate rehearsal leaders for each section. Bird had "straightened up" in McShann's words. He had begun writing by this time, and *Yardbird Suite* was in the book, although it had another title and was never recorded by McShann. But later Bird showed the members of the band how to get high on nutmeg by taking great quantities of it in milk or Coke.

The earliest recorded documents of Parker are not available to the public, although record producer–writer Frank Driggs hopes to make them so someday. There are six titles, recorded at a Wichita radio station in 1940. Parker solos on five. They are not lengthy, and far from his fully formed style, but the seeds of the past (the Lester Young influence) and the ready-to-ripen fruit are there to hear. His *Moten Swing* solo is part Pres, part Bird, with a sound that is not yet solidified; his entrance on *Honeysuckle Rose* is very Youngish, but the solo contains occasional significant departures; on *I Found a New Baby,* he exhibits his quickness—the pickups he employs at the beginning of phrases are a device he made extensive use of later; *Body and Soul* contains some typical runs—and a phrase he played ten years later on the same song at a restaurant in Sweden (issued on a Swedish label, Sonet); *Lady Be Good*, his longest solo—a complete chorus—is notable for its flowing lines.

When McShann did his first recording for Decca in 1941, Parker was featured on *Swingmatism* and *Hootie Blues*. The sides cut by the band a year later (July, 1942) in New York included *Sepian Bounce* and *The Jumpin' Blues*, both of which contain solos by Parker. The first four bars of his *Jumpin' Blues* solo emerged as part of Benny Harris' *Ornithology* a few years later.

In 1942, Bob Locke, reviewing the McShann band in *Down Beat*, wrote: "Charlie Parker offers inspired alto solos, using a minimum of notes in a fluid style with a somewhat thin tone but a wealth of pleasing ideas."

During the McShann years, Parker is supposed to have acquired his nickname of Yardbird because of his fondness for chicken. Parker himself was said to have traced it back to his school days and a series of transformations from Charlie to Yarlie to Yarl to Yard to Yardbird to Bird. Another story has Parker, underage, avidly keeping up with the music in the Kansas City clubs by sneaking into the backyards behind the buildings and listening—sometimes even playing along. However he got his nickname, it stuck. Some called him Yard; most called him Bird. Those who were aware knew that he had brought a new language to jazz.

While McShann was playing at the Savoy Ballroom in New York in 1941, Gene Ramey relates, people like Gillespie, Chubby Jackson, and Big Sid Catlett would come to sit in. At the same time, Parker was doubling at Monroe's, playing after-hours sessions. He spoke to Leonard Feather of these years later. "At Monroe's I heard sessions with a pianist named Allen Tinney; I'd listen to trumpet men like Lips Page, Roy, Dizzy and Charlie Shavers outblowing each other all night long. And Don Byas was there, playing everything there was to be played. I heard a trumpet man named Vic Coulsen playing things I'd never heard. Vic had the regular band at Monroe's, with George Treadwell also on trumpet, and a tenor man named Prichett. That was the kind of music that caused me to quit McShann and stay in New York."

Monroe's became Parker's main base of operations. In this period he also worked with Noble Sissle's band, doubling on clarinet. Some have reported that he was with Sissle for nine months, but the leader has placed the time as "maybe three or four weeks." Bird had but one solo in the book, and the relationship was not the most pleasant.

His next affiliation was much happier. At the urging of Billy Eckstine, Benny Harris, and lead altoist Scoops Carry, Earl Hines hired Parker for his band. (If you are familiar with Carry's solo on Hines's *Jelly Jelly*, you can hear that Bird listened to him with more than half an ear.) Since both alto chairs were filled, Hines bought him a tenor. For ten months in 1943, Parker played with the band; but due to the ban set by the musicians' union, no recorded evidence exists.

While Hines was rehearsing at Nola Studios in New York, the modern clique continued to jam at the uptown clubs. One night tenor great Ben Webster heard Parker at Minton's and took the instrument from his hands. "That horn," he said, "ain't supposed to sound that fast." But that night, Webster walked all over town telling everyone, "Man, I heard a guy—I swear he's gonna make everybody crazy on tenor."

Bird is reputed to have said of the tenor, "Man, this thing is too big." After the Hines days he returned to it for only two record dates, both with Miles Davis, in August, 1947, and in January, 1953. Perhaps he did not feel comfortable on tenor, but he played it convincingly, especially on the earlier Davis session, which produced *Sippin' at Bell's, Little Willie Leaps, Milestones,* and *Half Nelson,* and part of Bird's influence on Sonny Rollins can be ascribed to these sides.

Parker was brilliant on all the reeds. Anyone who had heard him play Charlie Ventura's baritone saxophone one night at the Royal Roost in December of 1948 would have to agree that he handled the large horn with the same ease as he did the alto, without sacrificing any tonal character.

Dizzy Gillespie tells of Parker on tenor with Hines. "He played superbly with that band," Diz is quoted as saying. "I remember Sarah Vaughan would sing *This Is My First Love* [probably *You Are My First Love*], and Bird would play 16 bars on it. The whole band would be turned to look at him. Nobody was playing like that."

Parker was not neglecting his alto either. He would bring it to theater engagements and practice between shows. This diligent attitude was not standard procedure, however. Often he would miss shows completely or fall asleep onstage. He wore dark glasses, and as Billy Eckstine has recounted, "Earl used to swear he was awake. He was the only man I knew who could sleep with his jaws poked out to look like he was playing."

Because of his bad feet, he often would take his shoes off during a performance. Once when Scoops Carry awakened him to take his solo, Bird ran out to the microphone in his stocking feet.

Many times the men in the band would gang up on him for a mass "lecture" regarding his dilatory actions, but heroin had a good hold on Bird by then and presented them too formidable a foe.

When Eckstine left Hines in 1943 he tried to make it as a single, but by 1944 he decided that he wanted a big-band setting again. He understood and supported the new jazz movement because he had been so involved with it in Hines's band. He also felt that the time was right for the public to receive the full impact of the innovations. He had picked up trumpet with Hines, but now he was playing valve trombone in an exuberant, if not particularly inventive, manner. In June of 1944 he formed his own band with the help of Budd Johnson, the man Parker had replaced in the Hines band. An effort was made to get as many of the Hines alumni as possible. Gillespie was one. Parker, who had played with Cootie Williams and Andy Kirk in the interim and was now working with Carroll Dickerson at the Rhumboogie in Chicago, was another. Both joined as the nucleus of a band that was to feature some of the best of the up-and-coming youngsters during the three years of its existence. Sarah Vaughan was one of them, and as with Hines, she sang *You Are My First Love*. Parker again played his solo, this time on alto. Art Blakey, Eckstine's drummer, referring to a Saturday night in Chicago, has said, "That man came out and took sixteen bars and stopped the show. The house was packed. People applauded so loud we couldn't go on. We had to do it all over again."

An October 1, 1944, review by Johnny Sippel in *Down Beat*, written while the band was at the Regal Theatre in Chicago, notes: "Driving force behind the reeds is Charlie Parker, destined to take his place behind Hodges as a stylist on alto sax. After hearing this band doing six shows during the week at the Regal, your reviewer didn't hear repeats on many of the choruses which

Parker did. His tone is adequate, but the individualizing factor is his tremendous store of new ideas."

Parker never recorded with Eckstine, for he did not stay with the band very long. His roots were in Fifty-second Street, where the new music now had its unofficial headquarters. Parker soon was leading his own trio, with Joe Albany on piano and Stan Levey on drums. Albany says that they played Monday nights at the Famous Door and that Baby Lawrence used to come in and dance with them. Levey places the club as the Spotlite and says, "This was Bird's first gig as leader, and it was also the first chance I really had a chance to hear him play. Oh, I'd heard his record of *Swingmatism* with Jay McShann, but that was all. My first impression of Charlie's playing was that he was a sort of Pied Piper. I'd never heard anything like it. I didn't really know what he was doing, but it made me feel good to listen to him."

On September 15, 1944, Parker recorded with guitarist Tiny Grimes for Savoy. "Bird used to come in and jam with me all the time," said Grimes, who worked extensively on Fifty-second Street between 1944 and 1947. "When I got this date, I called him to make it." With Parker and Grimes were Clyde Hart, an important transitional pianist in the early forties; Harold "Doc" West, a drummer who had been with Bird in the McShann band; and bassist Jimmy Butts. Grimes sings on two numbers, *Romance Without Finance* and *I'll Always Love You Just the Same*, and Parker solos convincingly on all four sides. These titles are far from the kind of original material that he was to record with Gillespie five months later. *Tiny's Tempo*, by Hart, is a riff blues, typical of the previous era, and Parker's *Red Cross*, based on *I Got Rhythm*, combines a *Mop Mop* figure (Leonard Feather has attributed the piece *Mop Mop*, copyrighted by Coleman Hawkins, to Parker) with a tricky run. Although his tone is not fully developed—it has not yet lost all its baby fat, so to speak—Bird's ideas suggest what he was going to do in the very near future. Undoubtedly, some of the freedom of his rhythmic phrasing is hampered by the more conservative time feeling of his mates.

In the company of Gillespie, Hart, guitarist Remo Palmieri, bassist Slam Stewart, and drummer Cozy Cole, some five months later, Parker played in the manner to which he later made us accustomed. The material recorded is more in keeping with the improvisatory inclinations of Parker and Gillespie, and naturally the playing that springs from songs like *Groovin' High* (based on the chords of *Whispering*) and *Dizzy Atmosphere* is more consistently representative. Even the standard ballad *All the Things You Are* is fitted out with a new introduction and coda. An insight into how the two sessions differ can be found by comparing the approaches of Grimes and Palmieri.

In May, 1945, a significant event took place. Parker and Gillespie appeared with their own quintet on Fifty-second Street at the Three Deuces. With them were Al Haig, piano; Curly Russell, bass; and Stan Levey, drums. When the group recorded for Guild Records, the versatile veteran Sid Catlett replaced Levey on the session that produced the swift, intricate *Shaw 'Nuff, Salt Peanuts*, and Tadd Dameron's beautifully integrated composition called *Hot House*. In addition, Sarah Vaughan sang a *Lover Man* that perhaps did not have the polish of her later singing but did have a pure beauty that her work has not always shown since.

Shaw 'Nuff and *Hot House* were definitive statements of the new music, recorded documents of the quintet's stay at the Deuces, and a culmination of the ideas that had been developing in the first half of the decade. Parker and Gillespie execute the unison work with fiery perfection and complement each other's solos marvelously. In an interview with Maitland Edey, Jr., Gillespie said, "I guess I probably played my best with Charlie Parker. He would inspire you; he'd *make* you play. And he always used to play before I did, so I had to follow him." Gillespie also traced his and Bird's ideas, and related how they became interdependent, from their first meeting in Kansas City. "At first we stressed different things," he said. "I was more for chord variations and he was more for melody, I think. But when we got together each influenced the other."

When he was asked the important differences between bebop and the jazz that preceded it, Gillespie put everything into perspective. "Well, chords," he stated. "And we stressed different accents in the rhythms. But I'm reluctant to say that anything is *the* difference between our music of the early forties and the music before that, of the thirties. You can get records from the early days and hear guys doing the same things. It just kept changing a little bit more; one guy would play a phrase one way, and another guy would come along and do something else with it. . . . Charlie Parker was very, very melodic; guys could copy his things quite a bit. Monk was one of the founders of the movement too, but his playing, my playing, and Charlie Parker's playing were altogether different."

Two other significant recording sessions took place in 1945. In June, an all-star date, combining older-style players like Teddy Wilson, Red Norvo, Slam Stewart, and Flip Phillips with Parker and Gillespie, was done for Comet and issued on two 12-inch 78-rpm records under Norvo's name. The titles are *Congo Blues, Hallelujah, Get Happy,* and *Slam Slam Blues* (other "takes" of both *Congo* and *Slam Slam* were later issued as *Bird's Blues*). The contrast in the styles of the players is marked, and Bird and Diz stand out in bold relief. At the same time, the group is homogenous, illustrating Gillespie's point about the similarity of the styles of the thirties and forties.

On *Slam Slam,* a slow, "down home" blues, Parker shows his blues roots quite directly and foreshadows his famous *Parker's Mood.* The faster *Congo* has no written opening line; the solos by Gillespie and Parker spring from interludes of Afro-Cuban rhythm into straight 4/4. (Incidentally, there has always been confusion over who the drummer is on the various tracks, Specs Powell or J. C. Heard. Heard told me, "I was doing a session in another studio in the same building. When I finished, I went to their studio to visit, and Dizzy asked me to sit in on *Congo Blues* and *Slam Slam Blues.*" Therefore, we can assume that Powell is on the other two.)

The other session took place on November 26 and still stands as a milestone in jazz history. It was the date for Savoy that included *Now's the Time, Billie's Bounce, Ko Ko,* and *Thriving From a Riff.* It was the first time that Parker was actually the leader on a record date, and on it he made two of his most durable masterpieces.

The simple blues riff *Now's the Time* later became a rhythm-and-blues hit under the title of *The Hucklebuck* (Parker did not get credit on the r&b version). Parker's solo combines the heritage of his Kansas City background with his longer-lined, more rhythmically complex flights. The naked beauty of this solo has stood up for twenty years without losing any of its impact as a piece of art.

The other blues line, *Billie's Bounce* (it should have read *Billy's Bounce,* as it was named for booking agent Billy Shaw), is a more intricate theme; its rhythmic contours are as representative of the new music as *Now's the Time* is of the old.

The second masterpiece is the virtuoso performance by Parker on *Ko Ko,* a whirlwind workout on the chords of *Cherokee.* Parker had been featured on *Cherokee* with McShann and had made extensive use of it in jam sessions from that time on. Its difficult progressions in the middle section were a stumbling block for a great many musicians. Bird not only negotiated them but played inventively as he whipped along. Martin Williams wrote of this recording: "*Ko Ko* may seem only a fast-tempo showpiece at first, but it is not. It is a precise, linear improvisation, for one thing, which has exceptional melodic content, and, incidentally, at times almost an atonality in its handling of the chord changes from *Cherokee.* It is an almost perfect example of virtuosity *and* economy: following a pause, notes fall over and between this beat and that beat—breaking them asunder, robbing them of any vestige of monotony—rests fall where heavy beats once came, now heavy beats come between beats and on weak beats. It has been a source book of ideas for fifteen years and no wonder; now that its basic innovations are more familiar, it seems even more a great performance in itself."

Musicians have called the last break that Parker takes at the close of the piece a condensed history of bop. "He says it *all* in there," has been a typical comment.

Warming Up a Riff, an incomplete, slower version of *Cherokee,* recorded while the musicians were running through the number, does not match the brilliance of *Ko Ko,* but it too is great and demonstrates the way Parker developed a solo—retaining, discarding, shaping with a spontaneity found only in the master players. *Meandering,* a ballad improvisation on *Embraceable You,* also cut with the musicians unaware, was not released until Savoy compiled an anthology of the entire date on an LP entitled *The Charlie Parker Story.* (This album is one of a series, issued after Parker's death, in which his entire output for the label, including incomplete takes, was issued.) Parker's ballad style, at least as of *Meandering,* had not developed to the full extent of breaking up a melody line as he was to do later on his Dial recordings. *Thriving From a Riff* (originally issued as *Thriving On a Riff*) is based on *I Got Rhythm.* Its theme later became known as *Anthropology.*

As a result of some liner notes by pianist John Mehegan on the back of the LP, confusion resulted concerning the correct personnel. Mehegan called the pianist Bud Powell and kept citing his introductions as "typical Bud intros," which they would not have been even if it had been Powell playing them. On the original 78-rpm issues, the label lists one Hen Gates as the pianist. It was assumed at the time that this was Dizzy Gillespie, and this is correct. (Later, a pianist from Philadelphia, Jimmy Foreman, used the same pseudonym in Gillespie's big band.) The evidence was corroborated in *The Jazz Review* by Sadik Hakim (known in the forties by his birth name, Argonne Thornton), who also revealed that he played on *Thriving* but that Gillespie was on piano for all other selections. A comparison of the piano solo on *Thriving* with Thornton's work on recordings with Eddie "Lockjaw" Davis, Dexter Gordon, and Lester Young substantiates his claim. His unique, dissonant, arpeggiated style is very recognizable.

Gillespie also plays the short trumpet passages on *Ko Ko*. It is not he on *Thriving* as the notes suggest. Miles Davis just played a more organized solo than the ones he took on *Billie's Bounce* and *Now's the Time*, but Davis' solos on these two numbers are not as "lugubrious and unswinging" as Mehegan says; they represent a young, nervous Miles, but nevertheless they have beauty. At that time, incidentally, Miles was heavily indebted to Freddie Webster.

In 1945, Parker also appeared on some recording dates as a sideman for the Continental label. Among his short solos and background comments are some unforgettable gems: the introduction and solo on *Mean to Me* with Sarah Vaughan; an obbligato to blues shouter Rubberlegs Williams' *4-F Blues;* a gorgeous melody statement and interpretation on *Dream of You* with trombonist Trummy Young; and a brilliant set of exchanges with Gillespie on Trummy's *Sorta Kinda.*

Besides working with Gillespie on Fifty-second Street in 1945, Parker later led a group of his own in the fall of the year at the Spotlite, a club hosted by Clark Monroe of Uptown House fame. Sir Charles Thompson was a member of the group, and in September the pianist used Bird and a third man from the combo, Dexter Gordon, together with trumpeter Buck Clayton, on a date for Apollo that produced *Takin' Off, If I Had You, 20th Century*

Blues, and *The Street Beat.* Parker is in typically swift form on *The Street Beat,* and *20th Century Blues* is a lovely vehicle for Bird's earthy expression.

At the very end of the year, Bird rejoined Dizzy, who had returned to a small group after an unsuccessful try at forming a big band. Together, they went to the West Coast for an engagement at Billy Berg's in Hollywood. California was not ready for them. Outside of a small circle of musicians and hip listeners, the reaction they received was hostile. Then, too, the price of heroin, according to Howard McGhee, was much higher than in New York. Parker did not always show up, and Gillespie had to hire tenor man Lucky Thompson to augment the band, which included Al Haig, Stan Levey, vibraphonist Milt Jackson, and bassist Ray Brown.

Ross Russell, who ran the Tempo Music Shop, a store that specialized in jazz, decided to form a record company and picked this group to do the first date. A rehearsal was scheduled, but the studio was overrun with visiting hipsters to the point of chaos. *Diggin' for Diz,* an original (based on the chords of *Lover*) by arranger-pianist George Handy, was committed to disc, however. According to Russell, Handy played piano on the date. Previously, Dodo Marmarosa was thought to be the pianist.

The actual session never came off as scheduled. When it came time to do the date, on February 7, neither Parker nor Handy was there. Gillespie and the rest of his group recorded five tunes, one of which was *Diggin' for Diz.* Thus Russell's Dial label was born. The version with Parker and Handy was released many years later and is a rare item.

I remember hearing Bird, Dizzy, and their band on Rudy Vallee's weekly network radio program during this time. (Crooner Vallee, who also plays alto sax, was Parker's boyhood idol, the man who supposedly inspired him to take up the alto.) Singer-pianist Harry "The Hipster" Gibson was appearing with Vallee on a fairly regular basis, and he was instrumental in placing Bird and Diz on the show. The reaction at Berg's got no better, however, and Gillespie decided to return to New York in February. Parker remained. Gillespie has explained this with, "They wanted to know why I left him in California. I didn't. I gave him his fare and he spent it and stayed on."

Drummer Levey has told it more explicitly. "When the time

came for the band to leave, I had all the plane tickets for the guys. But Charlie couldn't be found. He'd disappeared. For two hour that night, I took cabs all over town looking for him. Not a trace. I guess I must have spent $20 on cabfare. Finally, I gave up, rode out to Burbank airport, and took off for New York. Bird never made that plane."

This was the beginning of a slide that eventually put Parker in Camarillo. Bird was really scuffling. Howard McGhee tells of him coming to the club where McGhee was working in order to borrow money. Stories have it that he was living in a reconverted garage.

On March 28, close to two months after Gillespie's Dial date, Parker finally recorded for Russell. This was the session that included Gillespie's *A Night in Tunisia*, with Parker's famous four-bar break, into which he poured another miniature history of modern jazz; *Ornithology;* and two Parker compositions—the rhythmic *Moose the Mooche* and the melodic *Yardbird Suite*. Miles Davis had come out to the Coast with Billy Eckstine and was on the date, along with Lucky Thompson, Dodo Marmarosa, and guitarist Arv Garrison, among others. Parker is mellower here than he was later on in his quintet days, except for the fantastic break and driving solo on *Tunisia*. The relaxed delivery on *Yardbird Suite* and *Ornithology* (another master of this was released as *Bird Lore*) shows his link to Lester Young in spirit if not in exact style.

From January to April, Bird also appeared at several of Norman Granz's Jazz at the Philharmonic bashes, some of which have been preserved on record. JATP, as the series came to be known, was started by Granz, then a film editor at MGM studios, in July of 1944 at Los Angeles' Philharmonic Auditorium. His first tour with a JATP unit (through the Western states and Canada) was not too successful, but when albums recorded onstage at the Los Angeles concerts enjoyed wide sales, Granz was able to travel with a troupe all over the United States.

The basic unit usually consisted of a couple of trumpets, at least two tenor saxophones, a couple of altos, a trombone, and a rhythm section. Excitement, engendered by feverish solos backed by riffs from the other horns, was the main ingredient. In effect, JATP was a jam session moved from a smoky club to the concert stage. However, with the loss of the informality of jamming, there

was an air of hokey emotionalism, although this was not so prevalent in the early years as later. Whatever shortcomings JATP had,
there was always something of musical merit to hear, and often
the excitement was genuine.

Parker's work in the 1946 concerts contains some raggedy passages and a number of reed squeaks, and the background riffs are
sometimes as much against as with him, but nevertheless he manages to spin a few classics. His solo on *Lady Be Good* is one of
his grand statements; *After You've Gone* becomes a cyclonic wind
in his swinging holler; and the twists and turns with which he
negotiates *I Can't Get Started* contain a rare kind of acrid
beauty.

One West Coast altoist, Sonny Criss, was strongly moved during the short time Bird spent playing in California. His sound and
style were extremely reminiscent of the way Bird sounded in the
JATP recordings.

The strained edge in Bird's playing was reflective of what he
was feeling in California. Economically and mentally, things became worse for him. For a while he had a group with Miles
Davis, Joe Albany, bassist Addison Farmer, and drummer Chuck
Thompson at the Club Finale. He also sat in at an after-hours
place called Lovejoy's. After receiving a bad write-up in a local
paper, he told trumpeter Art Farmer, "Diz got away while the
getting was good, and I'm catching everything."

Things came to a head on July 29, during a recording date for
Dial with Howard McGhee, pianist Jimmy Bunn, bassist Bob
"Dingbod" Kesterson, and drummer Roy Porter. Bird was in a
state of anxiety that even a great quantity of straight whiskey
could not alleviate. He never forgave Russell for later releasing
the sides, but actually, although below his best, they are not quite
so bad as they seemed to many listeners when first issued.
McGhee recounts that "Bird was really disturbed. He was turning
around and around, and his horn was shooting up in the air, but
the sound came out fine. There were no wrong notes, and I feel
that the records are beautiful."

Perhaps McGhee is a bit overzealous in his praise, for *Max Is
Making Wax* is extremely chaotic, and Parker's short solo on
Bebop clearly shows the tension he was under—he is in and out
of the ensemble in an obviously unrehearsed manner. *The Gypsy*
is played almost straight, but it is not incompetent; rather, it is

more like a beginner who is content to just play his piece and risk no mistakes by being venturesome. The most famous of the four sides is *Lover Man*. What seems to be halting playing here was just Bird's way of breaking up a melody line, as he later showed with *Don't Blame Me* and *Embraceable You*. It is a performance of rare beauty. Charlie Mingus once chose it when asked to name his favorite Parker recordings. "I like all," he said, "none more than the other, but I'd have to pick *Lover Man* for the feeling he had then and his ability to express that feeling."

In all the numbers, you can hear tension and anguish in Parker's sound, for this is where a man's state of being is really bared. There is a pathetic air about *The Gypsy*, and the little whimper at the end of *Bebop* is unnerving.

There have been many reports and many interpretations of what happened to Charlie Parker at the *Lover Man* session, but the most plausible comes from an eyewitness who says that Parker had been taking the stimulant Benzedrine for several days and was in shaky condition as the effects of its prolonged use began to tell. A young physician present at the date observed Parker's condition and, knowing of his heroin addiction, mistook his symptoms for heroin withdrawal. Accordingly, he gave Parker a stimulant, assuring him it would help. It was the last thing that the altoist's physical and mental condition could stand, and it pushed him over the brink he had been skirting for months.

After the date, back in his hotel, Parker set fire to his room, presumably by falling asleep with a cigarette in his hand, and then ran down to the lobby without his pants. The police were called, and eventually he was committed to Camarillo State Hospital. Elliot Grennard, who wrote the short story "Sparrow's Last Jump," based on the recording session and its attendant incidents, felt that Bird's breakdown was due to lack of drugs, because as soon as the doctor gave him a shot of morphine, he became rational again.

Parker spent six months at Camarillo, where he was given psychiatric treatment. Bird was released in Russell's custody after much effort, many visits, and the employment of a private psychiatrist. Some of the people active in West Coast jazz circles helped stage a benefit for Bird and raised between $600 and $900. With the money, he purchased some clothes and two plane tickets back to New York. The other ticket was for Doris Sydnor, a girl he had known since 1944, who was to become his third wife in 1948. She had traveled to California to visit him in the hospital.

Before leaving for New York, Parker did two dates for Dial. The first was for the purpose of recording singer Earl Coleman, at Bird's insistence. Russell figured that if he did this, he wouldn't have to use Coleman on a farewell date he had planned, one that would include McGhee and tenor saxophonist Wardell Gray.

Erroll Garner was in Los Angeles working as a single. He had headed a trio including bassist Red Callender and Drummer Doc West, but none of the clubs would pay him enough to maintain it. As Callender and West were still around, the trio was engaged to accompany Parker and Coleman. It was agreed that the trio would do two sides, and *Trio* and *Pastel* were recorded.

Coleman, a disciple of Billy Eckstine, took two hours and twenty minutes of the three-hour session to finish his numbers, but he was better than Russell had given him credit for. In fact, *This Is Always* sold extremely well as a single, and *Dark Shadows* is a moving blues. Parker blows concisely and beautifully in his solo space. Part of his solo from the original issue of *Dark Shadows* was transcribed for Woody Herman's saxophone section in the band's arrangement of *I've Got News for You*. Bird's solos were new songs with melodies that were at once logical and disarming. Gillespie has recounted a story that illustrates the essence of this talent. "I saw something remarkable one time," said Diz. "He didn't show up for a dance he was supposed to play in Detroit. I was in town, and they asked me to play instead. I went up there, and we started playing. Then I heard this big roar, and Charlie Parker had come in and started playing. He'd play a phrase, and people might never have heard it before. But he'd start it, and the people would finish it with him, humming. It would be so lyrical and simple that it just seemed the most natural thing to play."

The quartet sides without Coleman are *Cool Blues* (one of the faster masters was released as *Hot Blues*) and *Bird's Nest*, an *I Got Rhythm* derivative. Parker and Garner are not ideally suited to each other, but there is no severe clash. To the contrary, the passage of time has been kind to their collaboration, and one finds much that is swinging and witty in spite of the variance of their time conceptions.

The Garner session was done on February 19. A week later, the septet date with McGhee, Gray, guitarist Barney Kessel, Marmarosa, and the rest took place. McGhee is credited with three tunes, *Cheers, Stupendous,* and *Carvin' the Bird,* although the latter, a blues, later showed up as *Swedish Pastry,* written by Kessel, on a recording by Swedish clarinetist Stan Hasselgard for Capitol. *Stupendous* is loosely based on Gershwin's *S'wonderful* and has the uncommon AABC construction. On *Carvin' the Bird,* Parker does the "carvin,'" as he is anchor man in the three-horn exchanges. Once he has said it, it is the final word.

Bird's one written contribution, supposedly ready weeks before the date, was, according to Russell, "scribbled in a taxicab on the way out." This is *Relaxin' at Camarillo,* a blues line, but one, like *Billie's Bounce,* that contains shifting accents quite unlike any blues from the past. At a rehearsal two days before the date, the entire time was spent, Russell once explained, "in everybody's trying to learn this sinuous twelve-bar line. Actually, they didn't get it down anywhere near cold by the end. I remember driving Dodo Marmarosa home later that night. He kept talking about this line. It was still bugging him. He hadn't been able to get it straight. It was only twelve bars, but he couldn't get it."

I remember talking with a young tenor saxophonist from Detroit in the summer of 1947. We had come from hearing Bird at the Onyx on Fifty-second Street. He hadn't played *Camarillo,* but Ralph Diamond brought it up because he knew I had just begun to play alto. "If you can play *Camarillo,* you've got the whole thing," he said. He wasn't implying that once you knew this tune you could use the licks interchangeably on any song and play bebop in six easy lessons. What he was saying made great sense: if one mastered this line, he would then have a grasp of the rhythmic nuances implicit in Bird's music that made it a new and vital force.

Kenny Clarke said of *Camarillo,* "It shows exactly how Bird felt about the blues and the odd sets of progressions he'd devise to prove that he knows more about the blues than any living musician."

When Parker came back to New York in 1947, he began his most creative period, one in which he led his own quintet in clubs across the United States and on several trips to Europe. First of all, he surrounded himself with sidemen who were in complete rapport with him, musicians who understood his music and knew how to complement it. Miles Davis had not yet reached full maturity (the years with Parker helped him greatly toward this goal), but he had improved tremendously since 1945. His light, middle-register sound was a perfect foil for Bird; if his solos were not up to Parker's on the very fast numbers, his personal lines were refreshing at medium tempo, and his tender, sustained-note ballad performances were an apt contrast to Parker's darting, intricate interpretations of standards.

Although Bud Powell was on the Savoy session that produced *Donna Lee* (long credited to Parker but said by Gil Evans to have been written by Davis), *Buzzy, Chasin' the Bird,* and *Cheryl,* the pianist who backed Bird most of the time in the rich years was Duke Jordan, a sensitive accompanist with a lyrical solo style. Together with bassist Tommy Potter and drummer Max Roach, Jordan helped form a rhythm section that was the ideal climate in which Parker could flourish. The recordings made for Dial and Savoy in 1947 and 1948 are the classic performances. As a body of work, they represent the refinement of a musical philosophy and the quintessence of small-band playing in their era just as Louis Armstrong's Hot Five and Count Basie's Jones-Smith Inc. were definitive in theirs.

There were so many facets to Parker's giant talent, and each is well illustrated by the recordings of this period. Vibraphonist Teddy Charles, in naming his favorite Parker recordings, categorized several from the 1947–1948 period in a neat little itinerary: "Bird the Pioneer, showing disciples the way, founding settlements and schools. Swingtown—*Scrapple from the Apple,* Bluesville—*Parker's Mood* and *Cheryl,* Counterpoint—*Chasing the Bird* and *Ah-Leu-Cha,* and Melodyburg—*Embraceable You.*"

Blues, always vital to Parker, are found in abundant variety, from the elemental *Parker's Mood* and *Bluebird* through the Latin-flavored *Barbados* and *Bongo Bop* to the sophisticated *Cheryl* and the blithe, buoyant *Perhaps.*

Another favorite jumping-off place for Parker was the *I Got Rhythm* chord pattern. As with the blues, he made his own variations, sometimes intermixing portions of *Honeysuckle Rose* and *I Got Rhythm*—as on *Scrapple from the Apple*—but, more importantly, interpreting these progressions in his own way. He made the multimeaning word "changes," the designation for chord progressions, seem especially appropriate. These numbers were usually driving, up-tempo outings with diamond-hard Parker, such as *Dexterity, Crazeology,* and the mercurial *Constellation.* Nor did he limit his breakneck tempos to the *Rhythm* pattern— *Bird Gets the Worm* (on *Lover, Come Back to Me*) and *Klaunstance* (on *The Way You Look Tonight*) are virtuoso performances of the highest order. The remarks made by French clarinetist Hubert Rostaing are relevant here. He called Parker "an incredible improviser, who exploits his virtuosity but does so almost unconsciously, because he has something to say and not because he has worked up a chorus that is hard to play. His instrumental technique is extraordinary, but personal; he plays such and such a figure because he 'feels' it (though sometimes he plays bits of phrases that 'fall under his fingers'), and the most complicated one always has a typical stamp that is his alone."

The selections mentioned in the immediately preceding paragraphs are all by Parker, save *Crazeology.* His compositions have the same clarity and spontaneity as his playing. Perhaps his best piece is *Confirmation.* Martin Williams feels this way and has described it as "a most delightful and ingenious melody. For one thing," he wrote, "it is a continuous linear invention. Most pop songs and jazz pieces have two parts, a main strain and a bridge, or middle strain. The main strain is played twice before the bridge and once after it. *Confirmation* skips along beautifully with no repeats (except for one very effective echo phrase) until the last eight bars, which are a kind of repeat in summary.

"Moreover, the bridge does not seem an interruption or an interlude that breaks up the flow of the piece but is a part of the continuously developing melody. Finally, if the chord sequence to *Confirmation* preceded the melody, then the melody became so strong as Parker worked on it that it forced him to alter the chords to fit its developing contours."

Parker's ballad playing created yet another atmosphere—it is definitely "love" music. His way of sculpting a melody line was completely unique. André Hodeir compared it with Louis Armstrong's way. "Louis transfigures the original melody by subtly distorting it rhythmically and by adding some extra figures," writes the French critic. "Bird encloses it and leaves it merely implied in a musical context that is sometimes fairly complex."

Citing the classic performances of *Don't Blame Me* and *Embraceable You,* he remarks, "Parker now and again lets the phrase-pretext put in a brief appearance, but at other times it can only be guessed at behind the garland of notes in which it is embedded and which, far from being useless embroidery, form by themselves a perfectly articulated musical discourse of which the theme, hidden or expressed, is merely one of the constituent elements."

The period 1947–1948 was the zenith of Charlie Parker's career and the time of his greatest influence. He shaped musicians of all instruments, but primarily this multifaceted player turned out hundreds of alto saxophonists for each of his sides. Every city had its "Bird." Most jazz fans have never heard of John Pierce (not the one who played with George Russell in the sixties), Art Whittecombe, Bill Spencer, Flaps Dungee, Bill Cannon, Johnny Carter, or Leo Douglas. Phil Woods, Charlie Mariano, Cannonball Adderley, Jackie McLean, and Charles McPherson are more familiar names. Each, in his own way, reflects Bird in general and in varying specifics. But no one has been able to get the whole man; each has had to be content with his own piece.

Three baritone saxophonists who achieved prominence were also strongly influenced by Bird. Leo Parker (no relation to Charles) played alto in his native Washington, D.C., and baritone in the Billy Eckstine band, but he did not begin to be widely known until he worked in Dizzy Gillespie's combo on Fifty-second Street in March of 1946. Though he was definitely a child of bebop ("I learned to blow from Charlie Parker," he told Barry Ulanov, as reported in the July, 1947, *Metronome*), actually he was more oriented toward Lester Young. The boppish runs were there, but the note-riding moments were more numerous. Both elements were delivered with a virile, deep-throated sound. An example of his tender handling of the large horn is his solo on *My Kinda Love* with Sarah Vaughan.

Leo Parker reached his peak of popularity with *Mad Lad,* an Apollo recording with Sir Charles Thompson. Then he recorded as leader (*El Sino*) and sideman (*Ice Freezes Red* with Fats Navarro and *Settin' the Pace* with Dexter Gordon) for Savoy and worked along Fifty-second Street. In 1948 he joined Illinois Jacquet's small band, but by the end of the decade he was less in evidence. His work had become infected with the honk, and he drifted more toward rhythm and blues, then finally out of music altogether. In late 1961, he made a comeback with two LP's for

Blue Note, but before a projected third could be done, he died of an apparent heart attack on February 11, 1962, at the age of 37.

The baritonist closest to Bird in style was Serge Chaloff, who died in July, 1957, about four months short of his thirty-fourth birthday—a victim of cancer, but long before victimized by the "horse" that so many rode. Chaloff, a Bostonian, was from a very musical family. His father played with the Boston Symphony, and his mother taught piano at the New England Conservatory. Dick Twardzik was one of many jazz pianists who studied with her.

Serge Chaloff gave a brief self-history on the back of his *Boston Blow-Up* album on Capitol: "I took lessons on piano and clarinet, but I taught myself baritone.

"At first I listened to Harry Carney and Jack Washington, the baritone men with Duke and Count. That's how I formed my first style. But it was an alto man, the great Charlie Parker, whose work made me change my style.

"In 1945 the new jazz was still pretty strange to everybody; I worked on developing my approach to it all through Georgie Auld's and Jimmy Dorsey's band. What evolved is the style I became identified with when I went with Woody's band in 1947."

With Woody Herman's band, Chaloff became one of the Four Brothers, his style marked by a lightness, fleetness, an excellent sense of dynamics, and the self-perpetuating bounce of a boulder rolling downhill. Besides *Four Brothers,* Serge was featured on *The Goof and I* and numerous other originals in the Herman book. He did some early recording on Dial with Ralph Burns and Sonny Berman (his solo on *Nocturne* with Berman is especially haunting); four sides with Red Rodney for Keynote; and four sides under his own name for Savoy, now included in the LP *Lestorian Mode.*

Chaloff, who won the *Down Beat* poll from 1949 through 1951 and the *Metronome* poll from 1949 through 1953, worked around the Boston area and taught at the Jazz Workshop there after leaving Herman. In 1955 he underwent a cure for drug addiction and then recorded some of his best work in *Boston Blow-Up.* His *Body and Soul* is a great testament to his ability. Bill Coss described it in the *Metronome Yearbook* of 1956 as "an almost frightening example of Serge's horn, moaning through a seemingly autobiographical portrayal of (his) *Body and Soul,* an enormously emotional jazz listening experience."

Chaloff's last two albums are also impressive documents of his playing. Of a quartet recording, *Blue Serge,* done for Capitol in Hollywood in March, 1956, Nat Hentoff wrote in his *Down Beat* review: "Chaloff continues to be one of the key modern jazz baritone saxists when he is at his best."

And Don Gold, in reviewing *The Four Brothers Together Again,* an LP made in February, 1957, for Victor's subsidiary, Vik, with Zoot Sims, Al Cohn, and Herbie Steward, wrote of Serge: "This, the last session before his death, represents the fervent expression of a fatally ill man. It is a kind of significant farewell, in the language he knew best."

The third baritone player influenced by Bird is Cecil Payne. Like Leo Parker, he started as an alto man. Born in Brooklyn, Payne first studied with the veteran Pete Brown and then made his recording debut on the alto with J.J. Johnson for Savoy in 1946. In that same year, he was playing baritone with Roy Eldridge's band at the Spotlite. It was then that Dizzy Gillespie heard and hired him. He remained with Diz until early 1949 and was featured in *Ow* and *Stay on It,* which were recorded. After leaving Gillespie, he worked with Tadd Dameron and James Moody, toured with Illinois Jacquet from 1952 to 1954, and then divided his time between helping his father in the real-estate business and gigging around New York. From 1958 to 1960, he was most often heard with pianist Randy Weston's groups. Later he was one of the several replacements who followed Jackie McLean into the off-Broadway theater success *The Connection,* and he also worked with Machito's orchestra. Payne and pianist Kenny Drew composed a new score for their time in *The Connection* and recorded it for the Charlie Parker label.

Payne's best recordings were done in the late fifties for the now defunct Signal company (some of these have been reissued on Savoy) and, with Weston, for Riverside. His first alto recordings show a curious combination of the swing style (the Pete Brown influence) with the later developments. The baritone solos with Gillespie reveal a deeper immersion in Parker, while the work on Signal points up a maturation into a personal groove within the Parker heritage. He has related that while rehearsing with Max Roach and Kenny Dorham in 1950, a change was effected in his style at their urging. He began to tongue more and to play more notes. His ability to play faster increased perceptibly. Payne assimilated this new skill into his over-all technique. Essentially a self-effacing man, he has a style that is, as one might expect, very light and nimble, with some fine baritone timbres and no bleats.

There was an alto saxophonist associated with Payne in Brooklyn and in the Gillespie band who also owed something to Bird, but perhaps not as much as most of his contemporary alto men. He was Ernie Henry, who, like both Parkers and Chaloff, failed to live out his thirties. Henry, who died at the age of 31 in December of 1957, first achieved recognition as a member of Tadd Dameron's group in 1947. He recorded with Dameron on both Savoy and Blue Note. *A Bebop Carroll, The Tadd Walk, The Squirrel, Dameronia,* and *Our Delight* all feature his singing, upper-register swing. He had his own sound and style of phrasing even then. Other recordings of his during this period include *Doubletalk, Boperation,* and *The Skunk,* with Howard McGhee and Fats Navarro on Blue Note.

In 1948 Henry joined Gillespie's orchestra and remained through 1949. He can be heard on the Victor recordings of *Duff Capers, Swedish Suite,* and, to especially good advantage, *Minor Walk.*

In 1950 and 1951 Henry worked with Illinois Jacquet. Then he returned to Brooklyn and was not heard from, except for reports of an occasional jam session, for several years. In 1956, he worked and recorded with Thelonious Monk. He also recorded under his own name and with Kenny Dorham and Matthew Gee for Riverside in 1956 and 1957. At the time of his death, he had been back with the then re-formed Gillespie band for almost a year.

Some of Henry's most passionate, expressive work is with Monk on *Brilliant Corners* and *Ba-lue Bolivar Ba-lues-are* in the Riverside album *Brilliant Corners.* Several critics rapped his own LP's for out-of-tune playing and faulty fingering. If he had lived into the sixties, I wonder how he would have been judged by the supporters of the "new thing."

Although Charlie Mingus mistook Davey Schildkraut for Parker in a *Blindfold Test,* it has most often been said that Sonny Stitt is "the closest thing to Bird." It is a cross he has had to bear throughout his career. At one point it turned him completely away from the alto to the tenor. Stitt has long insisted that he was playing his way before he had ever heard Parker. Miles Davis says he heard Sonny when Tiny Bradshaw's band came through St. Louis in 1942 and recalls that Stitt was playing in the same general style he employs today. Stitt himself says he did not hear the records Parker made with McShann until 1943. He was then 19 and was still with Bradshaw. He was anxious to meet Bird, and when the band's travels took him to Kansas City, he set out to find him. When he did, the two went to a club and jammed together for an hour. Stitt says that Parker then told him, "You sure sound like me."

The estimate is accurate if the word "sound" is emphasized. Sonny's sound and spirit are very close to Bird's, but there are some basic differences. Stitt attacks his notes differently. As Michael James has pointed out: "Even leaving aside structural differences—Stitt's style has been far more symmetrical, never so adventurous rhythmically . . . just as his choruses are much less complex than Bird's, so is the surface tension of his style considerably more uniform."

James's conclusion is also well-taken. "The material gleaned from Parker is not used to prop up some despicable piece of jerry-building but implements the basic structure of an edifice well designed in itself. That this is true in the earliest stages of his career is shown by his work on 1946 recordings such as *Royal Roost* (*Rue Chaptal*), *Epistrophy* and *Fat Boy*."

In 1946 Stitt also recorded excellent solos on *That's Earl Brother* and *Oop Bop Sh' Bam* with Dizzy Gillespie. In 1947, he was voted the new star on alto by the critics and musicians of a poll conducted by *Esquire* magazine. By this time, however, he was not around to receive the acclaim that went with this. He was in the Federal Narcotics Hospital in Lexington, Kentucky.

When he was released in late 1949, Sonny returned to the jazz scene on tenor saxophone. While he did not give up the alto completely, he certainly de-emphasized it. From 1950 to 1952 he co-led a small band with Gene Ammons. This unit recorded for Prestige, as did Stitt on his own. The tenor "battles" on *Blues Up and Down* and *Stringin' the Jug* with Ammons are creative as well as exciting. In the early sixties, Ammons and Stitt were re-united for a couple of club engagements and several records. By this time, however, Stitt was working on his own, but as a wanderer who would pick up a new rhythm section in each city he visited. Sonny also toured with JATP in 1958 and 1959, was reunited with Gillespie for three months in 1958, and played with Miles Davis in 1961.

In the sixties he was finally able to secure another cabaret card, the license that allows him to work in New York clubs. In a 1959 interview he told writer Dave Bittan, "I want to be in New York with my own combo. I'd like to get an apartment and make this city my headquarters. It was a long time ago when I got in trouble. I don't want to talk about it. It's a distasteful subject. I'm still paying for it. I was young. . . . I didn't know what it was all about. . . . My people were churchgoers and knew only the beautiful things in life. . . . They didn't tell me about the bad things."

Although born in Boston (in 1924), Sonny grew up in Saginaw, Michigan. His father, Edward Boatner, was a music teacher at Wylie and Sam Houston Colleges in Texas and led a one-thousand-voice choir at the New York World's Fair of 1939. He now teaches music in New York. Actor Clifton Webb once studied with him. Stitt's mother plays and teaches piano and organ. Sonny took the surname of her second husband, Robert Stitt. His brother Clifford, a concert pianist, and sister Adelaide, a singer, have kept the name Boatner.

In this musical family, young Edward (Sonny's given name) began to learn piano at the age of 7 but later switched to clarinet. Then came alto, tenor, and even baritone saxophone, on which he recorded some roaring solos in the early fifties. Now his playing time is divided between tenor and alto. He is equally adept on both, capable of high-velocity solos at medium and, especially, up tempos and of lyrical ballad expositions, although he does like to double-time on the latter. On tenor, his love of Lester Young shows through.

Stitt enjoys the challenge of a "cutting" session with another saxophonist, and he is a hard man to best in such horn-to-horn combat. Possessing a combination of stamina and inventiveness, he seldom loses. Those who were at the Half Note on a particular night in 1961 will attest that he fell before Zoot Sims on *Sweet Georgia Brown*, but this is the exception rather than the rule. He has a justifiable pride in his talent. Fellow saxophonist Stan Getz has said of him, "With Stitt, you've gotta work. He doesn't let you rest. You've *got* to work or else you're left at the starting gate. It's hard for me to say which horn he's better on, alto or tenor."

Al Cohn tells of an incident involving Getz and Stitt that is as illustrative as it is amusing. "Stan was playing at the Red Hill in Camden, New Jersey, and Sonny came by to sit in. He called a very fast tempo and took the first solo. By the time Stan got to play, the bass player's hand was about to drop off. As soon as the number ended, Sonny packed up his horn and split. Stan said, 'And he didn't even give me a chance to get even with a ballad.'"

Most of Stitt's recording has been for Verve, although he has recorded for a variety of other labels in the sixties. In his days as a peripatetic leader, he was fortunate to have his peers accompany him when it came time to record. The complaint against the trios that backed him on his stops all over the map was that they were afraid of playing with him. By the time relaxation and confidence set in, he would be off to another town.

One of his best recordings on alto was done for Roost in the mid-fifties with a small ensemble and Quincy Jones arrangements. A blues, *Quince,* and a heartfelt treatment of Tadd Dameron's *If You Could See Me Now* are not to be missed. *The Eternal Triangle,* a long track in a Verve album with Dizzy Gillespie and Sonny Rollins, demonstrates the kind of tenor heat he can generate when confronted with such a formidable saxophonist as Rollins. Perhaps a better over-all picture of his talent can be gained by listening to *Personal Appearance,* a Verve album in which he plays both his horns in a group of selections typical of his repertory.

In 1962 Stitt recorded on alto with a string section, as Parker had done almost ten years before. He revealed here a talent for composing pretty melodies, reminiscent of "popular" music before the advent of rock 'n' roll. To some of these tunes, he has written lyrics, but they are as yet unrecorded as vocals.

One very good album from the sixties is *Stitt Plays Bird* on Atlantic. Today it takes something out of the ordinary to inspire Stitt to his full powers, and the Parker-based material is just that. And *Ko Ko,* especially, is a performance of unrelenting drive that is thoughtful nevertheless.

An apocryphal story has it that several weeks before Parker's death, he met Stitt and told him, "Man, I'm not long for this life. You carry on. I'm leaving you the keys to the kingdom."

Several years later, Stitt's reaction to a magazine writer who tried to make him claim that he was the "new Bird" was one of hostility. "I'm no new Bird, man!" he cried. "And Cannonball Adderley isn't either! Nobody's Bird! *Bird died!*"

Parker's death occurred on March 12, 1955, but his physical decline had set in long before. In 1948 a doctor warned him about the dangerous condition of his health. As the forties became the fifties, however, he was still consistently in command of his powers. Kenny Dorham held the trumpet spot in his quintet after Davis, Al Haig replaced Duke Jordan, and Tommy Potter and Max Roach remained. In 1950 Red Rodney and Roy Haynes came in for Dorham and Roach; in 1951 it was Walter Bishop and Teddy Kotick who took over for Haig and Potter. On recording dates, the personnel was even more varied: Roach, Kenny Clarke, Davis, Rodney, and pianist John Lewis were among the sidemen.

This was the time that Parker began an association with Norman Granz, who was then affiliated with Mercury Records. Later, Granz formed his own companies, Clef and Norgran (these eventually became Verve), and continued to record Bird in a variety of formats. The most rewarding artistically was, as usual, the small group, which produced *Visa* and *Passport* in 1949 (although trombonist Tommy Turk intrudes heavily in *Visa*), *She Rote* and *Au Privave* in early 1951, and *Blues for Alice* and *Swedish Schnapps* in the summer of 1951. Then, too, there was the reunion with Gillespie in June of 1950.

For Granz, Parker first recorded some Afro-Cuban sides with Machito's orchestra in December of 1948 and January of 1949. His solos on *Mango Mangue, Okiedoke* (it should have read *Okiedokie,* one of his favorite expressions), and *No Noise* (Flip Phillips is also on this one) show his marvelous ability to remain himself and still fit into an alien format. In December, 1950, he and Phillips again played in front of Machito, this time in two sections of a Chico O'Farrill Afro-Cuban jazz suite. Both play separately on *Mambo,* but in *Jazz,* where the time is strictly 4/4, there are chase choruses in which Phillips, by preceding Parker, unwittingly helps demonstrate the pedestrian versus the sublime, as Bird makes silk purses out of sow's ears.

A Latin excursion of a different nature is the Parker LP *South of the Border,* recorded in two sessions (March, 1951, and January, 1952) with Benny Harris, Walter Bishop, and bongo and/or conga. The slight harmonic material and the clave combine to make this one of Parker's most earthbound sets, although he flies on *Tico Tico*, and because he played *My Little Suede Shoes* it became a vehicle for fellow musicians, who otherwise might never have discovered it.

Bird again rises above the ordinary and the trite in the LP *Charlie Parker Big Band*, which includes standards like *What Is This Thing Called Love?*, *Temptation*, *Autumn in New York*, and *Night and Day*, arranged by Joe Lipman for conventional dance orchestra (March, 1952) plus string section (January, 1952). Included in this album are *Dancing in the Dark* and *Laura*, two selections from a summer of 1950 *Bird with Strings* recording date. This ensemble, consisting of seven strings, oboe, French horn, harp, and rhythm section, was an amplification of a group used on a very successful album, the first *Bird with Strings* recording, made in November, 1949. In that one there were only four strings, harp, oboe, and/or English horn (played by Mitch Miller) in addition to the rhythm section.

The idea of casting Parker with strings came from *Repetition*, recorded in the summer of 1949 and first issued in an album called *The Jazz Scene*. Neal Hefti had written the piece for big band with string section but with no soloist in mind. Parker happened to be in the studio and was included strictly as an afterthought, and at his own request. Granz wrote in the notes to the album: "Parker actually plays on top of the original arrangement; that it jells as well as it does is a tribute both to the flexible arrangement of Hefti and the inventive genius of Parker to adapt himself to any musical surrounding."

Dizzy Gillespie told of how "Yard used to come and play with my big band. He'd never heard the arrangements before, but you'd think he'd written them. The brass would play something and cut off, and bang! Charlie Parker was there, coming in right where he was supposed to. It's a shame that when he was making those records with strings that the music wasn't up to his standards. There should have been a whole symphony behind him."

The *Bird with Strings* albums consist of standards like *Summertime*, *I Didn't Know What Time It Was*, and *Everything Happens to Me*, but the number most acclaimed is *Just Friends*, a less obvious piece of material, wherein Parker departs much further from the melody than on the others. It is one of his classic performances, one of the few of his own recordings he admitted liking.

Many people felt that strings were Granz's idea, that their purpose was to make Parker more popular. Doris Parker claims that it was really Bird's desire to play with strings and that Granz was merely satisfying his wish. Admittedly, the surroundings are extremely conservative and bland, but you cannot argue with the beauty of Parker's playing. He is compelling even when just stating a melody.

As a result of these recordings, a wider audience did materialize, and Parker soon was booked into Birdland (the club that had been named for him) for sixteen weeks with the string ensemble. Tours followed, but often this necessitated hiring local string and rhythm sections that usually were not up to the standard Parker was used to in his accompanying units. A typical incident took place in Rochester, New York, in 1952. After playing the first set with a horrible house-band rhythm section, Bird bemoaned his predicament to jazz enthusiast Lon Flanigan. He told him and his friends, "I need a rhythm section like old people need soft shoes."

Flanigan recounted the outcome to writer Robert Reisner: "Luckily, this happened on a Tuesday night, when most of the good local musicians were not working. Enough of them were in the house to provide Bird with a decent beat for the rest of the night. Bird took the manager of the place aside, and, with some help from us, convinced him that the house band did not play an appropriate style for a bebop musician. The next day, Art Taylor and Walter Bishop arrived by plane to salvage the rest of the week."

How many times Parker was not rescued by his regulars we do not know, but it must have been a source of great annoyance for him to have to play with inferior musicians at a point in his career when he should have been enjoying his greatest success.

Strings were not the only accouterments that Bird was surrounded with in the fifties. In May, 1953, Granz recorded him backed by flute, oboe, bassoon, clarinet, French horn, rhythm, and a vocal group headed by Dave Lambert. Gil Evans did the arrangements. All this proved to be a bit rich as an over-all musical diet, but Parker plays an idea-packed, kinetic solo on *In the*

Still of the Night, and just because he recorded *Old Folks*—like *My Little Suede Shoes*—his contemporaries also played it. A third number, *If I Love Again,* finds him in a happy, skipping mood.

Granz also recorded Parker with JATP again, when Bird made the 1949 tour with Norman's troupe. These numbers are *The Opener, Lester Leaps In, Embraceable You,* and *The Closer.* Bird is particularly good on the last two.

A studio jam session of June, 1952, which also included Johnny Hodges, Benny Carter, and Ben Webster, produced sides containing some excellent Parker in a swing atmosphere. J.J. Johnson, writing of Bird's solo on *Funky Blues* (the title tune of the album), said: "As advanced as Charlie Parker played, he never lost sight of tradition and 'grass roots' in jazz. I suspect he enjoyed playing with Hodges and Webster and company." I'm sure he did. Bird had a love of and respect for good music of any kind. In a *Blindfold Test* conducted by Leonard Feather, he reacted to Ellington's *Passion Flower* with "a beatific grin as he recognized the alto soloist," wrote Feather.

"That was Duke," said Bird, "featuring Johnny Lily Pons Hodges! I always took my hat off to Johnny Hodges 'cause he can *sing* with the horn; oh, he's a beautiful person. That record deserves all the stars you can muster."

On the same occasion, Parker said of George Wettling's *Heebie Jeebies:* "You want my honest opinion? Well, that's music—that's very good Dixieland." This was a period when the factions of jazz were at war, and Bird himself was subjected to some strong abuse from the "moldy figs," as the champions of modern jazz liked to call them.

Feather also played some classical music for Parker. Bird readily identified Stravinsky and said: "That's music at its best. I like all of Stravinsky—and Prokofiev, Hindemith, Ravel, Debussy and of course Wagner and Bach." Several years later he named Bartok as his favorite. In the forties, at the Roost, he would play the opening phrases of Hindemith's *Kleine Kammermusik* as a call to let his sidemen know that it was time for the next set. In the fifties, according to Bill Coss, "He never listened to jazz in his home. For that matter, he seldom listened to jazz anywhere unless he happened to be on a job. His main interest was in classical music, mostly the moderns. And when he was not devoting time to that he was watching Hopalong Cassidy or assorted other

Westerners, or, when the Parkers lived on Tenth Street and Avenue B in New York, he was in the neighborhood bars, arguing for hours with Ukrainian laborers and their women. No one sat in on these occasions. It rather defies the imagination to think of Bird in such an atmosphere, but it seemed to give him a great deal of pleasure no matter the amount of actual communication that went on. That he really wanted that companionship could be seen in the fact that he entered a roundhouse brawl in one bar one day over a small point of honor and emerged beaten and battered but, finally, accepted by the group."

In July of 1950, Parker married his fourth wife, dancer Chan Richardson. They had two children, a daughter, Pree, born in 1951, and a son, Baird, born the following year. He also thought of Kim, Chan's daughter from a previous marriage, as his own. (Leon, his son from his first, teenage marriage, was born in 1937 and was raised by Bird's mother until he was 10.)

Parker's ill health, always lurking beneath the surface of his dissipation, hospitalized him in early 1951, just after he had returned from some European engagements. He had a peptic ulcer; it was to plague him, along with heart and liver trouble, through the last years of his life. He suffered much pain in the form of periodic attacks and seizures. Observed one night shortly before his death, he was eating codeine pills as if they were candy.

His daughter Pree became ill and died of pneumonia, and Parker's spirits were severely depressed during 1953 and 1954. Apparently he had given up heroin (Dr. Robert Freymann, who attended him at the time of his death, said that his eyes and used-up veins indicated that he wasn't using drugs), but he was drinking excessively. He took on weight, much of it bloat. Pictures taken in his last years show why people thought he was much older than he actually was.

Parker must have had a tremendous constitution to be able to abuse his body for as long as he did. His drinking was prodigious. Howard McGhee tells of Bird's polishing off eight double whiskeys before he started his first set at the Los Angeles club in which they were working. One night at the Magpie (as the little bar above Birdland was then called) in 1953, I saw him consume eight Manhattan cocktails in a half hour with no apparent ill effects.

Then there was the Prestige recording session of January, 1953, for which Miles Davis was flanked by the tenors of Sonny Rollins and Parker. (When the sides were finally released in the late fifties, as part of an LP called *Collector's Items,* Parker was billed as Charlie Chan, the pseudonym he first used on the *Jazz at Massey Hall* album.) I was the A&R man for the Davis recording, and as a callow youth who still placed his favorite musicians on pedestals, I had quite a task trying to serve as buffer between record company and musicians on the one hand and musicians and engineers on the other. Things were progressing in a relatively smooth manner, after Davis' late arrival, when the refreshments arrived. Bird had asked for gin, which I ordered, along with some beer. It was customary to have a bottle on hand in case someone wanted a drink, but I believe I did as many sessions with sandwiches and coffee as with alcohol.

There were six musicians on the date, and the likelihood of anyone really getting loaded was not great because there were several people to share one fifth of gin. I hadn't reckoned with Bird. He assumed command of the bottle and emptied most of its contents into his mouth before finally surrendering it. Then he fell asleep for a while. When he woke up he was moving slowly and rather deliberately. At the end of the session, Miles berated Bird for having gotten himself into such a condition on his record date and told Parker that he (Miles) had never done that to him. Parker, sobered and alert by then, said, "All right, Lily Pons," and offered him some deliberate clichés, including "To produce beauty, we must suffer pain—from the oyster comes the pearl."

(One thing might be cleared up here about the session. After his stumbling on the second "take" of *The Serpent's Tooth,* Parker played a moving solo on *'Round Midnight,* which I described in the notes to the album as being "full of the pain and disappointment he knew too well." But I also gave him credit for playing the bridges at the beginning and end of the song. It wasn't until Danish writer Erik Weidemann pointed out that it was Rollins that I realized my mistake. In the years that had elapsed between the recording and its release, I had forgotten something that I may have specifically asked for in the studio.)

It has been said that "some weeks before his death," Bird passed a blind accordionist on Broadway and, dropping some money in his cup, asked him to play *All the Things You Are.* The event actually took place a week before the *Collector's Items* date. Bird had come over to Prestige to get an advance. Bob Weinstock had left a check for him, and Charlie wanted to know where he could cash it. Billie Wallington and I went over to the Colony Record Shop with him to facilitate matters. That is when we encountered the accordionist. When we left Colony, the accordionist was playing the song, and Bird praised the man for making the right changes. I don't remember whether Parker gave him any more money, but if he did, it was not "the last twenty-five cents in his old trousers," as one account of this incident has stated.

If he didn't wear old trousers, Bird often wore rumpled ones. The jazz musician has usually been known as a sharp dresser and often a style setter. Parker was the antithesis of this. In the late forties, his usual outfits were unpressed double-breasted pinstripe suits and loud floral-design ties. He paid a little more attention to clothes in the fifties—he was one of the first New Yorkers to wear a duffle coat—but clothes were never important to him.

Although he was not the natural clown that Gillespie is, Parker was a witty man. He used to introduce the trios that played opposite him at the Fifty-second Street clubs with an announcement that "put on" owner and audience at the same time. "The management has gone to grrrrrrrreat expense," he would intone, "to bring you the next group. Let's bring them on with a rousing round of applause." The last line would be delivered with rapidity in a descending arc, its cadences amazingly like a Parker solo.

Once Gillespie was heading an all-star big band at Birdland that was billed as Dizzy Gillespie's Dream Band. Parker was not playing with the group, but he was standing nearby, between sets, when someone asked Diz, "How's your dream band?" When Gillespie replied, "You mean my *wet*-dream band," Bird with his resonant voice, affected a mock-professorial tone, which he did so well on occasion, and inquired loudly, "Are you referring to somnambulistic ejaculation?"

A stranger aspect of his humor was revealed one night at the Open Door in Greenwich Village. He and tenor man Brew Moore, after playing at each other's behinds as they walked slowly around the dance floor in a musical "goosing" session, finished up by playing to a large spot of old chewing gum stuck to the floor.

The sessions at the Open Door were Sunday evening affairs run by Bob Reisner, beginning in April, 1953, and continuing through 1954. Bird was featured many times, and although the quality of his performances varied, there were supreme moments. Once Parker brought in two corny singers who did *Route 66* in a near-hillbilly manner while he took an intermission. Any members of the audience who left played into Parker's hands. The purpose of his little experiment was to get a turnover. He had a percentage deal with Reisner, and there were people waiting outside to get in.

On another occasion, after taking a solo, he sat down on a chair in the middle of the floor (the group played right on the dance floor, as there was no bandstand) with a handkerchief held to his face, fell asleep, and couldn't be awakened.

Reisner summed up the situation when he wrote: "The Sunday sessions were full of suspense and drama. Would he show? Was he well? Would he hang around or wander off? One night he disappeared, and I found out later that he had played across the street at another place called The Savannah Club for free, or maybe a couple of drinks. He felt he could not be bought. When he played free or for a few friends, he was at his best. His performances were uneven, but what seemed bad temper and perverseness—like falling asleep on the stand—is understandable, considering that he had advanced ulcers, dropsy, bad heart, and with it all, he could play like a dream and could melt and cow people and fell a two-hundred-pound man with a blow. Bird was the supreme hipster. He made his own laws. His arrogance was enormous, his humility profound."

At the end of the summer of 1954, Parker was booked into Birdland with the strings. On the stand he called one tune and came in playing another. After chastising and firing the group, he went home and attempted suicide by drinking iodine. Later he claimed that the whole thing had been a ruse to get himself committed to the hospital so that he couldn't be legally held accountable for debts he had incurred. On September 1 he was admitted to Bellevue and remained there for nine more days. On September 28 he returned of his own accord. The hospital report stated: "The patient committed himself to the Psychiatric Pavilion, stating that he had been severely depressed since his previous discharge, that he was drinking again, and feared for his own safety." On October 15 he was "discharged in his own custody."

Fifteen days later, he was presented in concert in Town Hall by Reisner. Parker played as well as he ever had, thrilling the large crowd. Unfortunately, the concert ended prematurely—it had started late, as many jazz concerts do—because of union regulations. The stagehands rang down the curtain while Bird was still playing. Leonard Feather has described Parker at the time of the concert: ". . . he looked healthy, talked sensibly, played magnificently and told me he was commuting daily between New Hope, Pa., where he and Chan had found a home, and Bellevue Hospital, where he was undergoing psychiatric treatment. He had dropped 20 pounds of unhealthy excess fat; he was like a new man, and New Hope seemed the right place for him to be living."

This happy state didn't last too long, however. Feather recounts meeting him at the bar above Birdland about a month before his death. He was "raggedly dressed. He said he had not been home to New Hope lately. The bloated fat was back. His eyes looked desperately sad."

Parker lived in Greenwich Village with friends in the last few months of 1954, occasionally traveling to nearby Eastern cities for short gigs. His last great recordings were a year behind him—sides made in August, 1953, containing *Chi Chi, I Remember You, Now's the Time,* and *Confirmation.* These four feature a rhythm section of Al Haig, Percy Heath, and Max Roach. (The Verve LP *Now's the Time* lists these men for all eight selections, but actually Hank Jones and Teddy Kotick, along with Roach, are on the last four—*Laird Baird, Kim, Cosmic Rays,* and *The Song Is You*—made in December, 1952.)

December, 1954, marked Parker's last record date. The two numbers taped were *Love for Sale* and *I Love Paris,* eventually used to complete a *Charlie Parker Plays Cole Porter* album. It is worth listening to, as is anything else he did, but it is a tired Bird, and the exceptional moments are few.

His last public appearance was at Birdland. On occasion he had been barred from the club despite the fact that it had been named for him. The first night of the job, March 4, 1955, was also the last. With Parker were Kenny Dorham, Bud Powell, Charlie Mingus, and Art Blakey, a formidable array, to be sure. There was a good crowd early that evening at the club, drawn by the exciting prospect of hearing these five play together. What followed instead was chaotic and depressing. Parker had arrived early, in bedroom slippers, but left for something and returned late. Dorham has given this account: ". . . the trouble started right away. . . . He had words with Oscar Goodstein, and when Oscar said go and play, Bird, indicating Bud Powell, who was in. no fit mental condition to, answered, 'What am I going to play when you give me this to play with?' Then Bud and Bird started to feud. Bud said, 'What do you want to play, Daddy?' Bird said, 'Let's play some *Out of Nowhere.*'

"Then Bud—that giant who was a shade below the caliber of Parker—asked Bird, who could play in any key and any time, 'What key you want it, Daddy?' Bird snarled back, 'S, Mother.'"

After this hassle, Parker played a few phrases and left the stand. He came back but refused to play. When Powell left the stand, Bird called his name repeatedly on the microphone. The troubles continued through the evening. Dorham did most of the soloing. Finally, Mingus grabbed the mike and told the audience that he didn't want to be associated with this and that these people were killing jazz. Bird got drunk and left the club. Someone saw him later at Basin Street, then located around the corner on Fifty-first Street, his face wet with tears.

Five days later, Parker stopped in at the apartment of his friend the Baroness Nica de Koenigswarter, called the Jazz Baroness, in the Hotel Stanhope. He was to leave for a job in Boston that night but became ill and started vomiting blood shortly after he entered the room. Nica called her doctor, and he advised that Parker be taken to a hospital. When Bird refused, they decided that he could remain there. The Baroness and her daughter ministered to his needs, and Dr. Freymann visited him several times a day. On the third day, Saturday, Parker seemed much better. The doctor gave him permission to sit up and watch television. While laughing at a juggling act on the Dorsey brothers' show, he had a seizure. By the time the doctor arrived, minutes later, he was dead. The autopsy cited lobar pneumonia as the cause of death, but Freymann said it was a heart attack.

The Baroness has explained that she wanted to let Chan, from whom Parker had been separated, know about his death before she found out from the radio or newspapers. Therefore she did not notify anyone until Monday night, when "Chan was finally contacted." Yet when Chan called Bird's mother in Kansas City to tell her, Mrs. Parker already knew—Doris Parker had called and told her. Doris Parker has said that Art Blakey had phoned her in Chicago and informed her of Parker's death.

The Baroness, who went to the Open Door on the Sunday night immediately following Bird's death, certainly hid well the bad news she carried so fresh in her mind.

On Tuesday the story broke in all the New York papers. It was then that errors and discrepancies in the circumstances of Parker's death were noted. Parker's age was given as 53, but by whom? Later the date of his death on his tombstone was marked as March 23 instead of March 12. (Why?) And why did Doctor Freymann refuse to sign the death certificate? Why did the body lie unidentified in the morgue for two days? These questions have remained unanswered.

The funeral was held on a gray day of downpour in New York at Adam Clayton Powell's Abyssinian Baptist Church. Once the coffin was almost dropped. Then the body was sent to Kansas City, where Bird had requested that it not go, for burial. Some musicians, such as Gail Brockman, came from as far away as Chicago for the funeral services. Other New York-based musicians were conspicuous by their absence.

Doris Parker, who had come to New York on hearing of Bird's death, won an early legal battle to become administratrix of the estate. This included the rights to privately recorded material that had not been released, as well as material from the Dial label that had been unavailable for a long time. In the early sixties these began to appear on the Charlie Parker label, a company started by Doris with Aubrey L. Mayhew.

The music on the LP *Bird Is Free* comes from a concert-dance of 1950. It contains some superb Bird, including a miraculous version of *Lester Leaps In*. More in-person Parker can be heard on *The Happy Bird*, recorded in 1951 in Framingham, Massachusetts. This is Bird in a relaxed, after-the-gig jamming atmosphere, with Wardell Gray on tenor.

Charlie Parker Records also took over the rights to three volumes first issued on a label called Le Jazz Cool. These consist of some very uninhibited air checks, mostly from the Royal Roost, circa 1948. They showed up as *Historical Masterpieces* in a boxed set on Charlie Parker with numerous errors in personnel. Miles

Davis is on several tracks for which Kenny Dorham receives credit. There were many other annoying mistakes in the company's product.

Martin Williams put together a comprehensive album of all the takes from the Red Norvo all-star session with Parker and Gillespie for Parker Records that was issued as *Once There Was Bird*, and an orderly reissue of all the Parker Dial material was planned, but soon after the first release, the label went inactive. The estate is tangled up once again—or, rather, it has never been completely untangled—and rare Parker material remains unreleased.

If the recordings that did come to light on the Charlie Parker label were to some a reminder of Parker's greatness, these people were probably among those whose memories did not need refreshing. For others, especially the younger listeners, Bird does not mean as much as he should, for jazz has failed to develop the kind of audience that appreciates its entire history. It is true that the music reflects the times, and it is natural for the new listener to concentrate on the present heroes, but it seems tragic that within five years after his death, a giant like Parker had become little more than a name to many young musicians.

Soon after his death, the words "Bird Lives" began to appear on buildings, fences, and subway steps and walls—and through his music, he does live. But for all the sincerity found in these graffiti, they were also symbolic of his deification by beatniks, many of whom really knew little about his music.

His life inspired Bob Reisner to compile a documentary that is the source of many of the anecdotes and facts in this chapter. The book, *The Legend of Charlie Parker*, published in 1962, was adapted into play form in 1965. Bird-like musicians have also been the central characters in two novels, *The Sound* by Ross Russell and *Night Song* by John A. Williams. In 1965 a film version of the latter was produced, with Dick Gregory playing the part of Eagle.

Bird was a man who would try to shortchange his sidemen because he *needed* money but would back down when his bluff was called; a man who at the end was at the constricting mercy of his "judges," as he called his booking agents; a man who could pick up any old saxophone, fitted with a strange mouthpiece and a worn-out reed, and make music for eternity.

Charlie Parker's greatness is demonstrated by the body of his recorded art, but what made him great can be heard in even the abbreviated phrase of an individual solo. Listen, for example, only to the end of his first solo on the alternate take, initially un-issued, of *Parker's Mood* on the LP *Charlie Parker Memorial* on Savoy. You'll hear the soul of a giant.

Recommended Listening

CHARLIE PARKER

First Recordings, ONYX 221

NOTE: Warner Bros. issued a limited edition boxed set of all Parker's Dial material but this is probably not in general circulation. The same recordings can be found on Spotlite 101-106. A Warner Bros. two-record set also contains some of this material, 2WB 3198.

The Complete Savoy Studio Sessions, SAVOY S5J 5500
Master Takes, SAVOY SJL 2201
Encores, SAVOY SJL 1107
Encores, Volume 2, SAVOY SJL 1129
Bird at the Roost, SAVOY SJL 1108
Summit Meeting at Birdland, COLUMBIA JC 34831
Bird with Strings Live at the Apollo, Carnegie Hall and Birdland,
    COLUMBIA JC 34832
The Verve Years (1948-50), VERVE VE-2-2501
Norman Granz Jam Session, The Charlie Parker Sides, VERVE
    VE-2-2508
One Night in Chicago, SAVOY SJL 1132
One Night in Washington, ELECTRA-MUSICIAN E-1-60019
International Jam Session, XANADU 122

(see also Gillespie)

SONNY STITT

Genesis, PRESTIGE P-24044 or *Bud's Blues,* PRESTIGE 7839
Stitt Plays Bird, ATLANTIC 1418
Tune-Up, COBBLESTONE 9013
Constellation, COBBLESTONE 9021

(see also Gillespie, Navarro)

2

DIZZY GILLESPIE
AND THE TRUMPETERS

LATE IN PARKER'S LIFE he met with Dizzy Gillespie at Basin Street, the New York club. Gillespie has related: "He spoke about us getting together again. He said it in a way that implied '. . . before it's too late.' Unfortunately, it was already too late. If it had happened, it would have been the greatest."

Gillespie obviously meant that it would have been a wonderful thing to have been reunited with Parker, but it also would have been the "greatest" from a musical standpoint; for whenever these two giant talents combined forces, history was made. First, there were the early collaborations dating from 1945. After the California fiasco, Dizzy and Bird were never to play together on a regular basis. There were four occasions after 1946, however, when they did perform together. One was a studio recording session; two other instances were concert performances; and Parker and Gillespie played together at Birdland in March, 1951, with Bud Powell, Tommy Potter, and Roy Haynes (four titles, *Blue 'N Boogie, Anthropology, 'Round Midnight,* and *A Night in Tunisia,* were recorded from a broadcast, but are not available to the general public).

On September 29, 1947, the Gillespie big band gave a concert at Carnegie Hall. Part of the evening's program was given over to a reunion between Gillespie and Parker, backed by the rhythm section of the big band—John Lewis, Al McKibbon, and Joe Harris. The results were recorded and issued on a bootleg label, Black Deuce, but were later made available legitimately on Roost. All the excitement of that evening is captured in *A Night in Tunisia, Dizzy Atmosphere,* and *Groovin' High.*

In early June, 1950, Norman Granz recorded them for Mercury with a rather incongruous rhythm section of Thelonious Monk, Curly Russell, and Buddy Rich. Although Rich's drumming swings strongly in its own way, his accents are at odds with the rhythmic conceptions of Parker and Gillespie. Nevertheless, the LP has only improved with age; the musical statements of *Bird and Diz* (as the album is now titled) are rich with ideas. The additional "takes" on *An Oscar for Treadwell, Mohawk, Leap Frog,* and *Relaxin' with Lee* are especially enlightening. The other titles, in single "takes," are *Bloomdido* and *My Melancholy Baby.*

Three years later, on May 15, 1953, the famed concert at Massey Hall in Toronto, Canada, took place. With Bud Powell, Charlie Mingus, and Max Roach, Parker and Gillespie did *Perdido, Salt Peanuts, All the Things You Are, Wee, Hot House,* and *A Night in Tunisia.* The proceedings, highly charged as they were, were recorded and released by Mingus' company, Debut, but are now available on Fantasy (*Jazz at Massey Hall*). Parker appears under the pseudonym Charlie Chan.

Both the Carnegie Hall and Massey Hall concerts were battlegrounds of the ego for Bird and Diz according to observers. Ross Russell, reviewing the Roost LP, maintained that because of Parker's unreliability he was an "added starter" for the Carnegie concert and that he showed up "really bugged—hopping mad, offended at having been passed over, and loaded with aggression for his old friend and protector. The concert, with its *auld lang syne* overtones, developed into something more than scheduled; not so much a formal presentation of the new music, as an embittered duel between its two leading exponents."

Bill Coss, in his liner notes to the first edition of the Massey Hall LP on Debut, wrote: "In Toronto, the quintet performed brilliantly, with asides for individual temperaments. And, fortunately, there was a tape machine present to record most that came to pass. The asides are often more felt than heard: Chan's unusual amount of interpolations on *Perdido;* Chan blowing Bud off his back on *Things;* Chan seemingly furious on his early choruses of *Peanuts,* as if he were scolding the clowning Gillespie, whom he had announced before the number as 'my worthy constituent.' One can wonder if the use of the word was deliberate or not."

The tensions described by Russell and Coss were not imaginary. There is, however, a natural tendency to read into these accounts a more glamorous encounter than actually took place. If the animosities between Parker and Gillespie were there, they were of short duration. Gillespie, in explaining the essentially divergent paths he and Bird took, said to me, "When two people are developing, it has to go the way of a leader. It's good for a guy to develop under somebody and then go out on his own. We never had any serious breach." I might add, when you have two leaders, you must have two bands.

Of Parker's reputation for strange behavior, Gillespie stated, "He wasn't weird to me. He wasn't weird at all. I hear them tell stories on me, and I *know* they're not true—right in front of my face, so you know what they do behind your back."

Dizzy, as his nickname implies, had quite a reputation for eccentric behavior. But for all his youthful zaniness, John Birks Gillespie has always been acutely aware of what was happening to him and around him. As someone once observed, "Yeah, Dizzy's crazy—crazy like a fox."

Diz's sense of humor—and the various paths it takes—is one of the things that set him apart from the other musical giants of his circle. Writer Ralph J. Gleason, sketching Gillespie the man in a set of liner notes for the Verve album *An Electrifying Evening with Dizzy Gillespie,* compared him with George Bernard Shaw in that they both discovered that "you can tell the public the truth, the total truth, but only if you can make them laugh."

A part of Gillespie's ability to make people laugh comes from his curiosity and a kind of enlighted innocence. Also, there is a lack of bitterness in his humor. Dizzy can be highly satirical and sometimes quite cutting, but basically his wit springs from irony rather than from hard cynicism.

Sometimes his antics have caused people to lose sight of his prodigious talent. In 1950 his dynamic big band, formed in the forties, dissipated its power and finally was dissolved. In *Down Beat,* Dizzy complained that many of his men lacked showman-ship and said, "If you got enough money . . . to play for your-self, you can play anything you want to. But if you want to make a living at music, you've got to sell it."

He formed a small combo. First it included Milt Jackson on vibes and piano and Percy Heath on bass; later, with singer Joe Carroll, the group placed its emphasis on vocal novelties and devoted less time to creative jazz playing. Baritone saxophonist Bill Graham, while an accomplished musician, was hardly an in-spired soloist. An audience might wait in vain for Dizzy to cut loose, while he seemed content to play conga drum and sing *Oo-*

Sho-Be-Do-Be and *The Umbrella Man*. Adverse criticism was strong in this period, and many accused him of selling out. British critic Michael James wrote: "There is no contesting the fact that much of the band's production was poor by any musical standards. The rhythmic pulse was never absent, perhaps, but much of the improvisation was obviously inspired by commercial factors." James then quoted Gillespie's comments during a European tour with this group: "I'm not interested any more in going down in history. I want to eat."

In 1962, when I asked Dizzy about this period and the criticism he received, he said, "It didn't bother me. I wasn't making too much money, but I was having a good time."

Whether it bothered him or not, that time did hurt his standing with the jazz public and many of the critics. Musicians who know, however, were not misled. It was in the midst of this time of "selling out" that Miles Davis told me, "Diz is it! Whenever I want to learn something, I go and listen to Diz."

In 1956, when he reorganized his big band for a State Department tour of the Middle East, Gillespie began to regain some of his prestige among the doubters. The opportunity to lead a big band for the first time in six years seemed to breathe new life into his playing. If Gillespie was not really a "born leader" of a big band, he certainly grew up in the big-band era and received his formative playing experience in this kind of setting. The combination of the Gillespie personality and the environment of the large swing orchestra helped to produce one of the most important leaders jazz has ever had.

John Birks Gillespie was born in Cheraw, South Carolina, on October 21, 1917. His father was a bricklayer, but his sideline was music. As the leader of a local band, Dizzy's father was also the custodian of the instruments. "All those instruments sticking up around there," is the way Dizzy describes it. "My father wanted somebody to be a musician in the family. My mother told me that he used to make my older sisters and brothers take piano lesssons —and he used to make them practice—but none of them had no eyes. I was only ten when he died, so he didn't know about my playing, but I imagine he'd be pretty proud now to have one of his children as a musician." Dizzy started on trombone but didn't stay with it for long. "My arms weren't long enough to go down to the seventh position," he explains.

Gillespie was 14 at the time. Nine months later he began borrowing a trumpet from a neighbor, James Harrington. "The guy next door, his father bought him a trumpet. There it was, so I practiced on his."

Although he gave up the slide instrument, trombonists had an influence on his early development. Gillespie sorely felt the loss of his boyhood buddy Bill McNeil, who died as a result of racial violence. "He was a rough player, like J. C. Higginbotham," says Diz.

He also talks of his distant cousins, trombonists Norman and Ralph Powe. (Powe was his mother's maiden name.) Ralph, a lawyer, who played his way through Tuskegee Institute, taught Norman, and he in turn taught Dizzy to read music.

One of "those instruments sticking up around there" also was an early aid to Gillespie's musical education, but it was of a limited nature. "My father had a bass violin," Dizzy (quoted in *Metronome*, March, 1958) explained to a musicians' panel at Music Inn in Lenox, Massachusetts, in the summer of 1956. "Ever since I could remember he had it. My father probably got the bass viol around 1911, or something like that. My mother sold it when I was in school. Well, it was reddish looking.

"It never had over one string on it. We played it in B-flat. I wanted to show my cousin how to play rag, in B-flat, you know. So I would tell him how to tune up the bass. I made a mark on the fret for B-flat; where he could put his finger on this and turn the thing up until it gets to B-flat. So, he played that one string. You know, we played all over South Carolina with that one string."

Even though he couldn't read a note and could play in only one key, at the age of 15 John Gillespie was known as "the best jazz trumpeter in Cheraw."

Dizzy told the panel: "Now there was this boy, one of the guys that had been up North to Philadelphia and Charlotte, North Carolina. His name was Freddie Mathews. Well, he came back to visit his family. Well, his family were piano teachers, music teachers. His mother was a very well-known piano teacher there, and so naturally he could read. He was up there playing orchestrations and things. So when he came back, he wanted to meet the trumpet player, this young boy, the trumpet player. So I take this school horn and go out to meet him. He got on this new

song . . . you know, *Nagasaki*. I said I don't know it, but I'll try
it. He sat down at the piano and started off in C. I couldn't find
one note for *Nagasaki*. I was so embarrassed because I was supposed to be a trumpet player. I said, oh, oh, I got to learn it. But
I never knew there was any key except B-flat."

Gillespie's education continued because of his musical talent.
He received a scholarship to Laurinburg Institute, a Negro indus-
trial school in North Carolina. He took up theory and harmony,
as well as "farming for a couple of years—vocational agriculture.
A lot of my classmates are big farmers down there."

When he was 17, Gillespie got the first trumpet he could really
call his own. His family had moved to Philadelphia, but he
waited until the end of the school year to join them. (He didn't
get his degree, however, until 1947, when he played at Laurinburg with Ella Fitzgerald and was given his diploma and football letter in a special ceremony.) It was then his brother-in-law
bought him a horn from a pawnshop. Dizzy entertained the idea
of attending Temple University, but, he explains, "I got a job as
soon as I got there, and I've been working ever since."

The job was with a local band whose arrangements gave the
young trumpeter trouble. "I could read manuscript—printed
music," said Gillespie. "Then I got in this band, and they had
special arrangements that were written in pencil. Couldn't see it.
I was reading the tail on the eighth notes. They thought I
couldn't read. Bill Doggett was the bandleader–musical director.
The whole band quit over some stolen money. Then I went
with Frank Fairfax."

The trumpet section of the Fairfax band included Charlie
Shavers, Carl "Bama" Warwick (later to work in Gillespie's
orchestra), and Jimmy Hamilton (destined to become a fixture in
the Duke Ellington saxophone section). "I used to call him Joe
Trump," says Gillespie of Hamilton. "I *still* call him Joe Trump.
He was practicing clarinet all the time."

In those days, Dizzy was a disciple of Roy Eldridge and played
Little Jazz's style to the hilt. The broadcasts made from New
York's Savoy Ballroom by Teddy Hill's band, featuring Eldridge
and tenor saxophonist Chu Berry, had an impact on Gillespie.
"We used to listen to the lady's radio next door—'Saturday Session
at the Savoy,' " he said. "I wanted to play with that band, and then
I came to New York and got right with the band."

Gillespie actually came to New York for a prospective job with Lucky Millinder's orchestra. When it didn't materialize, an opening with Hill did.

Hill told Leonard Feather how this came about: "First time I heard Dizzy was in Philadelphia. At that time I had Roy Eldridge and Chu Berry in my band. Then Roy and Chu left to join Fletcher Henderson in Chicago. Dizzy had come to New York in the meanwhile, and along with a lot of other trumpet men he spoke to me about getting Roy's chair. I asked him to come to the next rehearsal.

"I called the brass section for rehearsal a couple of hours before the reeds. I'd been using Bill Dillard on first trumpet, Shad Collins on second and Roy on third. I switched Shad to third and gave Dizzy the second book. He got up on the bandstand with his overcoat on, gloves on and everything. I asked him his name; I'd forgotten it.

" 'John Gillespie.'

" 'Oh, sure, the same John Gillespie I met in Philly.' "

Feather went on to report: "Dizzy stayed up there with his overcoat on—in fact he did everything in an unorthodox fashion, says Teddy. Embarking on a new arrangement he was as likely as not to start reading an interlude or the last chorus instead of taking it from the top. 'Boy,' said Teddy, 'you're really dizzy.' 'Yes,' said John cheerfully, 'that's right.' 'Think I'm going to call you Dizzy,' mused Teddy; and that's the way it's been."

(In a 1957 "Cross Section" feature, Dizzy himself told *Down Beat*'s Don Gold: "The guys started calling me that in '35 in Philly, as indicative of my impetuous youth.")

His antics with the Hill band served to make the nickname a permanent one. He was observed dancing in the middle of someone else's turn in a stage show or putting on his metal trumpet derby and facing the backdrop instead of the audience. "If Dizzy put his foot up on a chair and was reprimanded, he'd remove the foot and place it on a music stand," Feather wrote. "If Teddy again complained, he'd say, 'But you told me not to put my foot on the *chair*.' "

Gillespie once described his father as a "real man" who, when he talked, "roared," and added, "I got a beating every Sunday morning." By way of explanation, he continued: "At school I was smart, but I didn't study much. I'd fight every day. Ev-er-y day I'd fight. I was *al*-ways bad, you know."

The naughty boy seemed to persist as a part of the Gillespie personality. Some people enjoyed Diz's humor; others were exasperated. "Some of the fellows resented Dizzy," Teddy Hill told Feather. "When the possibility of a European tour came up, there was talk of getting a man with more of a reputation. Some of the men even threatened to leave if Dizzy was kept in the band. I thought Diz had possibilities, so I called their bluff and told them to go ahead and leave. They stayed."

So did Dizzy. He was an unobtrusive member of the Hill band as it provided background music for the acts of a Cotton Club show that played at London's Palladium and in Paris during the summer of 1937. "Nobody paid me no mind," he said. "I was just having a good time." His good time consisted of sitting in with the small group at an after-hours jazz club called The Nest and beginning his collection of international headgear with a British regimental busby.

When the band returned to the United States, Gillespie applied for membership in New York's Local 802. While waiting for his transfer time to expire, Diz worked weekends, including one job with a bassist who doubled on musical saw.

"After getting his 802 card, Dizzy rejoined Teddy," wrote Feather. "He was now able to make a steady living, and out of the $45 a week earned at the Savoy by Hill's sidemen, plus a few extras when the band went on one-nighters or theaters, Dizzy managed to save a little and send money to his family in Philly. He even made frequent loans to other men in the band, just to avoid throwing his money away. Dizzy was not the type to use up all his loot on liquor and chicks, despite his other wild characteristics. He was still a kid at heart. Teddy Hill's house was his home away from home, a playground where he could romp with Teddy's little girl, Gwendolyn, telling her that candy wasn't good for her and then eating it all himself."

Dizzy was doing more than playing nursemaid to a six-year-old, however. In May, 1937, during a Hill record date, he played solos on *King Porter Stomp* and *Blue Rhythm Fantasy* that clearly showed the Eldridge influence, especially the one on *King Porter*. This tendency was reinforced by the band's first alto saxophonist, Howard Johnson, who wrote out some of Roy's solos for him to copy. Then Gillespie's individuality began to assert itself. His style didn't change immediately, but he did begin to help initiate ideas for "head" arrangements and would set choruses for the production numbers they used for theater stage shows. One of these, according to Feather, was "entitled *The Dizzy Crawl* . . . used for background music by the dancing line at the Apollo. Diz never bothered to copyright it; later it acquired some momentum in the Count Basie band under the title *Rock-a-Bye-Basie*, the composer credit going to Basie, Lester Young and Shad Collins, the trumpet player who had been Gillespie's neighbor in the Teddy Hill brass section."

Later neighbors in Hill's trumpet section were Al Killian and Joe Guy. By this time (1939–1940), Dizzy was playing first trumpet and helping the new men with their reading. In this period, he played with the band in a facsimile of the Savoy Ballroom set up at the New York World's Fair. He also worked with pianist Edgar Hayes and met drummer Kenny Clarke, who was also to play with him in Hill's band. "I used to shuffle between Edgar Hayes and Teddy Hill, backwards and forwards," said Diz. "When one had a job, I'd play with him.

"When I was with Hayes," he continued, "Rudy Powell made an arrangement on some tune there that was very fascinating.

"I could always play the piano, see," he digressed by way of explanation, "so that was an advantage, because you get things from the piano. You can't get them from the trumpet or any one-note instrument.

"It was something in this arrangement that almost changed my whole playing around. It was like when you go from C-sharp to C . . . of course, Roy had been doing a couple of things like that, but this was really—it had a melody. Just one bar, maybe two bars or something in this arrangement. I used to *like* when we'd get to that arrangement, and I started playing that same thing in other things—you know, putting it in different places and it evolved around it." The "it" that evolved was the incipient Gillespie style, which, although it still contained strong attachments to Eldridge, began to take on characteristics that were soon to be identified as unmistakably Diz.

In September, 1939, Gillespie was in fast company on a Lionel Hampton date for Victor: Benny Carter on alto; Coleman Hawkins, Ben Webster, and Chu Berry on tenors. His opening muted solo on *Hot Mallets* showed, according to Leonard Feather, "a definite trend away from the Eldridge style and a slight hint of the typical Gillespian cascades of eighth notes that eventually marked his work."

In 1940, Hill, unable to work at the Savoy because of a disagreement with the booking office over the scale at the World's Fair Savoy, dissolved his band. It did not bring to an end, however, the relationship of Teddy and Dizzy. Henry Minton, an ex-saxophonist, reconverted a run-down dining room in the Hotel Cecil on West 118th Street, reopened it as a jazz club known as Minton's Playhouse, and eventually brought in Hill to manage it. (It is still a jazz room—called simply the Playhouse, but often referred to as Minton's. Henry Minton has passed from the scene, but Teddy Hill is still the manager.) Kenny Clarke has described its development as a focal point as rather swift. In late 1940 it had been a quiet, nondescript gathering place for Minton's old friends. (Minton had been the first delegate from Harlem to Local 802.) For a while, the music consisted of a little band in the back room led by tenor saxophonist Happy Cauldwell. Then Hill became the manager in 1941 and hired Clarke, the same man he had fired from his own band, several years earlier, for playing too modern.

With Hill and Clarke in attendance, the character of the music changed. Teddy provided an outlet for the new music at a time when jazz jobs in general were not too plentiful. According to Clarke, Hill never tried to influence the musicians as to what to play, and this helped them to go in their own direction.

Clarke's band included Joe Guy, Thelonious Monk, and bassist Nick Fenton. This was the basic unit at the after-hours sessions at Minton's. When their regular gigs were over, men like Don Byas, Georgie Auld, Ben Webster, Hot Lips Page, Earl Hines, Lester Young, and Jimmy Blanton would come in to jam. Occasionally Benny Goodman would drop in. Charlie Christian was such a regular after-hours jammer there that he left a spare amplifier at the club so that he could just come by and plug in. Gillespie was another frequent sitter-in.

Bassist Milt Hinton, who was Dizzy's band mate in the Cab Calloway orchestra, an organization that Gillespie joined in late 1939 and stayed with until 1941, has said of the 1939 to 1943 period: "Dizzy was everywhere at the time. He was a mischievous guy, and he was also trying so hard to accomplish what he eventually did. Diz at the time was practically ignored by the veteran musicians. Their accent was on good intonation and good tone—this he reached later. He was trying for harmonic evolution, and his tone was very thin and weak. He improved it later. But his ideas were sound, and they got sounder. It was the beginning of modern jazz."

Trumpeter Benny Harris, known then as Little Benny, met Dizzy when the latter first came to New York in 1937 and promptly fell under his influence. Gillespie was instrumental in getting him a job in Tiny Bradshaw's band. Harris told Richard Hadlock that "Dizzy had gotten away from Roy Eldridge's influence pretty well but he had some trouble with his chops. Mario Bauza, Cab's lead man and a fine all-around musician, was a big influence on Dizzy at that time. Mario showed him how to blow correctly. And Dizzy got some of his first feeling for Afro-Cuban music through Bauza too." Bauza was the man responsible for bringing Gillespie into the Calloway band.

A home recording made by Jerry Newman at Minton's in May of 1941 and issued on an Esoteric LP in the fifties offers Gillespie solos on two versions of *Star Dust* and on a number called *Kerouac,* based on *Exactly Like You*. These tracks are good examples of the "harmonic evolution" Hinton mentioned. The Eldridge influence is still present, but the personal Gillespie nuances that were soon to be widely imitated are in evidence too.

Dizzy has always had a great enthusiasm for jamming. "In 1937, when I first came to New York," he told me, "Charlie Shavers, Little Benny, Bobby Moore, and Bama, we used to go around and play at seven, eight, nine different places. We'd wait for the union man to come, and when he'd cut out we'd play. We used to gang up on Red Allen and the older trumpet players— play eight bars apiece. All of us used to sound alike—like Roy Eldridge—anyway."

Gillespie decries the lack of communication through jamming among today's young musicians. "They don't get the experience that they got when I was coming up—like the experience of big bands and going around jamming with all these different guys. If a guy comes up today and says he wants to sit in with you, the cats look at him. And that used to be a common thing. Chick

Webb used to let me sit in his band in Taft Jordan's place, and the [Savoy] Sultans used to let me sit in. I was the only guy they'd let sit in, though.

"That was the swingingest band I ever heard in my life, let me tell you. They'd swing so much, they'd stomp the Savoy down. The beams broke in the Savoy one time, coming through the poolroom downstairs.

"I used to be the extra trumpet player that played the Apollo Theatre with them—1937 and 1938. I was with Teddy Hill at the time, and we were playing the Savoy the same time they were. Boy, them cats sure could swing. Rudy . . ." He paused as he reflected about Rudy Williams, the Sultans' teenage alto saxophonist, who in the early fifties played tenor with the Gillespie small group. "And then Charlie Parker came to New York and ruined Rudy," he added, referring to the stylistic havoc Bird wrought. "He had a nice style going—Rudy—for him. Very rough. Now both of 'em are dead."

Kenny Clarke has talked of the afternoon get-togethers in which he, Gillespie, Monk, and Guy would work out different chord progressions for the purpose of freezing out undesirable sitters-in at night. Dizzy has corroborated this, telling how he and Monk would invent chordal variations to keep away the "no-talent guys," although he admits that eventually they became more involved with their musical experiment for its own sake.

Gillespie remembers that in this period Monk was already playing the song that he eventually recorded for Prestige in the early fifties as *Bye-ya;* Thelonious also had collaborated with Clarke to produce *Epistrophy.* "Monk reminds me of Billy Strayhorn," Diz says. "They do the unexpected. Where everybody else goes this way, they go in the opposite direction."

While granting Monk his personal harmonic conception, Clarke feels that Gillespie was the most advanced member of Minton's inner circle, pointing out that Gillespie was the first musician he heard play *How High the Moon* in other than its original ballad tempo. That was 1941. Of course, the up-tempo *How High the Moon* later became the anthem of Fifty-second Street.

At the time that Minton's became important as an incubator of the new music, Gillespie was with Calloway. Within the band, he found another workshop. Bassist Milt Hinton, who remembers how angry Calloway would get when Dizzy would get ad-

venturous and end up missing a high note, used to accompany
Gillespie in off-the-bandstand "woodshedding" sessions. Some of
these took place on the roof of the Cotton Club, between the
rigorous two-and-a-half-hour shows that the band had to do. Hinton would "walk" for Gillespie as the latter tried out different
chords and progressions. Guitarist Danny Barker occasionally
participated in the events at the open-air laboratory and was
ready whenever Milt and Dizzy incorporated their findings into
their Calloway performances. Gillespie would solo, Hinton sup-
porting him harmonically. When Diz's work went against the
grain of the arrangement, Hinton would direct a look at Barker,
who would help to make it blend. Although he personally found
them fascinating, Barker says that Gillespie's departures annoyed Cab and several members of the band.

This activity caused Cab to tell Dizzy, "I don't want you playing that Chinese music in my band." But Calloway did give
Gillespie solos on quite a few numbers, including *A Bee Gezindt,
Calling All Bars, Hard Times, Bye-Bye Blues, Chop-Chop Charlie
Chan, Boo-Wah, Boo-Wah,* and *Cupid's Nightmare.* There was
also *Pickin' the Cabbage,* composed and arranged by Gillespie.
"A minor key tune in the two-bar riff tradition of the swing era, it
nevertheless went far enough within this stale pattern to acquire
a personal tone-color and a fine sense of dramatic construction,"
Leonard Feather wrote of it in *Inside Jazz.*

In the June 1, 1940, issue of *Down Beat,* the magazine's record
reviewer of that time, one Barrelhouse Dan, wrote, in comparing
Pickin' the Cabbage with its flip side, that it was "better, with
Dizzy Gillespie's trumpet taking the go parts. The theme is weird
and at times smacks of the Duke."

Although at times Dizzy's antics exasperated Calloway, Cab
did appreciate him enough to feature his playing and record his
arrangements. However, Cab's tolerance came to an end in September, 1941, at the State Theatre in Hartford, Connecticut.
During a stage show, Calloway thought Gillespie had thrown a
spitball at him. When the band came offstage, an argument and a
scuffle between the two men followed. When it was all over, Cab
had to have ten stitches taken on his posterior. The headline in
Down Beat read: "Cab Calloway 'Carved' By Own Trumpet
Man." The article that followed stated: "Men in the band claim
that a paper plane used by members of the band in the act struck

Cab and this is what enraged him." Hinton tells it differently. He explains that after he took a solo, he would look to Dizzy for a critical appraisal. When it was positive, it would be indicated by a nod of the head; when negative, by the age-old gesture of fingers pinching nostrils shut. In this particular stage show, Hinton was soloing in the spotlight with the Cab-Jivers, a small unit within the band. He looked back over his shoulder for Dizzy's opinion. It was negative. As Gillespie put his fingers to his nose, Jonah Jones threw a spitball, which landed in the spotlight. Calloway, in the wings, saw it. When the curtain came down, Cab began to berate Dizzy. Calloway had seen Gillespie's arm move but hadn't seen Jones throw the spitball and thought Dizzy had done it. Although Gillespie, being blamelesss, was resentful, he wouldn't reveal Jones, and Jonah had already left the theater. In the argument that followed, Cab swiped at Dizzy, and Dizzy retaliated with a knife. Hinton grabbed Gillespie's hand, but Diz was more powerful. Before they could be separated, Calloway sustained a cut. He didn't realize this until he returned to his dressing room and saw blood. Then he confronted Gillespie and gave him immediate notice.

On the heels of this sudden notoriety, Gillespie worked with Ella Fitzgerald's band (Ella had taken over Chick Webb's outfit after Webb died) for a few weeks. Then he joined Benny Carter's six-piece band on Fifty-second Street, and in November of 1941 he played a concert with Carter at the Museum of Modern Art. During the holiday season, Gillespie left Carter to go on the road with Charlie Barnet for a few weeks, but he returned to Carter for a couple of months at the Famous Door and Kelly's Stables before the combo disbanded in February of 1942. At this time, he was also involved in the sessions that Harry Lim was running at the Village Vanguard.

Gillespie's next stop was the band of Les Hite, whose California organization Louis Armstrong had fronted and recorded with in the early thirties. This edition was, to quote Leonard Feather, a "hazardous Eastern venture with the help of a wealthy backer who was running the band as a somewhat unprofitable hobby. Walter (Gil) Fuller was writing for the band and there was some music. The leader and most of the sidemen regarded Diz with a mixture of amusement, irritation and respect. That the respect was justified can be heard clearly in Dizzy's half-chorus on *Jersey*

Bounce . . . probably the first example of pure bebop on record. By now Dizzy's style was clearly formed, his tone excellent and his ideas faster-flowing than ever."

After leaving Hite, Gillespie did some work with Lucky Millinder, including one record date; then he took a job with pianist Calvin Jackson. Michael James has described his two 12-bar choruses on *Little John Special* with Millinder as "extrovert, well-organized, and exciting"; they "emphasize the rapid strides he was making: the last four bars are exceptionally impressive for his technical mastery."

Generally speaking, however, not too much was happening for him. So he went back to Philadelphia and headed his own group at Nat Segall's Down Beat Club, with Johnny Acea, piano; Oscar Smith, bass; and Stan Levey, drums. It was during this period that Monte Kay was running Sunday-afternoon sessions at Kelly's Stables. "After the third month, the bop people started coming in," says Kay. "Bird started sitting in. Dizzy came to lots of them. He used to come from Philly and pay six dollars' fare to make a ten-dollar job. But he wanted to be seen there."

Dizzy remembers meeting Bird while playing at a hotel in Kansas City. Parker was then with McShann. Although their paths crossed at the Harlem sessions, it wasn't until early 1943 that they were together in a band, that of Earl Hines. Gillespie was a member of a trumpet section that included Benny Harris, Gail Brockman, and Shorty McConnell. All three eventually recorded as soloists in small-band contexts in the late forties with prominent tenor men: Harris with Don Byas, Brockman with Gene Ammons, McConnell with Lester Young.

Trombonist Bennie Green, who had joined the band in 1942, by his own admission wasn't playing too much jazz at the time. When Gillespie joined, Green began to listen closely to Diz from his seat right in front of him. Many of the men in the band who couldn't understand Dizzy's conceptions nevertheless admired his technical proficiency. Green was one of these, but he also liked what he had not yet fathomed.

Dizzy took him to his house and showed him, on the piano, alternate chords and various other techniques and ideas. "It was like going to school," Green has said. "I remember starting to ad lib around an eight-bar thing he'd written up. It opened up a new era for me. Then I started practicing things he'd tell me, and before I knew it, I was ad libbing more and more."

One of Green's features in the Hines band was to carry the melody statement of an exotic, minor-key composition and arrangement Gillespie had written a couple of years earlier. Titled *A Night in Tunisia* by Earl, it became a jazz classic, one of the most recorded of jazz "originals."

"There was a lot of freedom in the band," Benny Harris has said. "Earl never came to rehearsals, and Scoops Carry, who rehearsed the band, was sympathetic to what we were trying to do. Earl played wonderful piano, but I'm not sure he knew what was going on."

In September, 1943, Gillespie left Hines and came to New York to play with Coleman Hawkins. In October, he took Shorty Baker's place (Shorty didn't have a Local 802 card) in Duke Ellington's brass section for an engagement at the Capitol Theatre. His only solo work in the three weeks he spent with the band was limited to backgrounds for dancers. Musicians in the band have said that the Ellington-Gillespie combination was not the most compatible at the time. As the years passed, however, Ellington and Gillespie developed a mutual-admiration society that resulted in Diz's recording with Duke in 1959 and then doing a tribute to him, backed by clarinets and French horns, in 1961. The first-mentioned work is a guest appearance in *Ellington Jazz Party,* wherein Dizzy solos on the blues *Hello Little Girl* and is featured on Billy Strayhorn's *U.M.M.G.* Expanding on his feeling about Strayhorn's doing the unexpected, Dizzy said, "Like when I made that record with Duke—the way he jumped into that A-flat minor-seventh bar, jumped out of a clear blue sky. I wasn't down there to make the record date. I just stopped by, and he pulled that out of the book."

When Gillespie recorded his *Portrait of Duke Ellington* for Verve, with arrangements by Clare Fischer, he included *U.M.M.G.* and two other Strayhorn pieces, *Johnny Come Lately* and *Chelsea Bridge.*

In 1944, The Street, as Fifty-second Street was affectionately known, began to become the center of the modern movement. The block between Fifth and Sixth Avenues was the home of the Three Deuces, the Downbeat, the Famous Door, the Spotlite, Kelly's Stables, the Yacht Club, and the Onyx; between Sixth and Seventh there stood the Hickory House and the Club 18, which later became the Troubador. From the end of Prohibition to the late forties, The Street flourished, but during the middle years of the forties—the war and immediate postwar years—it reached its peak. The April, 1948, *Metronome* carried an article by Leonard Feather entitled "The Street Is Dead." As reasons for The Street's demise as a jazz center, Feather cited the high cost of living; lack of talent with sufficient drawing power; the high price put on the drawing cards by their managers and agents; the clip-joint tactics; and the bad reputation brought about by the presence of dope peddlers, dope addicts, pimps, and prostitutes. These conditions existed, but they continued after the Downbeat and other clubs became strip joints and the Troubador was converted into a Chinese restaurant. (Some wag wrote: "Fifty-second Street is being strangled by a G-string dipped in chop suey.")

Jazz on The Street did not die until the Fifties, when many properties were razed and large office buildings were constructed in their place. (Jimmy Ryan's, the lone Dixieland outpost, held out until 1962.) But jazz was a rarity after 1948. The Three Deuces lasted longer than most, and early in 1950 there was a last gasp for the modern when Miles Davis, Bud Powell, Wardell Gray, and Sonny Stitt played briefly at the Orchid, a new name for the Onyx. What happened was that the scene had moved to Broadway, to clubs like the Royal Roost. In the forties, jazz was dying on The Street, but the audience for the music labeled bebop was growing, and people were ready to fill larger clubs that had a policy of an admission price for a "listening section," where one was not forced to drink. In its heyday, the Roost, dubbed the Metropolitan Bopera House, had crowds waiting outside in subfreezing temperatures.

In late 1943, however, The Street was ready to serve as the downtown incubator for bop. Oscar Pettiford gave this account to Robert Reisner: "Dizzy Gillespie and I went looking up and down 52nd Street for work in 1943. We turned down $75 a week apiece offered by Kelly's Stables. I had worked at the Onyx club before, and I was good friends with the owner, Mike Westerman, so I asked if I could be re-engaged. I was welcomed back gladly. I said, 'Make it a Diz group.' And Diz said, 'Make it your group because you got the job.' So we made it the Gillespie-Pettiford group. We wanted Bird to come in the group, but he didn't have a union card."

The band was "originally four pieces," says Gillespie, "just one horn and three rhythm. . . . Don Byas came in the club to work

as a single. When we'd rehearse, he'd be there too. So he just
went right in. He wanted to play with us."

With his regular job, Dizzy still found time for jamming.
Trumpeter Jerry Lloyd (then Jerry Hurwitz), one of the first
white musicians around New York to pick up on Dizzy, recalls
nights of meeting him after the job ended at 4 A.M., waiting until
studios like Nola's opened at 9 or 10 A.M., and blowing all day.

Lloyd, who had lung trouble from an early age, recorded with
George Wallington and Brew Moore in the late forties and with
Zoot Sims in the fifties, but for the most part he has not earned
his living from music. Wallington was the pianist with the
Gillespie-Pettiford band, which received a mention in the February 1, 1944, *Down Beat*. They did no recording while they were
together, but a year later Gillespie, Byas, and Pettiford, along
with trombonist Trummy Young, pianist Clyde Hart, and drummer Irv Kluger (Shelly Manne was credited, incorrectly, on the
label), did *Good Bait, I Can't Get Started, Salted Peanuts* (the
same as *Salt Peanuts*), and *Be-Bop* for Manor.

I Can't Get Started was especially startling to some people; it
drew inevitable comparisons with a trumpet version of the song
that was one of the most popular in jazz—Bunny Berigan's. To
others, it was a perfect introduction to Gillespie's music—they
were able to hear what he was doing within a framework familiar
to them. Dizzy has talked about the coda he did on *Started*, relating it to the influence his contributions to jazz have had: "First I
did it on the end of *I Can't Get Started*, and then I made that for
the introduction on *'Round Midnight*, same thing. I've been doing
it in and out of arrangements. And I notice that this thing, it
comes through to me from a-a-a-all this music. One guy down in
South America wrote a who-o-ole symphony off that one phrase.
All the guys that play *'Round Midnight*, they use my introduction, and they use my ending."

Although the Gillespie-Pettiford group did not record while on
Fifty-second Street, Dizzy, Oscar, Don Byas, and Max Roach
took part in a date for Apollo Records on February 16, 1944,
headed by their "neighbor" Coleman Hawkins. Generally recognized as the first bop record session, it included Vic Coulsen and
Ed Vandeveer, trumpets; Leonard Lowry and Leo Parker, alto
saxophones; Byas or Ray Abramson, tenor saxophones; Budd
Johnson, baritone saxophone; and Clyde Hart, piano. Three num-

bers are strictly ballad vehicles for Hawkins (inspired performances, I might add); the others are a blues called *Disorder at the
Border*, Budd Johnson's *Bu-Dee-Daht*, and Gillespie's *Woody'n
You*. Dizzy had originally written the latter for Woody Herman,
whose band played it behind dancers but never recorded it.
Gillespie's solo is soaring, harmonically intricate, and contains
many of his characteristic pyrotechnics.

After leaving the Onyx (Pettiford stayed on with his own
group), Dizzy took Budd Johnson and Max Roach across the street
with him to the Yacht Club for a brief engagement, then became
a part of the John Kirby sextet at the Aquarium Restaurant on
Seventh Avenue. As the story goes, Kirby was not completely
convinced of Diz's reliability and had Charlie Shavers come in
whenever the band did a broadcast. It was at this time that Billy
Eckstine was putting together his big band and began tapping
the talent he had come to know so well in the Hines band. He
wanted Gillespie to serve as musical director as well as' play
trumpet. This he did, even filling in occasionally on piano and
drums when a sideman was missing for a particular performance.
The band, which played its first public engagement in June, 1944,
was reviewed in *Down Beat* by Johnny Sippel when they played
Chicago in August. "The handsome 'sepia Sinatra,'" wrote Sippel,
"is proving a versatile front man . . . not far behind the leader is
ever-mugging Dizzy Gillespie. Record collectors have long
watched for the ex-Calloway trumpeter's advanced ideas of improvisation."

Record collectors soon had some new examples of Gillespie's
improvisational skill when Deluxe began to issue records of the
Eckstine band. The introduction and coda used by Gillespie and
Parker on their February, 1945, *All the Things You Are* made
their first appearance on record as the intro to *Good Jelly Blues*.
Gillespie, who undoubtedly was responsible for this, does not
solo, but on a second Eckstine vocal from this April, 1944, session,
I Stay in the Mood for You, he comes through in what was soon
to become one of the most widely imitated styles in jazz. A December date for the same company produced *Opus X*—credited
to the band's pianist, John Malachi, but really an updating of
Lunceford Special—which features altoist John Jackson but contains some telling licks by Dizzy; and the exciting tenor battle between Gene Ammons and Dexter Gordon on *Blowin' the Blues*

Away, which is climaxed by Gillespie's horn screaming above the ensemble.

The Eckstine band continued into 1947 before the singer-leader decided to go out again as a single. (He had done so without too much success in the period between leaving Hines and forming his band, but this time he was ready. He and Sarah Vaughan both became big jukebox favorites in the late forties.) Gillespie, however, had left long before. The February 15, 1945, *Down Beat* (published in January) reported him, Benny Harris, Trummy Young, and Johnny Bothwell in Boyd Raeburn's band at the Apollo Theatre. Now based in New York, Dizzy began to record often, both as sideman and leader.

In January, he was featured with Raeburn's band on *March of the Boyds* and the first recording of his *A Night in Tunisia.* (The latter was called *Interlude,* with *A Night in Tunisia* as the subtitle.) On February 7, he soloed on *In the Middle,* along with Georgie Auld and Erroll Garner, in an Auld-led all-star band, and in March, with Auld's regular band, he was featured on *Co-Pilot,* a Vanig Hovsepian (a guitarist also known as Turk Van Lake) arrangement of a minor-key theme. Throughout these solos, Diz contrasts subtlety with bravado; intricate figures, piquant, gracenoted phrases, and explosively fast runs are artfully blended into entities that then were delightfully startling to some, jarring to others, but now can be savored as lasting statements of high musical value. The two-note phrases that seem to say "be-bop" crop up from time to time.

Although his range was very good at the time, Gillespie's "chops" weren't always a match for the challenging places that his fertile, highly adventurous mind would take them. The "mistakes" noted by his severe critics were actually part of a new musical language, but Dizzy was even then such a resourceful soloist that he was able to convert a seeming "clam" into a highly useful part of an idea pattern. He does this very convincingly at the end of *My Melancholy Baby,* made with a most incongruous group of musicians under clarinetist Joe Marsala's name for Black & White in January, 1945. (The quintet, which included modern guitarist Chuck Wayne and stride pianist Cliff Jackson, also recorded *Cherokee.*)

In February, two days after the first Auld date, Dizzy did his first recording as a leader. The *Groovin' High* he did with Dexter

Gordon and Chuck Wayne was never issued, but another of his lines, *Blue 'N Boogie,* was the other side of the *Groovin' High* he made with Parker at the end of the month. This session also included the *All the Things You Are* mentioned earlier and *Dizzy Atmosphere,* which contains a marvelous written variation on its theme, stated in unison by Bird and Diz, that melds deftly back into the original line to close the piece. Like *Blue 'N Boogie* and the May, 1945, sides *Shaw 'Nuff, Hot House, Salt Peanuts,* and *Lover Man,* all were cut for Guild. (Many were issued and reissued on the Musicraft label, which took over the Guild masters, and on a variety of LP's, including Allegro, Vernon, and Savoy. *Groovin' High,* a Savoy LP, includes all the titles except *Shaw 'Nuff* and *Lover Man.*)

In 1945 Gillespie also appeared as a sideman behind singers Albinia Jones, Rubberlegs Williams, Trummy Young, and Sarah Vaughan. The last three dates included Charlie Parker, as did a June session with the Red Norvo all-stars. Before all these records were actually issued, Gillespie and Parker appeared at the Three Deuces in May and were the featured attractions at Town Hall concerts in May and June.

Dizzy was beginning to achieve a degree of popularity through his combination of personality and talent. His name was cropping up with greater frequency every day in music circles. It was then that his manager, Billy Shaw, decided it was time to put him at the helm of a big band. With people like trumpeter Kenny (then Kinny) Dorham, tenor man Charlie Rouse, and Max Roach, the band set out on a tour of the South as part of a unit called the Hepsations of 1945. Others in the package included the Nicholas Brothers, comedians Patterson and Jackson, and vocalist June Eckstine (Mrs. Billy Eckstine). The problems confronting a Negro band touring below the Mason-Dixon line soon effected a turnover of the original personnel of the band. Then the promoters told Dizzy that people couldn't dance to his music, and the trumpeter had to lock his best arrangements in the trunk. Leonard Feather reported that at first "Dizzy was not yet experienced enough, either, to be successful fronting a big band. Always light-hearted and at ease in earlier jobs, he seemed to tighten up with the responsibility now confronting him. He would take stiff, awkward bows and generally showed no signs of the comic, personable Dizzy of the past."

At the end of 1945, Gillespie was in California with Parker and the group that played Billy Berg's. Before the unhappy sojourn on the Coast ended, Gillespie had recorded several sessions. The one for Dial included the Bird-less *Diggin' for Diz, 'Round Midnight, When I Grow Too Old To* (some of the Gillespie humor in both title and vocal rendition), a new version of *Dizzy Atmosphere* (issued in two takes as *Dynamo A* and *Dynamo B*), and Parker's *Confirmation.*

He and Bird also recorded for a small Coast label, Beltone, with their co-attraction at Berg's, Slim Gaillard. These sides— *Slim's Jam, Popity Pop, Flat Foot Floogie,* and *Dizzy Boogie*— are now available on a Parker memorial album on Savoy.

A recording in Hollywood of a Jerome Kern memorial album, featuring the trumpeter backed by strings for the Paramount label (no connection with today's ABC-Paramount), was never released because the controlling powers of the Kern estate felt that Dizzy had strayed too far from the way the composer had written the songs. However, Gillespie did appear in person and on record with Jazz at the Philharmonic for Norman Granz at the end of January, 1946 (*Crazy Rhythm, Sweet Georgia Brown, The Man I Love*). This impresario had been quoted in *Down Beat* some six months earlier as saying: "Jazz in New York stinks. Even the drummers on 52nd Street sound like Dizzy Gillespie."

Back in the friendlier environment of Fifty-second Street, Gillespie opened with Milt Jackson, Al Haig, Ray Brown, and Stan Levey at the Spotlite in March of 1946. In place of Charlie Parker was baritone saxophonist Leo Parker. This group never recorded intact. At the end of February, Diz had recorded for Victor's *New 52nd Street Jazz* album (*Anthropology, A Night in Tunisia, 52nd Street Theme, Ol' Man Rebop*) with Don Byas, guitarist Bill De Arango, drummer J. C. Heard, and his own men —Jackson, Haig, and Brown. In May, for Musicraft, with De Arango out and Sonny Stitt and Kenny Clarke replacing Byas and Heard, they cut *Oop Bop Sh'Bam, That's Earl, Brother, One Bass Hit,* and *A Hand Fulla Gimme,* the latter a vocal by Alice Roberts. These eight sides contain superlative Gillespie. His tone is fuller and fatter, his intricate melodic journeys more assured.

It was at this point in his career that Dizzy turned again to an orchestral format. Although the band did not receive overwhelming acceptance at first, the audience was there this time, and it continued to grow. Unlike the Hepsations orchestra, this one was represented by records. And Dizzy became a public figure. Magazine articles in national publications, although full of inaccuracies and often snidely slanted, pointed up this arrival.

Although Parker was acclaimed by the inner circle as the key figure of the era, Gillespie was the man the people thought of immediately when the word "bop" was mentioned. He was the clown, with his beret (he had wanted headgear that he could stuff in his pocket without crumpling it beyond reuse), goatee (he didn't care to risk shaving close to his lips), and an occasional leopard-skin jacket. The heavy horn-rimmed glasses he wore became known as "bop glasses," the floppy polka-dot bow ties became familiar as "bop bow ties." Berets became *de rigueur;* with peaks added, they became "bop caps." "Bop glasses," or simply "bops," were affected by many, often with tinted "windowpane" lenses. (I remember buying a pair of sunglasses in St. Louis that featured the heavy black frames. An acquaintance there told me, "Those shades are cool, but why don't you get a pair of bops to hide behind for the nighttime?")

Goatees were sprouting among many musicians, especially trumpeters. Shorty Rogers described his sparse growth with, "Mine shouldn't happen to Hitler." Some fans who couldn't even raise hair one were pasting on false beards. To many, the beret, glasses, and goatee were badges to identify the wearer as one completely dedicated to Gillespie, the musician and the person. When his picture was taken with several buttons at the bottom of his sport shirt undone, some of the more extreme followers began wearing theirs in this manner. It is a wonder that they did not ape Gabriel (as Dizzy was billed for contractual reasons) when he appeared on the inside cover of the Dial *Bebop* album with his pants zipper accidentally at half-mast. Singing scat and leading his band with his rump, Diz cut quite a distinctive figure, and the general public was perhaps attracted more by all those accouterments than by his musicianship. Granted that his style is flamboyant, it is also highly musical. Even the seemingly nonsensical syllables he employs in scatting convey the valid rhythmic licks a drummer might play or inventive lines identical to what comes out of his trumpet. For all his showmanship, Dizzy is no joker when it comes down to the music. In 1948, he was quoted in *Down Beat:* "Too many people take this bop rage as a lark.

There's a lot of publicity. . . . But too many kids studying music are letting it blind them. . . . If the kids get so hip they frown on everything that isn't out-and-out bop, we're going to wind up with a sad bunch of musicians 10 years from now. They have to learn all their rudiments."

More than ten years later, he responded to Gene Lees's observation that his humor had cost him respect and money in some areas with: "It's a possibility, all right. Especially among people who are so *serious* about this.

"Now to come into the serious part of this *music,* that's something else. Serious as far as the *music* is concerned. But as far as your actions are concerned, that has nothing to do with your seriousness about jazz. Because I'm extremely serious about the music.

"I don't put music on.

"But a lot of people can't tell the difference. I get a lot of write-ups saying, 'If only he wouldn't do such-and-such a thing, if he wouldn't make people laugh. I read a lot of articles like that, here and in Europe.

"But I think I have a definite commitment to do things and let people feel good, and put them in the right vein to accept the music. There's no B.S. about the music. The music is extremely important."

Gillespie is superb in either a large- or a small-group setting, but he really seems to bloom with a big band behind him, especially when it is his own. Parker gained experience with big bands, as we have seen, but once on his own he gravitated toward the small combo. Gillespie's band experience as a sideman was much more extensive, and when he became a leader it didn't take him a year before he was in front of an orchestra. If he had a choice today, he would direct a group of seventeen or eighteen pieces. "I'd like to have a big band again," he told me in early 1962, "but I don't want to go through that," referring to the economic hazards inherent in such an undertaking today. "If you think about it— where you gonna play if you had one? There's no place to play. Outside of New York, you can forget it. You see, to have a big band, you must have the band together for a long time before you get any kind of identification for it. As you play things, new things come into the arrangements."

Dizzy considers his last band—the one that toured for the State

Department in 1956 and stayed together until 1958—his best. "The last one had something the other ones didn't have. It had— well, the other ones had a lot of enthusiasm, but they were a little rough around the edges. The last one had both," he said, alluding to the spirit and polish that come with two years of togetherness.

Critic Michael James wrote: "The records made by the band do not compare with those made by the orchestra he led in the second half of the Forties insofar as verve, attack and originality of ideas are concerned; yet the section playing, though not quite so fierce, is superior by academic standards."

The second Gillespie band, formed in the spring of 1946, played at the Spotlite and recorded for Musicraft. Thelonious Monk was with it for a short while, and then John Lewis came in on piano to join his former Army buddy Kenny Clarke. It was here, with Milt Jackson, that the seeds for the Modern Jazz Quartet were planted. This band recorded Tadd Dameron's *Our Delight;* another version of *One Bass Hit;* Brown's *Ray's Idea,* a collaboration with Gil Fuller; and the volcanic *Things to Come,* a Gillespie-Fuller brainchild. Ray Abrams was heard on tenor saxophone, and young Dave Burns was a carbon copy of his leader in the trumpet section. Jackson's vibes were not the best set in town, technically speaking, but already he was becoming the new voice on his instrument. He is featured on *Things to Come* and a blues, *Emanon,* which also spotlights James Moody on tenor, as well as soaring Gillespie. The trumpets here and on *One Bass Hit* sound like they are playing Gillespie solo passages orchestrated for the section. Recorded along with *Emanon* was Gillespie's haunting ballad *I Waited for You,* with a vocal by Detroiter Kenny "Pancho" Hagood, an Eckstine-Vaughan disciple who was an important part of the band until he left to work at the Royal Roost with Parker and Dameron in 1948. These two sides were done in November, the others in June and July. (Many of them are in the *Groovin' High* album on Savoy.)

This was a rough band but a fiery one. James has written: ". . . the band's appeal stemmed in the main from its blatant force and seemingly inexhaustible power. This can be attributed only to the temperaments of the sidemen; such is their power of instant involvement that one is persuaded to believe they would have been incapable of a more restrained or modulated performance."

By 1947 the personnel had shifted and solidified. James Moody was the featured tenor soloist, and Cecil Payne was the baritone anchor for the reeds. The band had become more polished. Hagood was doing *Time After Time* and the popular novelty *South America, Take It Away,* the latter prefaced by Gillespie's original solo from *Congo Blues.* But *Things to Come* was still there in all its molten fury, enhanced by superior execution, and new things like Gillespie's *Ow!* were being added. In August, the band appeared at the Downbeat on The Street. Dizzy drank Scotch in milk at the bar during the intermissions while the saxophone quintet practiced informally and uproariously in the upstairs dressing room. Sometimes Moody and Milt Jackson would race to the corner of Sixth Avenue from the club's awning, a half block away, in their own Fifty-second Street Olympics.

In late August, the band recorded the first session under its new affiliation with Victor: *Ow!;* John Lewis' *Two Bass Hit,* featuring Brown (not McKibbon as has sometimes been written); Tadd Dameron's *Stay on It;* and *Oopapada,* a scatting duet between Dizzy and Pancho that exemplifies a combination of humor and valid music.

The highly successful Carnegie Hall concert followed in September, and the band was really on its way. The primitive power of Chano Pozo's conga gave the band a new dimension. It brought into full play the Afro-Cuban influence that had been in Gillespie's mind for a long time. The Havana-born drummer, who spoke very little English, can be heard inspiring the band on the Victor recordings of *Algo Bueno* (a new version of *Woody'n You*), *Manteca,* and George Russell's *Cubana Be, Cubana Bop,* all recorded in December. The latter work was Chano's feature. As one who saw him stalking around the stage of Town Hall in a concert on December 27 (five days after *Cubana Be* was cut), I can attest that he was as effective visually as he was rhythmically.

Named by *Metronome* as Band of the Year, the Gillespie orchestra was launched into 1948 with great momentum. In January, the group sailed across the Atlantic for a tour of Sweden and Denmark. The public reaction was excellent, but the Swedish promoter proved to be crooked. By the time the band got to Belgium, the promoter was behind in his payments and things were getting desperate. Billy Shaw flew to Sweden and found that the man was guilty of forgery and misuse of funds. Due to his mismanagement, dates in Switzerland, Holland, and Czechoslovakia fell through. A London date was canceled when the British Ministry of Labor overrode the British Musicians' Union. Then French jazz critic Charles Delaunay took over the tour, and the Brussels concert was marked by great audience fervor.

Dizzy returned to Paris, eleven years after he had first been there—almost anonymously, with Teddy Hill—and sold out three concerts at the Salle Pleyel. The first of these, on February 22, was recorded and eventually issued on the French Swing label. The band played club and theater dates in Paris, went on to Marseilles and Lyons, then returned to Paris for a final few days at the Ambassadeurs club. Although the French part of the tour was hastily arranged, it was a financial success and enabled the band to return to the United States in March in a comfortable manner.

A highlight of 1948 was an August concert for disc jockey Gene Norman in Los Angeles. Unlike the Salle Pleyel recording, which never was distributed in the States, this affair was eventually released here on Norman's own GNP label. These "live" performances of the band's staple repertoire illustrate the group's tremendous spirit and enthusiasm. Gillespie is in rare form, whether flying high on *Emanon,* with its *Shaw 'Nuff* introduction, or waxing tender on *'Round Midnight* and *I Can't Get Started.* All through the concert, his playing is seemingly effortless—even in the upper register, to which he often ascends.

The featured soloists besides Dizzy are Moody, Payne, and alto saxophonist Ernie Henry. It was Pozo's last recording with the band. In December, a year after joining Gillespie, he was fatally shot at the Rio Café, a Harlem bar, for what was rumored to be negligence in paying a bill. Although Gillespie continued to use the conga as a permanent part of the band, the men who came after Pozo did not have his fire.

During 1949, the material that the band employed was spotty; and when the group shifted from Victor to Capitol, it reached its lowest ebb artistically. Many of the old guard had departed. It was like a giant machine suddenly running down. The hazards of keeping a big band together were becoming greater; in 1950 Count Basie disbanded, and Dizzy followed suit.

Everyone was burying bop. But while the faddish aspects were over, the music continued as a dominant influence through the fifties in various new settings. Many of the older critics, who had been among bop's greatest detractors during the forties, became jazz producers and soon began recording modern musicians extensively. In 1950, however, things were not popping for Gillespie. He recorded with Parker for Norman Granz, and in the fall he followed Parker's lead of a year before by recording with strings for Discovery. From the remnants of his big band, he put together a small unit.

In 1951 he tried another venture. George Hoefer, in his column "The Hot Box," wrote: "No one suffered professionally more than Dizzy Gillespie as a result of the recent fiasco made of modern progressive jazz by the 'Bop for the People' campaign indulged in by the Capitol and RCA record bigwigs. The type of tunes given Diz to record at Capitol were as ridiculous as giving Pee Wee Hunt an assignment to wax *Groovin' High*. . . . Nor did the Dizzy with strings experiment bring forth anything of note musically or, as was true in the case of Bird, a wider listening audience, which all brings us to the current development, the Dee Gee record company."

Dee Gee was Gillespie's joint operation with Detroiter Dave Usher and was based in the Motor City. The two had met when Usher, a student at Admiral Farragut Academy in New Jersey, used to go to hear Gillespie on Fifty-second Street in early 1946. In October of that year, when Dizzy's band was playing at the Paradise Theatre in Detroit, there was a gasoline strike on. Dave, whose family was in the oil business, had cans of gas in his car and saw to it that Dizzy was not in need during his stay. They became friends, and in 1951 Dave, who had had some experience with the short-lived Emanon label in the late forties, decided to take some money he had made driving oil trucks for his father and go in with Diz on Dee Gee. The first sides were *Birks Works*, a medium-tempo, minor-key blues, and *Tin Tin Daeo*, an Afro-Cuban number dedicated to Chano Pozo, who had had a hand in writing it. John Coltrane, who had played alto saxophone in the last Gillespie big band, was on tenor but was not heard in solo. Solo space was left to Milt Jackson, guitarist Kenny Burrell, making his recording debut at 19, and, of course, the leader. Several people commented on how Dizzy was concentrating on the middle register which they found unusual. He also created a delightful, muffled tonal effect by the use of a felt-beanie mute.

During the company's first year, the numbers with Joe Carroll —*Lady Be Good, School Days,* and *Oo-Sho-Be-Do-Be*—were very solid single sellers. Indeed, the latter was in the hit category, and Dee Gee was moving nicely. Then distribution difficulties set in, and the masters were sold to Savoy. A lot of the material can be heard in an LP called *The Champ*—after its exciting title number, on which Diz is in combustible, high-altitude form.

Although their business venture ended prematurely, the two men have continued their friendship. Usher describes Dizzy as a "very warm guy. He gets absorbed in something," says Dave, "and you don't think he's with you, but he refers to it later. He gets on different kicks—wheat germ, food supplements—and he digs collecting things—alligator shoes, chess sets."

Gillespie the collector is well known for his meerschaum pipes and his hats. The chess sets are not merely for show; Diz plays the game with more than passing skill. "Max [Roach] plays a very good game," he was quoted as saying in a *Down Beat* feature in January, 1958. "But after I've read some of the tournament play and pull some of those moves on him, I get him every time."

The combination of the sophisticated city dweller and the un-affected country boy that is Dizzy comes out in Usher's early-sixties musings. "He digs sports, current events—he's concerned with the racial situation. He's really 'down home.' The kids from the neighborhood come in to see him—a natural guy. He doesn't call attention to a lot of the good things he's done."

The neighborhood is Corona, Long Island, where John Birks and his wife, Lorraine, live in a modest frame house; they occupy the main floor and basement, and they rent the two apartments on the upper floors. The basement is Dizzy's lair, for it is here that he has his stereo equipment, motion-picture projector, and piano. It is a playroom that doubles as a workshop where the Gillespie quintet rehearses.

Dizzy and Lorraine celebrated their silver wedding anniversary on May 9, 1965. They met when he was playing with Teddy Hill at the Howard Theatre in Washington, D.C., and she was dancing in the show. While waiting out his Local 802 card, he courted her by cooking elaborate meals and taking them to the Apollo Theatre, where she was working.

Lorraine is a devout Catholic who, Usher says, "has been a stabilizing influence on him. He listens to her, and she's been responsible for a lot of his moves. She's an aware person but shuns the business when the band travels overseas—but, then, she's with Dizzy, not the band." Dizzy, a Baptist, has shown interest in many religious philosophies.

Leonard Feather once wrote that Lorraine Gillespie's "visits to her husband's places of business are circumscribed by her almost total lack of enthusiasm for the branch of music in which he is engaged," and he recounted that during 1956, on a trip to the summer jazz colony at Music Inn in Lenox, Massachusetts, she remained in her room the whole time, playing records by Andre Kostelanetz and Frank Sinatra.

"There's no decline in his excitement for life," says Usher, "but Diz has calmed down a lot." He fights his tendency to put on weight by telling his tailor to make his pants two inches smaller than his waist measurement.

Usher also mentioned Dizzy's concern for the future. "He wants to be straight," said Dave, referring to finances, "so that he doesn't have to work too hard when he gets older—but he'll play for playing until he's done."

The beret of the forties is no more, and the heavy horn-rims have been replaced by a less ostentatious model, but Gillespie's individualism has been represented by another trademark—the upswept trumpet—since 1954. How it came about is another fascinating piece of Gillespiana, one that reveals that his inventiveness works even in the face of disaster.

At a birthday celebration for Lorraine in 1954 at Snookie's on West Forty-fourth Street, many musicians and entertainers were performing. When Dizzy left to make an appearance on a disc-jockey show, he left his horn on the stand. While he was gone, the comedy-dance team of Stump and Stumpy managed to knock over and bend the instrument in the course of their act. As Dizzy has told it: "So Illinois Jacquet, he left! *Immediately!* He said he don't want to be there when I get back."

Gillespie was mad, but after playing for a bit he started to revel in his newly bent horn. The next day, however, he had it reconstructed to its original shape. After several weeks, he wrote to the Martin company and asked whether it was possible for them to do on purpose what Stump and Stumpy had done by accident.

Dizzy felt that he could hear himself better with his bell at a 45-angle. Only once since then, while waiting for a replacement after someone had stolen his special horn, has he played a conventional model. In 1956 the entire trumpet section of his band was supplied with the tilted bells. Dizzy reasons that when the men are reading, they play toward the floor and the full impact of the sound is lost. On the other hand, he points out that if a full section is playing right at an audience, the sound can be somewhat piercing if it is not diffused.

At the time he first became involved with his special horn, Gillespie wanted to corner the market on skyward sound. He had visions of mass-producing these tilted instruments. His hopes of becoming a trumpet tycoon were quickly squashed when he tried to patent his idea. Someone had beaten him to the punch by 150 years.

Through the bop years, Gillespie and his Long Island neighbor Louis Armstrong had a mild feud going. Armstrong recorded *The Boppenpoof Song*—a version of *The Wiffenpoof Song* that put down bop—in retaliation for a Gillespie parody of Louis called *Pop's Confessin'*. But although Armstrong called bop "jujitsu music" and Gillespie in turn often demeaned the abilities of Louis' colleagues, they usually had good things to say about each other's playing. There was talk of a collaboration on LP a few years ago, but the idea was never realized. So far, their only get-togethers have been social.

In a 1947 *Blindfold Test*, Gillespie reacted to Armstrong's solo on *Savoy Blues*, done in 1928, with: "Louis *always* sounds good to me." In the "Afterthoughts" section of the same article, he said: "I like all kinds of music and musicians, all styles of trumpet players. I like Harold Baker, Ray Nance, Taft Jordan, Roy [Eldridge], Shavers, Bobby Hackett, Billy Butterfield, Freddie Webster, Karl George, Leonard Hawkins and lots more. For technique, Rafael Mendez. I like Clark Terry in St. Louis."

In 1962 Dizzy talked to me of trumpeters. "I used to like Dud Bascomb," he said. "Very tasty. Most of these modern trumpet players, a lot of the things they play—like a lot of the things that Clifford Brown . . . the way he phrased notes—Dud Bascomb was doing some of that. 'Bli-bli'—grace notes. He was a terrific trumpet player. We used to talk quite a bit when I was with Teddy Hill and he was with Erskine Hawkins." Bascomb was the featured soloist on Hawkins' Bluebird records of *Hot Platter, Gin Mill Special, Tuxedo Junction* (I've heard Miles Davis quote from this one), and others, for which Erskine was generally credited.

Diz also, in remembering the men with whom he toured the Harlem sessions from 1937 on, recalled Bobby Moore. "Little Bobby—he was the best of the crowd, the best of the younger trumpet players." He added, sadly, "He's in an insane asylum." (The March 1, 1940, *Down Beat* carried the item: ". . . former Count Basie trumpeter Bobby Moore judged insane at Bellevue.")

The forties presented a trial by fire to the musicians who were deeply dedicated to the new music and enmeshed in its theater of operations. The seeds of self-destruction came easily to fruition. Gillespie is one who retained his physical and mental health. The same can be said of J.J. Johnson and Milt Jackson, among the giants who have dominated their instrumental divisions since the end of that decade. There are others who made the journey more or less intact, although they traveled a rockier road. The list of those who died or were left stranded by the wayside—functioning far below their capabilities or in obscurity—is depressingly imposing, particularly among the trumpeters.

Freddie Webster, who was born in Cleveland in 1917, died in Chicago in 1947. He was heard in the orchestras of Lucky Millinder, Earl Hines, Benny Carter, and Jimmie Lunceford in the forties. He recorded some isolated solos with Millinder (*How About That Mess* and *Savoy*) on Decca and with Hines (*Yellow Fire* and *Windy City Jive*) on Bluebird. His own tune called *Reverse the Charges* twice served as a longer solo vehicle for him—with Sonny Boy Williams on Decca and with Frankie Socolow on Duke. He also did *Rubber Bounce* with vocalist Williams.

Perhaps Webster's most widely known work is on Sarah Vaughan's recordings of *You're Not the Kind* and *If You Could See Me Now*. This is gorgeous ballad playing, showing off Webster's wide-vibratoed, singing tone. Dexter Gordon recalls that when Webster was with Lunceford on a theater date, "he played the first few notes of his solo toward the wings" for dramatic effect. Dizzy calls his sound "the best I ever heard" and recounts that Freddie once gave him some mechanical help. "One time I had a Blessing mouthpiece. He took it and cut off the end. Not only that, but he made a bigger hole—the back bore. He pulled my coat to that—the shorter mouthpiece. You get to the note quicker."

Webster did not have a swift, multinote style like Gillespie's, but harmonically and in spirit he was one of the early players in modern jazz. "Freddie was a tremendous trumpet player," Benny Harris has stated. "He had it all, and I think he influenced Miles quite a lot."

As we have seen, Harris was also in the vanguard of the modern movement. Dexter Gordon has mentioned him as the "first cat I met in New York. He was into it already at that time. He was telling me about Bird." A native New Yorker (born in April, 1919), Harris played French horn in a youth band sponsored by the now defunct *Daily Mirror* when he was 12. In the mid-forties, Benny was on the Fifty-second Street scene with Coleman Hawkins, Don Byas, Oscar Pettiford, and Clyde Hart. With Hart he recorded his own *Little Benny* (later known as *Ideology* and *Crazeology* and recorded by Bud Powell as *Bud's Bubble*) and Denzil Best's *Dee Dee's Dance;* with Byas he was heard on *How High the Moon.* In the fifties, he recorded with Charlie Parker on Bird's *South of the Border* album, but by then his lip was not in good shape. What had once been a promising career was suffering from the demon that had killed Webster.

In 1961 Harris turned up in San Francisco, but after an interview with Richard Hadlock, quoted from here, he evaporated back into the obscurity that had cloaked him for most of the fifties. The most lasting of his contributions have been his songs. In addition to *Ornithology,* he wrote *Reets and I,* stretched over the chords of *All God's Chillun,* its melody based on the "little dab'll do ya" phrase that Powell played on his first version of that song; and the line on *Perdido* that appeared under its correct title, *Wahoo,* on a Tadd Dameron Jazzland LP of "live" performances from the Roost. *Wahoo* refers to Harris' Indian lineage. His father was a full-blooded San Blas tribesman according to Leonard Feather, who wrote that Benny "has title to islands, pineapple, chocolate sources, etc., but says, 'I have no eyes for the woods.'"

A 1946 recording of *Perdido* on the Keynote label incorporates *Wahoo* as a countermelody to the original Juan Tizol theme. Dave Lambert and Buddy Stewart scat Harris' line, and Red

Rodney states *Perdido*. The label reads "Red Rodney's Be-boppers," and the young man from Philadelphia certainly was a bebopper. Red began in a drum-and-bugle corps of the Boy Scouts, took up the trumpet at 13, and while still in his teens appeared as a Harry James-styled player in the bands of Jimmy Dorsey and Jerry Wald. Then he began playing at the Down Beat club in Philly, where he heard Gillespie and Parker. When he played at a Fraternal Clubhouse session in the fall of 1945, the 18-year-old Rodney was a Dizzy disciple right down to the point of his orange goatee.

While in Gene Krupa's Band, Red soloed on several Columbia records: *How High the Moon*, a Gerry Mulligan arrangement that contains some strains from *Ornithology; Just the Other Day;* and *It's Just a Matter of Opinion*, wherein he informs everyone, "I'm on a Dizzy kick." The same year, 1946, he sat in with Buddy Rich's band for its Mercury record of *Oop Bop Sh'Bam*. All this activity landed him in a tie for twenty-second place with Taft Jordan in the results of the 1946 *Metronome* poll, published in that magazine's January, 1947, issue. This was the same poll in which Gillespie captured the top spot for the first time.

Rodney recorded with his Be-boppers again for Keynote in 1947, this time without Lambert and Stewart. Allen Eager and Serge Chaloff were the other horns. They did Mulligan's *Elevation*, Al Cohn's *The Goof and I, Fine and Dandy*, and *All God's Chillun*. With Claude Thornhill, Red had solos on *Yardbird Suite* and *Donna Lee*. In 1948, with Woody Herman, he blew on *Lemon Drop* and *That's Right*.

At the end of the decade he became Charlie Parker's trumpeter, remaining with him into 1951, with a few months off to play with Charlie Ventura's big band. By then he had absorbed his Gillespie influence and integrated the nuances of Miles Davis that had affected him. If he was close to anyone, it was Fats Navarro.

In the fifties, Rodney's newly acquired heroin habit kept him in and out of hospitals, jails, and music. When he did record, for Signal in 1957 and for Argo in 1959, he showed that he was still a fine player, with a real *trumpet* sound and great facility. His Argo recording of *Shaw 'Nuff*, a tune not attempted by many, is exceptionally good. After playing around the San Francisco area in the early sixties, Red worked in Las Vegas in the summer of 1965.

The gambling center has become a haven for many white former big-band musicians. There is work in the hotel lounges and clubs in an abundance to be found nowhere else in the United States. Red Rodney is not the ordinary band musician. He was in Las Vegas to play while recuperating from a serious automobile accident. As 1965 drew to a close, he had passed the junior bar examination and was in New York, pursuing further studies toward a new career as a lawyer. He later moved back to the Coast.

Another Gillespie follower in the forties was Doug Mettome (pronounced *met*-o-me), who sometimes sounded quite a bit like Rodney. He was one of the few white musicians to work in the Billy Eckstine band (1946–1947), and he was featured in the Benny Goodman band of 1949, when Goodman had a short flirtation with bop. Mettome has a brash, high-note solo on *Undercurrent Blues* with the big band and more thoughtful, but no less swinging, improvisations on *Blue Lou* and *Bedlam* with the sextet.

Mettome played with Herbie Fields from 1948–1952 and then with a variety of big bands, including those of Herman, Pete Rugolo, Johnny Richards, and Tommy Dorsey. He was inactive in 1958 due to illness, but he worked around New York in the early sixties. One night at the Roundtable, I heard him play in an eclectic style that was away from Gillespie's but incorporated that of Eldridge, who first influenced Doug, as well as elements of Bobby Hackett and Billy Butterfield. He later returned to his Salt Lake City birthplace, where he died, a month short of his thirty-ninth birthday, in February, 1964. It was reported that he had suffered an allergic reaction to medication administered at a local hospital.

Saul "Sonny" Berman wasn't even 23 when he died of what was termed a "heart attack" on January 16, 1947. Berman's death was a tragedy built upon a tragedy. An older brother who was a promising musician was killed in a diving accident at 17, and Sonny took up the trumpet. "He was supposed to be one of the greatest," said Sonny. "Everybody around New Haven, all the old-time musicians said so. He didn't live, so I had to play."

Sonny was with the bands of Louis Prima, Sonny Dunham, Tommy Dorsey, Harry James, Benny Goodman, and Georgie Auld between 1940 and 1945. In May, 1944, he recorded his first solo, a chorus on *Taps Miller* with Auld for Apollo. Eldridge seems to be the main influence, but there are slight overtones of

Gillespie. In a *Metronome* profile of Woody Herman's men, the writer noted: "Louis Armstrong is [Berman's] man," and then he quoted Sonny: "And Roy and Dizzy, too, of course. You dig me?"

With Herman from February, 1945, until shortly before his death, Sonny was featured most prominently on *Sidewalks of Cuba* (with a parody of Harry James's *Flight of the Bumble Bee* for openers) and *Your Father's Mustache,* but he can also be heard on *I Wonder* (a Cootie Williams growl behind Herman's vocal); *A Kiss Goodnight* (Roy-ish); *Uncle Remus Said;* a V-disc of *Don't Worry 'Bout That Mule* (one of his best, little-known solos); *Let it Snow!;* and a Woodchopper set that includes *Igor, Pam, Someday Sweetheart, Fan It,* and *Lost Weekend* (Dizzy-ish on the last two).

In January, 1946, Jerry Newman, who had recorded Gillespie and Christian at Minton's and Monroe's in 1941, put on discs a jam session at his apartment in which Hermanites and future Hermanites participated. Issued on an Esoteric LP (*Sonny Berman—Jazz Immortal*) in the late fifties, it consists of four long selections—*Down With Up!, Ciretose, Hoggimous, Higgamous,* and *The Slumbering Giant.* The first is the early incarnation of Sonny's *Woodchopper's Holiday,* which he did for Dial, and *Hoggimous, Higgamous* is his number the Herd used to play as *They Went Thataway,* which was eventually recorded by the 1950 Herman band for Capitol as *Sonny Speaks.*

While the Herman band was on the West Coast, a Dial date on September 21, 1946, produced, in addition to *Woodchopper's Holiday,* Shorty Rogers' *Curbstone Scuffle* and Ralph Burns's *Nocturne.* Two days later, Sonny played a solo on Burns's *Introspection,* an orchestral side that is part of Norman Granz's *Jazz Scene* album.

In a letter to me a few years ago, critic Harvey Pekar, a great admirer of Berman, made some points about Sonny's playing he considered notable: "He was versatile and could evoke a wide range of emotions. His muted *Woodchopper* solos are exquisite; he is very forceful and wild on *Your Father's Mustache* (which is one of the funniest solos I've ever heard) and *Sidewalks of Cuba.* He had an essentially lyric style though.

"He had a very advanced harmonic conception. He would change keys unexpectedly, implying bi-tonality—*Father's Mustache* and *Slumbering Giant,* for example. He had a good concept of tension and release, and his solos were well constructed. In *Someday Sweetheart* every phrase sets up the next one." (*Let It Snow!* is another good example of expert construction.)

Pekar also believes that Jewish religious music influenced Berman. "Listen to a good cantor and then listen to his solos on *Introspection* and *Pam*," he wrote. (*Nocturne* can justifiably be added to these.) "Pay attention to his intervals, inflections and the way he will trail notes off at the end of a phrase (*Pam*)."

Barry Ulanov, then editor of *Metronome*, eulogized after Berman's death: "Dead long before his time, this boy was well on his way to a mark in jazz beside the handful of titans on his instrument, until the ways of his world caught up with him."

Pete Candoli was the high-note trumpet with the 1945–1946 Herman band. Sometimes he would come running out in a Superman costume to climax *Apple Honey* in a theater presentation. He named Rex Stewart as his favorite trumpeter in 1945, but he also dug Dizzy. His specialty seems to obscure the fact that he is a good soloist in other registers as well. However, it is his younger brother who really is the jazz soloist in the family. At 16, during his summer vacation, Conte Candoli played briefly with the Herman band. After graduating from high school, he again did a short stint with the band before going into the Army. At that time (August, 1945), he took a solo on the record *Put That Ring on My Finger* that shows he had a liking for Eldridge and some parallels with Berman.

After Army service, Conte played on Fifty-second Street with Chubby Jackson and made the Swedish trip with the bassist's sextet. His *L'Ana* (co-written with Jackson) and *Crown Pilots* were both recorded by Chubby. In this period, Conte was a strong Gillespie man. He worked with Stan Kenton in 1948 and with Herman in 1950. In between, his solos were more frequent in Charlie Ventura's small group of 1949. Since the fifties, when he was heavily recorded, Candoli has made the Los Angeles area his home base, appearing at the Lighthouse in Hermosa Beach with Howard Rumsey and then for quite a while as a member of Shelly Manne's group. Miles Davis and Clifford Brown were influences that were added to his playing during this time.

We have seen that, like Gillespie, many of the men Dizzy influenced were first under the spell of Roy Eldridge. This was true of two of the most important trumpeters of the forties, Howard

McGhee and Fats Navarro. In 1943 they both were members of Andy Kirk's orchestra. Navarro, five years younger than McGhee, was quoted in 1947 as saying of Howard, "He was the influence. I used to go and jam with him all the time."

Bill Coss quotes McGhee as saying that "Fats and I, when we were with Kirk, used to go hunt up Roy. He killed us. He had a style of, like, running on trumpet. . . .

"You know, it's Roy and Louis who were my favorites; then Dizzy and Miles. From the older school I guess I like Red Allen the best now. He is *a* great. He's always trying. From the modern, it's got to be Dizzy. Diz is one of the most wonderful trumpet players I ever heard. He has so much at his disposal. He can travel as fast as he wants. In the old days, he would turn Fats and me around every night."

McGhee was born on February 6, 1918, in Tulsa, Oklahoma, but grew up in Detroit. His half brother, who played guitar, taught him the fundamentals of music. He heard Eldridge and Armstrong. "I never heard a G so pretty as Louis played it," McGhee told Coss.

"I went to a teacher and asked to play trumpet, but I got a clarinet. Now I know that was all right. It taught me a faster articulation."

McGhee played with territory bands from 1936 to 1940, and after returning to Detroit, he led his own twelve-piece unit there, at the Club Congo in 1941. He joined Lionel Hampton in September but left shortly before the band made its first recordings. Then it was on to Andy Kirk—and Howard's first recording, his own *McGhee Special*, in July, 1942. This side clearly shows his strong interest in Eldridge.

A year with Charlie Barnet produced nothing on record due to the AFM ban, and when McGhee returned to Kirk in 1943, neither he nor Navarro was given solos on the record dates in which they participated.

When he did *McGhee Special* with Georgie Auld's band in a stage show at Chicago's Regal Theatre in 1944, a *Down Beat* reviewer noted: "McGhee's performance differs from the Decca record by Kirk in that he has accelerated the tempo and features more and more faster slurred runs."

McGhee could play high and fast, and in his tenure with Coleman Hawkins' quintet, from November, 1944, to March, 1945, he showed that he could also play "modern." He had obviously been listening to Gillespie and had added new harmonic dimensions to his playing. Coss says: "McGhee was best known in the earlier days, after the modern took hold in him, as a master of the middle register of the horn. His chief contribution, according to many, was that he slowed down the rapid delivery common then to bop and made the characteristic augmented chords and whole-tone melodies familiar to those who never realized they doted on Debussy."

The Hawkins group was based in California, and the records made in early 1945 for Asch (*Bean Stalkin', Sportsman's Hop, Night Ramble, Ladies Lulllaby*) and Capitol (*Rifftide, Hollywood Stampede,* etc.) are good examples of this McGhee approach. At the same time, Howard recorded an excellent solo typical of the new bebop style on *Northwest Passage* with Chubby Jackson for Keynote. (McGhee and Jackson had been together in the Barnet band three years before.)

While in Los Angeles, McGhee apppeared with Hawkins in a movie called *The Crimson Canary* (playing *Hollywood Stampede*). This was also the time of the first Jazz at the Philharmonic concerts, and McGhee took part in several, including the first one to be issued with *How High the Moon.* He then had his own band and recorded for Dial with Charlie Parker and on his own. In 1946 there was a session with tenor man Teddy Edwards and pianist Dodo Marmarosa (*Midnight at Minton's, Dialated Pupils, High Wind in Hollywood,* and *Up in Dodo's Room*) and a quartet date (*Trumpet at Tempo, Thermodynamics*). McGhee left Los Angeles in 1947 and formed a group with James Moody, Milt Jackson, and Ray Brown, who had recently left the Gillespie band. This group recorded for Dial in New York in December. McGhee also found time to record a relaxed solo on *El Sino* with Leo Parker on Savoy. He was listed on the label as Maggsi Evounce for contractual reasons.

After touring with JATP, McGhee took a band, including Jimmy and Percy Heath, to the Paris Jazz Festival in 1948. He recorded with Navarro for Blue Note in 1948, and the next year he did a particularly rewarding date for the same company with J.J. Johnson and Brew Moore (*Lo-Flame, Fuguetta, Fluid Drive, Meciendo, Donnellon Square, I'll Remember April*). He and Moore were featured in front of Machito's orchestra on *Cubop*

City for Roost. He won the *Down Beat* poll in 1949 (readers couldn't vote for leaders of permanent groups at that time, so Gillespie was ineligible), and things were going well for Maggie, as he is known to his friends.

The fifties marked a big slide, however. After a USO tour with Oscar Pettiford in the winter of 1951–1952, it was downhill all the way. When McGhee and Charlie Parker were together, briefly, in Billy Eckstine's band in 1944, Howard noticed that Bird had a clarinet case full of capsules. When he asked what they were, Parker replied, "Man, you don't want to be bothered with that."

For a long time, McGhee wasn't bothered—but not long enough. McGhee virtually disappeared through most of the fifties. But unlike many others, he came back. In the early sixties, he played with Duke Ellington and since then has led his own combo in person and on record. One record is a reunion with Teddy Edwards for Contemporary entitled *Together Again*. Those who heard him at Newport in 1963 knew that Howard McGhee had gotten himself together again.

Navarro's story is again one on the tragic side of the ledger. He was born in Key West, Florida, on September 24, 1923, of mixed Cuban-Negro-Chinese parentage. His third cousin is Charlie Shavers, whose abilities he greatly admired. Shavers was "the greatest, but *not* for his jazz," Fats once was quoted as saying. "He's a real trumpet player."

Navarro began his study of the trumpet at 13. By 1941, after high school, he had left Key West for good to join Sol Allbright's band in Orlando. (He had played some tenor saxophone with Walter Johnson's band in Miami.) "I didn't like Key West at all. I'll never go back," said Fats.

With Allbright he traveled to Cincinnati, studied with another teacher there, and went to Indianapolis to join Snookum Russell, in whose band he met J.J. Johnson. He was with Russell from 1941 to 1942 and went to Andy Kirk in 1943.

In 1945, when Gillespie was about to leave Eckstine, he told Billy to go listen to Navarro as a possible replacement. "He had a lot of Spanish influence in his playing. His phrases were like those of the bullring," says Dizzy. "He was great. I liked the way he put phrases together, and he had a good attack."

Nat Shapiro and Nat Hentoff quote Eckstine as saying that he "went out to the club, and the only thing Fats had to blow (because Howard McGhee was the featured trumpet player) was behind a chorus number. But he was *wailing* behind this number, and I said to myself, 'This is good enough; this'll fit.'

"So I got Fats to come by and talk it over, and about two weeks after that he took Dizzy's chair, and take it from me, he came *right* in. Fats came in the band, and great as Diz is—and I'll never say other than he is one of the finest things that ever happened to a brass instrument—Fats played his book and you would hardly know that Diz had left the band. 'Fat Girl' played Dizzy's solos, not note-for-note, but his ideas on Dizzy's parts and the feeling was the same and there was just as much swing."

Navarro was with Eckstine for eighteen months, leaving him in June, 1946. The only recorded evidence of his stay is *Long, Long Journey* and *Tell Me, Pretty Baby*, two blues vocals by Eckstine. His bit on the former consists in a short suspended ending with a high-note climax; the latter contains a beautifully realized chorus that finds him much closer to Gillespie than he was later.

In New York, he began recording as a sideman. On September 5, 1946, he did a date with Kenny Clarke for French Swing that produced *Rue Chaptal* (reissued later as *Royal Roost*), *Epistrophy*, *52nd Street Theme*, and *Oop Bop Sh'Bam*. The following day, virtually the same group (Sonny Stitt and Kenny Dorham were on both dates) recorded *Webb City, Fat Boy*, and *Everything's Cool* for Savoy. Navarro was already an extremely convincing soloist on these sides, with long melodic lines in excellent control. Before the year was out, he did two sides with Coleman Hawkins for Sonora, *Bean and the Boys* and *I Mean You* (he is listed under his legal name, Theodore Navarro). Although the solos are shorter than the extended (for that time) workouts on the Savoys, they are also marvelous pieces of playing.

Navarro did not make bad records. He told Ulanov: "I'd like to just play a perfect melody of my own, all the chord progressions right, the melody original and fresh—my own." This he did, but the similarity of his work on various "takes" of his Blue Note recordings with Dameron led people to think that perhaps he was preparing his solos before he came to the studio. On the other hand, maybe he knew what he wanted to say on a particular tune after his first interpretation and was satisfied to polish it rather than depart on another idea pattern as Parker did. Certainly his choruses on *Sweet Georgia Brown* and *High on an Open Mike* from WNEW's "Saturday Night Swing Session" (recorded in April, 1947, and last available on a Counterpoint LP) were not worked out beforehand, and they are as brilliant as his other work from this period.

In 1947 he worked with Illinois Jacquet, with whom he recorded a half chorus on *Jivin' with Jack the Bellboy* under the pseudonym Slim Romero. In December he again recorded with Hawkins, this time for Victor. His playing on *Jumpin' for Jane* is fine, but *Half Step Down, Please* is exceptional even for him.

The same year, Fats recorded under his own name for Savoy such notable sides as *Fat Girl, Eb-pob, Ice Freezes Red* (a line based on the chords of *Indiana* that made use of the *I Get the Neck of the Chicken* phrase that the boppers were interpolating quite often in those days because Parker had used it), and *Nostalgia* (his own lovely melody on *Out of Nowhere*). There was also a date with Dexter Gordon for Savoy. Max Harrison has written of him: "His sense of logical musical development is clearly illustrated by his use of the high register. He had an impressive command of the upper reaches of his instrument, but reserved it for climaxes that were always the result of increasing musical intensity. The *Eb-pob* solo also shows how, once a climax was reached—in this case just before the chorus' half-way mark —he would release the tension gradually."

In December, Navarro and tenor Don Lanphere backed Earl Coleman on a Dial date. One instrumental came out of this session, a very fast version of Denzil Best's *Move;* here a muted Navarro and Max Roach combine their wizardry in a duet at beginning and end.

The year 1947 also marked the beginning of an association with Tadd Dameron's small groups. They recorded for Savoy (*The Tadd Walk, A Bebop Carroll*) and for Blue Note (*Dameronia, The Squirrel, Our Delight, The Chase*).

Another edition of the Dameron group played at the Roost in 1948–1949. This band recorded for Blue Note (*Lady Bird, Jahbero, Symphonette*) and can also be heard on two Jazzland LP's, issued in the sixties, comprising broadcasts from the Roost. All contain superb Navarro, especially his breathless double-timing on *Good Bait,* a number in which he never failed to excel.

In 1948 he also recorded a date with McGhee for Blue Note. Included was *Double Talk,* a trumpet battle originally issued as a two-part 78. If McGhee had been the "influence," here his younger colleague surpassed him in harmonic awareness and all-around handling of the horn. (Incidentally, contrary to the liner notes on *The Fabulous Fats Navarro* LP, Navarro has the first solo chorus and McGhee the second.)

Navarro also can be heard to advantage on four sides made with Bud Powell for Blue Note: *Wail, Bouncin' with Bud, Dance of the Infidels,* and *52nd Street Theme.*

Two unusual recordings in which he participated are a 1949 Metronome All-Star date for Victor (on which he engages Dizzy Gillespie and Miles Davis in exchanges on *Overtime* and blows a half chorus on *Victory Ball*) and a 1948 sextet number of *Stealin' Apples* with Benny Goodman for Capitol (on which he blows what might be termed a perfect solo, even for Fats).

He rehearsed with Goodman's big band but never appeared with it. His last big-band stay had been three months in 1948 with Lionel Hampton. As he told Barry Ulanov: "I must play in small bands. You can't learn anything in big bands. I hope I never work in one again. You know—no chance to really play— no progress."

Fats had a love of interpolating phrases of other songs in his solos. Swing-era players had done it earlier—Art Tatum in completely his own manner—but the boppers really brought it to the fore. In the hands of some, this was banal, but Navarro integrated his quotes artfully. British critic Michael G. Shera commented on this: "Examples are to be found in *Nostalgia* (Savoy) where he begins his second chorus with a quote from *Rockin' in Rhythm; Anthropology* and *The Squirrel* (both Jazzland) where he quotes from *We're in the Money* and *It Might As Well Be Spring,* respectively. In each case, the quote is amazingly apt, and fits perfectly into the melodic line of the solo."

Navarro's tremendous talent inspired awe in his contemporaries. Dameron told me, "I used to try to get other fellows to play with me, and they'd say, 'Oh, is Fats in the band? Oh, no!' It got to the point where I had to pay him so much money that I told him he should go on his own. I said, 'Once you start making this kind of money, you need to be a leader yourself.' But he didn't want to quit. He didn't have security because of his habits." The "habit" was, of course, heroin addiction, acquired after he came to New York.

Gillespie reminisced about him. "He was sweet. He was like a little baby. Very nice. Fats was playing with Bud [Powell] at the Three Deuces. Bud used to bug him all the time."

One incident to which Dizzy alluded occurred at a Leonard Feather-organized jam session at the Three Deuces. Feather describes it on the back of *The Fabulous Fats Navarro:* " . . . the tension between the two was aggravated as Bud chided Fats between sets. At the beginning of the next set Fats reached the bursting point. While the audience looked on in silent, terrified tension, he lifted his horn and tried to bring the full weight of it crashing down on Bud's hands. He missed, thank God, but the strength of the blow was enough to buckle the horn against the piano; Fats had to borrow a trumpet to play the set. The incident, however, failed to affect the close friendship and mutual admiration between Bud and Fats."

Navarro's last year was marked by a diminution of activity as his health began to decline. The sides with Powell were made in August, 1949. In September he recorded his last date as a leader, for Prestige (*Wailing Wall, Stop, Go, Infatuation*). If not equal to his best, it is certainly fat-toned, assured, exciting playing.

Then the decline really set in. I saw him at Birdland in 1950. His double-breasted suit hung on him in folds. His once cherubic face was terribly drawn, his neck was away from his shirt collar, and his playing, punctuated by fits of coughing, echoed his beaten, tired bearing. [Incidentally, I question the May, 1950, dating of records made of his broadcasts with Charlie Parker from Café Society (*Ornithology, Move, Cool Blues, The Street Beat, Perdido*). His playing seems too vibrant for the man I had seen at Birdland, too alive for a man who would be dead of tuberculosis on July 7. A chronological clue is that the same rhythm section that is on the 1949 Powell sides—Tommy Potter and Roy Haynes—is most likely the rhythm section on the Parkers.]

Trumpeter Don Ferrara, analyzing trumpet styles in a series of magazine articles, had this to say in praise of Navarro: "Harmonically his playing was closer to Bird's. Chords never trapped him, but rather, he could get right into them and play good melodic ideas. Fats was the only trumpet player I ever heard who dared to play Bird's great solo on *Ko Ko*. This solo, one of Bird's best, is extremely difficult to play, so difficult that few saxophonists have attempted it. When Fats played it, it flowed out of him, technically perfect, and with tremendous feeling and vitality. He really understood it."

Dameron summed up Navarro the man this way: "He was pretty quiet, soulful, sensitive. He never found himself, really. He was always searching. I don't know what he was looking for—he *had* it!"

Navarro influenced a number of trumpeters in his short life. Through Clifford Brown, with whom he played in Philadelphia on several occasions, Fats reached many of the young hornmen in the fifties who were too young to have heard him in person. Brown made something personal out of his Navarro background. In the forties it was Kenny Dorham who did this.

McKinley Dorham (he was first known in jazz as Kinny, but he gave in eventually to the more common, mistaken spelling) was born in Texas, played horn around the Oakland area after his Army discharge in the early forties, and eventually migrated to New York. He was in Gillespie's first band ("He's got a whole lot of musical knowledge," says Diz) and then, in 1946, was a member of Billy Eckstine's organization. He had written arrangements of *Okay for Baby* for Lucky Millinder and of Benny Carter's *Malibu* for Cootie Williams. With Eckstine he did a catchy bop theme entitled *Dead End*. Later, in 1948–1949, when Dorham was with Charlie Parker, Bird featured it quite regularly.

Like McGhee and Navarro, Dorham had once played a reed instrument (tenor sax), and this may help explain the rapid delivery common to all three. Dorham's execution on his earlier recordings, however, left much to be desired. His "running" style stumbled a bit then—on *The Jitney Man* with Eckstine, *Webb City* and *Fat Boy* with Navarro, and the Sonny Stitt Quintet sides on Savoy, for example. But through the uncertainty, a talent could be perceived. A muted solo on *Kool* with Mary Lou Williams contained further indications, and in 1947, with the first version of Art Blakey's Jazz Messengers, Dorham played convincingly on *The Thin Man,* his own composition.

With Parker, Dorham improved even further, and by the time he left the group, he had really tightened up the loose ends of his delivery. While in France for the 1949 Paris Jazz Festival, the Parker group, with James Moody subbing for Bird, recorded *Prince Albert,* a Dorham–Max Roach melody based on the changes of *All the Things You Are.*

In the fifties, Kenny was heard extensively with Art Blakey, Max Roach, and his own groups. Gillespie and Navarro had not overpowered him, and he had developed into one of the best trumpeters in modern jazz and perhaps the most personal stylist after Gillespie and Miles Davis.

The sixties found Idrees Sulieman as one of the large contingent of American expatriate musicians in Europe. In the forties, as Leonard Graham, he was one of the early sitters-in at Minton's and was heard on Fifty-second Street with Sid Catlett's band. He recorded with Ben Webster, Bill De Arango, and Catlett (*Jeep Is Jumpin', Dark Corners*) for Haven and revealed a style strongly influenced by Gillespie. Later in this period, he also recorded with Monk (*Suburban Eyes, Humph,* and his own *Evonce*) and Mary Lou Williams (*Knowledge, Tisherome*), revealing that he had been listening to Fats and Kenny. Before leaving for overseas at the end of the fifties, Sulieman was an active participant on the New York scene, especially with the group that pianist Randy Weston led. By then, Clifford Brown had further shaped Sulieman's playing. In Europe, he reversed the McGhee-Navarro-Dorham procedure by doubling on saxophone—alto, in this case.

In bop's heyday, the Gillespie horn drew many trumpeters under its bell. But virtually the only young trumpeter today who plays directly in his style is Lonnie Hillyer, heard most often with Charlie Mingus and Barry Harris. The mark of a musician is not how many players he influences but, rather, how he affects the whole music. What Gillespie did in the forties had a profound bearing on the history of jazz, but because of his tremendous power as an individual, he has continued to be an important force since the time that people were writing about the "death of bop" in 1950.

Although some of his colleagues in his small groups of the early fifties were below his level, Dizzy also recorded in other settings. In late 1953 he began an association with Norman Granz. His recordings included a jam session with the likes of Johnny Hodges, Ben Webster, and Lionel Hampton; albums with his first inspiration, Roy Eldridge; an LP with Stan Getz, another with Sonny Stitt, a third with Getz and Stitt. During this time he also toured with JATP.

In 1956 Gillespie had the young arranger Quincy Jones help him put a big band together. Jones and Joe Gordon were in the trumpet section, along with Bama Warwick, Dizzy's buddy from the Frank Fairfax days; Phil Woods was on alto, Billy Mitchell on tenor, and Melba Liston on trombone. From March to May they toured the Middle East, Yugoslavia, and Greece for the U.S. State Department. It was the first time the government had subsidized jazz. The trip was such a success that in the fall of that year, the band visited Latin America as "ambassadors" from Washington, D.C. Even the severest critics of the Eisenhower Administration would have to credit it for this.

Dizzy kept the big band together until January, 1958, except for some time spent with JATP. The later edition included Lee Morgan, then an 18-year-old trumpeter, tenor saxophonist Benny Golson, and pianist Wynton Kelly. Gillespie has always unselfishly fostered new talent. What other trumpeter-leader would have given Morgan the featured spot on *A Night in Tunisia?* Gillespie did, and he had earlier done the same for Gordon.

Diz has continued to hire youngsters for the small groups with which he has worked successfully since the big band was dissolved. First he had pianist-composer Lalo Schifrin; more recently Kenny Barron has filled the same role. Junior Mance, who preceded Schifrin, has said, "Working with Dizzy is the best schooling a jazz musician can get." The improvement of bassist Chris White and drummer Rudy Collins during their time with Gillespie is a case in point, and reedman Leo Wright certainly benefited from his years with Gillespie (1959–1962).

Wright's replacement, James Moody, was, of course, returning to his alma mater for postgraduate seminars. The Gillespie quintets of the sixties, as compared with those of the early fifties, have been commercial without necessarily trying to be—and their musical level has been much higher.

Gillespie is not generally known for his arranging talent, but those on the inside of jazz know and respect his knowledge. "The last big band," says Diz, "I had about eight arrangements. I'm pretty lazy." His compositions, played by many others, are more instantly recognized. Dizzy's erudition is especially keen in the area of the beat. On some occasions in the Eckstine band, he had subbed on drums in an emergency. "I don't know how to play the drums," he says, "but I know how drums should sound."

He held forth on the subject during a *Down Beat Blindfold Test* in 1962, first bringing to light the failure of today's young drummers to utilize the bass drum more extensively. "I come from the old school," he told Leonard Feather. "I imagine I do

sound pretty old now, saying that—but when I first started playing, the leader of the band I played with in South Carolina was a
bass drummer, and he played it not with his foot but with his
hand. I didn't think too much about it at the time, but he was the
leader, and after all, there is always a certain natural anathema
between a sideman and leader; but as I grew older and I didn't
hear this anymore, I realized that this guy was actually great on
that bass drum. He had his knee up against the bass drum, to
make different sounds—yes, the same idea as the elbow on the
snare the way they do it now. Of course, we had a snare drummer
in the band, too."

Gillespie likes the way Buddy Rich is able to integrate all the
different components of the drum set and yet still keep the bass-
drum rhythm going. He mentions drummers like Art Blakey, Al
Jones, Specs Wright, and Stan Levey, men who have played with
him at various times through the years, and explains that all
seemed to come to him with a conception of using the bass drum
for accenting. Needless to say, Dizzy gave them his own brand of
instruction. He feels that each part of the set is an instrument
unto itself and that all must be skillfully tied together. He speaks
from personal preference and what he thinks most soloists like.

Dizzy told Feather: "This thing didn't start with Philly Joe
[Jones]. Long before his time, back in the early 52nd Street days
when Max played with me, the brushes and the bass drum had to
go right together, and Max played that way with me."

Three years later, in an interview with Dan Morgenstern, Gillespie reiterated these ideas in discussing his current drummer:
"When I hired Rudy Collins, I had my choice of two or three
drummers," he said. "I picked Rudy because I noticed that he
played on his bass drum, too. So few drummers do, nowadays.
There was a guy with King Curtis I heard at Birdland; he really
knocked me out. I'm a rhythm man, you know. I used to play for
dancers."

He then talked of playing behind his wife: "She used to be a
dancer, and I still try to phrase like that. I loved to play for that
chorus line at the Cotton Club! One night—I had just joined
Teddy Hill—I was playing something that really made that line
step, and Bill Robinson was watching in the wings. He turned
around to somebody and asked: 'Where did that little bastard
come from?' I'm still a rhythm man."

Anyone who needs proof of Dizzy's way with rhythm should

listen—and feel—the infectious excitement he generates with a tambourine on *No More Blues* (in the LP *Dizzy on the French Riviera*). To *see* him play the tambourine is another stimulating experience. Utilizing his hands, elbows, and knees in striking the instrument, he is a swinging sight as well as sound. And then there are his accompanying dance steps. Gillespie the singer is not bad either. Without the greatest vocal equipment in the world, he can still convey a message. And he can shout the blues, as *Dizzy's Blues* (*Cripple Crapple Crutch*) lets us know.

Dizzy has always been someone to see as well as hear. The unorthodox methods he employs to achieve his surging power at times make him look like a large bullfrog. His cheeks distend as if they are harboring rubber balls, and his neck swells inside his outsize collars to twice its normal size.

Gillespie realizes the value of keeping his chops in shape. Once he was taught this the hard way. "A while back," he told writer Harry Frost, "I laid off for two weeks and then opened at Birdland. I'll never do *that* again. When I picked up that horn, I couldn't do half the things I wanted to. There were layers of dead skin on my lip. That's what happens when I don't play. So I *have* to play—almost every day."

Dizzy related to Frost how he warms up his embouchure in taxicabs by using just his mouthpiece. "Sometimes the cab drivers turn around and look at me like I'm crazy," he said. "They can't imagine what I'm doing and I have to explain, 'This is a trumpet mouthpiece, not a duck call. I'm preparing myself for the job.'

"I can make a sound like a police siren, and one night in Central Park there was a car ahead of us, and he wouldn't let us get past, and I was late for the job. So I took the mouthpiece and leaned out the window and made this sound like a siren. The car pulled right over."

The Gillespie humor takes many forms. Even when he is on the bandstand, one can never be sure what to expect. At the end of a particularly burning opening-night set at Birdland in the fall of 1964, he quickly dropped to his knees and gave a remarkably accurate impression of the club's diminutive but vociferous announcer, Pee Wee Marquette. Pee Wee, handling the lights at the time, immediately plunged the bandstand into darkness.

Although some of his bits have become familiar to his audiences, he has retained them because of their acquired classic

stature. For instance, there is his apology for tardiness at the beginning of a set: "I'm sorry we're a little late getting started this
evening, but, you see, we just came from a very, very, important
show. The Ku Klux Klan and the John Birch Society were giving
a benefit for the Catholic Youth Organization and the B'nai
B'rith. It was held at the Harlem YMCA . . . so you can see
we're very lucky to be here at all this evening."

Another evergreen routine finds Dizzy telling his audience that
he would like to introduce the members of the band—and then
his bandsmen all begin shaking hands and telling one another
their names.

Gillespie explained why he enjoys "putting people on" to Gene
Lees: "Oh, that's just a characteristic of the human race. Every-
body wants to put people on, I think. And get away with it!
That's the thing about it: put people on and get *away* with it.
That's a science in itself."

Professor Gillespie does this with aplomb and *élan*.. Sometimes, in Nigerian robes, with an African tarboosh atop his head,
he assumes the identity of one Prince Iwo. In 1963 he arrived at
San Francisco's International Airport thus attired, with band
members White, Barron, and Collins, dressed in diplomatically
dignified black suits, attending him at a respectful distance. After
throwing the airport into confusion, they got into a taxi. According to Patricia Willard: "To their white cabby they presented a
slip of paper bearing the name of a hotel where they held reser-
vations, and proceeded into a violent and extended argument
among themselves in pseudo-African double talk all the way
there. The driver began to show signs of nervous uneasiness. At
the hotel, the passengers looked uncomprehendingly when the
fare was quoted. Everybody 'Ungawa'-ed. The cabby began rais-
ing his voice and pointed to the meter. The passengers got more
excited and more confused. In desperation, the man held up eight
fingers and slowly counted them to indicate the dollars owed.

"'Man, why didn't you say so in the first place?' Diz smiled
warmly as he handed him a ten dollar denomination in United
States currency and gestured that no change was necessary."

That is one Gillespie. There is also the man who, while in
Karachi, Pakistan, in 1956, "persuaded a doubtful snake-charmer
to play a duet in his room," according to Marshall Sterns. "To the
flustered management he countered, 'The man's a musician, isn't

he?' You could hear the native bellboys hissing the news. In Ankara, Dizzy declined to play at a lawn party unless the urchins crowding outside the walls were admitted. 'I came here to play for all the people,' he murmured."

Ralph Gleason ended his liner notes for the LP for *An Electrifying Evening with the Dizzy Gillespie Quintet* by writing: "I have a button one of his booking agents sent out once as a gag. 'Dizzy Gillespie for President' it says. I'm not kidding when I tell you he's got my vote any time he runs."

In 1964 Gleason's wife, Jeannie, actually mounted a campaign for him. The cover of the November 5, 1964, *Down Beat* has a picture of Gillespie being sworn in by "Supreme Court Justice" White as "Justice" Collins looks on. It is captioned: "Dizzy's Dream Inauguration Day, 1965." Inside is an interview with the "candidate" that is a mixture of the serious and humorous insight that typifies Gillespie's outlook. One of the lighter moments occurs in his listing of potential Cabinet officials and ambassadors: "Gov. George C. Wallace: Chief information officer in the Congo . . . under Tshombe," said Gillespie.

Even though Dizzy did not win, one of his California supporters, Ramona Crowell, has made sure that his image stays before the public. She sells sweat shirts with a smiling likeness of John Birks adorning the front, like the Bach and Beethoven items of a few years ago.

Gillespie, now in his forties, is far from ready to be consigned to antiquity. A story told by saxophonist Zoot Sims about an incident involving Woody Herman in the forties is still representative of the Gillespie of today: "Once the band's [Herman's] Pullman car was stranded in Salt Lake City by a snow storm. Meantime, Dizzy Gillespie's band, which was scheduled to play there, was stuck in Denver—which was where the Herman band was supposed to be.

"We played their gig and they played ours," Zoot related. "But Dizzy had made it to Salt Lake by flying, and he sat in with us. That was a ball. He played with the section, and was featured in front of the band on different numbers. You know Dizzy—he's never at a loss for what to do."

Or at a loss for what to say, I might add. On an April, 1965, program of ABC-TV's "Nightlife," Gillespie was a guest, along with a doctor who was explaining his theory for freezing human beings and then reviving them at a later time when the disease that had killed them could be cured. Slyly but trenchantly, Gillespie asked, "But what are they going to do about our souls?"

One can write about Gillespie and talk about him for hours on end, for he is a fascinating man as well as a great musician. But he can never be captured completely this way. As Dave Usher says, "Dizzy is more to live with than talk about. He has to be experienced—like jazz."

Recommended Listening
DIZZY GILLESPIE

Charlie Christian (with Thelonious Monk), EVEREST FS-219
The Development of an American Artist,
    SMITHSONIAN COLLECTION R004
In the Beginning, PRESTIGE P-24030
The Greatest Jazz Concert Ever, PRESTIGE P-24024
Dizzy Gillespie and His Big Band, GNP 23, GNP CRESCENDO
Manteca, QUINTESSENCE 25211
Dizzy Gillespie, Dee Gee Days, SAVOY SJL 2209
Diz and Getz, VERVE VE-2-2521
The Sonny Rollins/Sonny Stitt Sessions, VERVE VE-2-2505
Oscar Peterson and Dizzy Gillespie, PABLO 2310740

(see also Parker)

FATS NAVARRO

Mr. B. and the Band, SAVOY SJL 2214
Prime Source, BLUE NOTE BN LA 507-H2
Fat Girl, SAVOY SJL 2216
First Sessions 1949/50, PRESTIGE P-24081
Fats Navarro (with Tadd Dameron), MILESTONE M-47041

(see also Parker, Powell)

3

BUD POWELL AND THE PIANISTS

PERHAPS the most erratic of all the great talents to come to light in the forties was pianist Earl "Bud" Powell. Charlie Parker was hampered by his personal problems, but they usually did not prevent him from functioning at close to his top level. Powell, on the other hand, is a tormented soul whose musical effectiveness was impaired for long periods in the forties and fifties. In the early sixties, he lived in Paris as an expatriate, playing, and sometimes playing very well, but seldom reaching the musical heights that once were his. After being hospitalized for a year with tuberculosis, he returned to the United States in August, 1964. A year later, he was again seriously ill and in a hospital.

To have heard Bud Powell at his zenith was one of the most exhilarating experiences in jazz. One night at the Three Deuces in the summer of 1947, Charlie Parker's group was on the stand when Fats Navarro and Powell came in and replaced, for one set, the regular trumpeter and pianist, Miles Davis and Duke Jordan. The tune was Thelonious Monk's 52nd Street Theme, played at an intensely fast tempo. Parker and Navarro played well, but what Powell did clearly eclipsed their work that night. For twenty or twenty-five choruses, he hung the audience by its nerve ends, playing music of demonically driven beauty, music of hard, unflinching swing, music of genius.

The man achieving this fantastic expression was one with the music itself: right leg digging into the floor at an odd angle, pants leg up to almost the top of the shin, shoulders hunched, upper lip tight against his teeth, mouth emitting an accompanying guttural song to what the steel fingers were playing, vein in temple throbbing violently as perspiration popped out all over his scalp and ran down his face and neck.

This was the young, tigerish Powell who had already influenced countless pianists, as well as many players on other instruments. It was also the Powell whose trips to mental institutions numbered five between 1945 and 1955.

The Powell of Paris, 1961, according to alto man Jackie Mc-
Lean, was "quite well—very, very heavy. He looks like Art
Tatum . . . when he's at the keyboard now. He doesn't have
that slender look that Bud used to have. He really has the old
master look, sitting back and nothing moving but his fingers."

Powell also tried singing. "It's kinda sad—I mean pitiful—to
watch Bud sing," said Jackie, "because his choice of tunes is so
closely linked with his life, like *I Should Care*. And he doesn't an-
nounce it or anything like that. He just pulls the mike over and
starts singing in a very quiet voice. It fits."

McLean's other comments about Powell's playing in Paris did
not make one think of an "old master." From what I gathered,
most of the time he was just going through the motions. "He
didn't seem to want to play too much at the Blue Note club,"
McLean said. "He didn't get inspired to play there, but just when
someone he knew would come in. I know whenever I would go
in—and it wasn't very often, 'cause I was working myself—Bud
would open up and stretch out. Or when any musicians that were
visiting, coming through Paris, would come in to see him, he
would stretch out."

The only other time Powell seemed to regain his old form was
at concerts. McLean said, "He plays a very commercial-type
piano in the club, but when he gets on a concert he really
stretches out into fabulous Bud Powell, and you know he can be
fabulous when he wants to be. If you catch Bud at a concert over
there, then you really get a chance to hear him."

Proof of this is heard in the album released in the United States
by Epic titled *Blakey in Paris*. This concert, recorded at the Thé-
âtre des Champs-Élysées in 1959, features Art Blakey's Jazz
Messengers, French saxophonist Barney Wilen, and, on one half
of the LP, Powell, sitting in for Walter Davis, Jr., the Messengers'
pianist of the time. Two Powell originals from the late forties,
Dance of the Infidels and *Bouncin' with Bud*, are explored at
length, with Powell playing some of his best piano since the early
fifties—long, building choruses with that marvelous brand of
connection and continuity he once displayed regularly. Also convincing are his trio tracks and solos with Coleman Hawkins at the
Essen Jazz Festival in 1960.

If his European performances were not generally up to the best
Powell standard, he was a better adjusted man than he was in the

States. When he took up permanent residence in Paris in the spring of 1959, he was in bad shape. His wife, Buttercup, related it this way to writer Robert Perlongo: "Nobody gave him much longer to live. Not even me, for a while there. His liver, you know, was very bad. He had to keep taking these vitamin B-12 tablets all the time. And his emotions—well, let's just say he was not a very well person."

Then she described the Bud Powell of 1961: "For one thing, I guess you'd say he's more mellow than he used to be. You know how Bud always was: tender, but so persistent, just so persistent. Like a horse with blinders that only knows straight ahead and nothing else. Bud back home was never in command of the situation—except at the piano, when he became a different person altogether."

Powell was born in New York City, September 27, 1924, and began playing the piano at the age of 6. His grandfather was a musician; his older brother, William, plays trumpet and violin; and his father, William Powell, was a pianist. Bud credits his father with giving him "much advice, inspiration, and encouragement." According to Jackie McLean, William Powell, Sr., is now the superintendent of an apartment building in Harlem, but he still plays. McLean describes him as a "fine, old-time stride-piano player" and remembers hearing him "really make the piano sing—he filled the room with sound."

For seven years Bud studied the works of Debussy, Beethoven, Liszt, Chopin, Schumann, and Bach. Pianist Elmo Hope was a childhood friend, and the two used to listen to classical recordings together. In his early teens, Bud became interested in jazz; his first influence was Billy Kyle, pianist with the John Kirby group.

Powell attended DeWitt Clinton High School in the Bronx for three years and quit when he was 15. After working with his brother Bill's band, he began gigging at small Coney Island clubs. Then he played for singer Valaida Snow and in a band called the Sunset Royals. He played in actor Canada Lee's Chicken Coop Restaurant in Harlem and then at The Place in Greenwich Village. He would head uptown after work and tour the Harlem bars and would usually wind up at Minton's.

It was at an uptown bar that he met pianist-composer Thelonious Monk, who first took him to Minton's. Bud was shy, introspective, and in awe of Monk and the other figures who graced this gathering place. He was not generally accepted, but it was through Monk's endorsement that he began to get some recognition. The first time he went to Minton's, Powell sat in a chair and put his feet up on the fresh white tablecloth. When a waiter started to throw him out, Monk intervened with, "Don't do that. That kid's got talent." Monk has said of Powell: "He wasn't playing much then. He didn't know the advanced chords. He wasn't hep to much harmony. I was the only one who dug him. Nobody understood what he was playing."

Young Bud appreciated the approval and also the music of his benefactor. Jackie McLean told me, in relating his experiences with Bud in the forties, "He spoke of Monk quite a bit. He really loves Monk. He would always play Monk for me." Powell was one of the few to play Monk publicly at a time when that genius's music was misunderstood and not in vogue. He first recorded Monk's *Off Minor* in 1949. In 1961 he did it again in a Paris session, eventually released on a Columbia LP as *A Portrait of Thelonious.* The album also includes *Ruby, My Dear, Thelonious,* and *Monk's Mood,* all written by Monk. There is no doubt that harmonically Monk had an effect on him. The earliest glimpse we have of Bud on record is *Reverse the Charges,* the Freddie Webster number, on the obscure Duke label. It comes from 1942, according to tenor man Frankie Socolow, who was the leader of the date. Bud's allegiance to his earliest influences is obvious, but there are a couple of phrases that hint at an incipient bop style. He is much more advanced on *Blue Garden Blues* (actually *Royal Garden Blues*), recorded with trumpeter Charles "Cootie" Williams' orchestra in August of 1944 for Hit Records, but the material and the band's performance elicit from him nuances of swing-style playing and dictate an over-all feeling that is not in keeping with the new music in which he was to play such an important role during the next ten years. He does not solo on the first recording of Monk's *'Round Midnight,* done at the same date.

Among the eight sides cut for Hit in January of 1944 by a sextet from the Williams band, Powell has several solos that contain fully formed ideas in the new style. The four-pocket 78-rpm album is entitled *Echoes of Harlem* and has been unavailable for many years. On *My Old Flame* Bud has a flowery solo with a

Tatumesque run; *Sweet Lorraine* has a similar flourish, but he points vaguely toward his personal style. On *Do Some War Work, Baby* he backs Cootie's vocal with boppish obbligatos and takes a short solo in the same vein. *Honeysuckle Rose* begins with his bop-inflected intro and later shows him off in a solo of definite bebop material. However, this solo is played on the beat, whereas his eight-bar bit on *I Don't Know* reveals the intricate double-timing that is a Powell hallmark, and the half chorus on *Floogie Boo* is completely idiomatic. Set against the older styles of Williams, tenor saxophonist Eddie "Lockjaw" Davis, and alto saxophonist Eddie "Cleanhead" Vinson, Powell's style stands out all the more.

Bud was with Williams in 1943–1944. Then he became part of the Fifty-second Street scene, working with John Kirby, Dizzy Gillespie, Don Byas, Dexter Gordon, J.J. Johnson, Allen Eager, and Sid Catlett. He appeared on many Savoy records in the next few years, backing Gordon, Johnson, Sonny Stitt, and as a member of an all-star group billed as the Bebop Boys. His solos on *Long Tall Dexter* (a blues recorded in January, 1946) and on *Jay Jay* (an *I Got Rhythm* variant done with Johnson in June) directly foreshadowed, respectively, longer, more intense solos on *Fat Boy* and *Webb City* with the Bebop Boys in September of the same year. *Webb City* is Powell's tune. Pianist Freddie Redd says of Bud's *Webb City* solo, "*That's* Bud Powell!"

Another Powell original from this period was *Serenade to a Square,* based on the chords of *Cherokee.* The first recording was by Sonny Stitt, with Powell accompanying him, on Savoy. I have always felt that there was something missing, as there is an abrupt jump from Bud's frantic introduction right into Sonny's improvised choruses. Later, when Bud recorded *Cherokee* in a trio performance (for the album called the *Jazz Scene*), he used the same introduction and phrased his variation of the melody in a shifting, chordal statement. This obviously was the theme, the "head," removed from the Stitt record for reasons of space. Dave Lambert has said that this tune was used by Parker and Powell in the "weeding-out process" in which "the men were separated from the boys."

Powell made only one studio recording with Parker, and that was in June of 1947, the Savoy session that produced *Donna Lee, Chasing the Bird, Cheryl,* and *Buzzy.* The other Powell-with-

Parker on record consists of some tracks on the Jazz Cool label and the *Jazz at Massey Hall* set on Fantasy. The former are "live" performances taped either off the air or at a club and include marvelous solos on *'Round Midnight*, with Monkish touches and perfectly timed, typically Powellian runs, and *Ornithology*, with the kind of blazing continuity that only Bud could produce.

Parker and Powell probably wouldn't have played together much more often even if Bud hadn't spent so much time in hospitals. As Walter Bishop has been quoted as saying: "Bird's and Bud's personalities clashed. Bud was leader status himself."

There *were* clashes, the final one taking place at Birdland on Parker's last appearance there. But any of Powell's leaders had his hands full. In the Cootie Williams band, during a dance, Cootie called a certain number. Powell told him that he didn't want to play it. As reported in *Ebony* by Allan Morrison: "Cootie, by this time used to the pianist's peculiarities, pursed his lips impatiently and repeated the title of the tune. Bud folded his arms over the keyboard and stared at the ceiling. 'I won't play it,' he told Cootie. Cootie finally compromised on another tune."

Owing to his trips to the hospitals and the shifting nature of small groups generally, Powell did not spend a lot of time with any one unit in the forties. There was one fabulous but short-lived group that really deserved the "all-star" title that was so often indiscriminately thrown around. Besides Bud, there were Miles Davis, Fats Navarro, Lucky Thompson, Dexter Gordon, Kai Winding, Milt Jackson, Oscar Pettiford, and Kenny Clarke. They played at the Clique (later Birdland) as Christmas opposition to a show at the Royal Roost in 1948. When Bud played, the front line turned around and faced the piano in order to listen more closely. Once, after a particularly great solo, Powell walked off the stand, applauding himself as he went, and Jackson had to finish the number at the piano.

In the late forties, Powell did trio work with Curly Russell and Max Roach. They recorded for a company called Three Deuces, after the Fifty-second Street club, but the eight sides (including *Off Minor*) eventually were issued on Roost. This is vintage Powell, with some typical up-tempo flights on *Indiana* and *Bud's Bubble* (really Benny Harris' *Crazeology*). Just before this, Powell had recorded a fine trio set for Norman Granz on Mercury with Roach and Ray Brown. It included *All God's Chillun Got*

Rhythm, a favorite Powell vehicle. It was numbers like this that
caused one hipster to call him "hammerfingers," not because Bud
bludgeoned the keys but because of his touch, the way he articulated each note in the rapid lines he put together at very fast
tempos.

I remember the impatience with which the inner circle in New
York waited for the issue of *All God's Chillun.* It was later transferred to a Verve LP (*Bud Powell: Jazz Giant*) and is note-
worthy not only for excellent Powell and a well-integrated trio
but for several examples of his ability as a composer of well-
constructed lines: *Celia, Tempus Fugue-It,* and *Strictly Confiden-
tial.* The unaccompanied piano solo called *I'll Keep Loving You* is
Bud's lush and highly emotional interpretation of *You Are Too
Beautiful.*

Before the trio version of *All God's Chillun* came out, Prestige
Records issued a version featuring Sonny Stitt on tenor, backed
by Powell, Russell, and Roach. This was done at a December 11,
1949, session and led to another date with the same personnel on
January 26, 1950. (During the month of January, Stitt and Powell
worked together at the Orchid on Fifty-second Street.) The sides
from both recording dates are remarkable for the unrelenting
swing of the entire quartet and the unflagging flow of the two
principals. There are not many pianists who can compete with a
hard-blowing hornman like Stitt, but the "amazing Bud Powell"
(as he was later to be billed) does it, and he manages to domi-
nate the proceedings at many points.

Powell, who was a great needler and taunter, was on the receiving end at the December Prestige recording session. Stitt kept
intoning in an extremely sarcastic way, "The great Bud Powell
. . ." If anything, this spurred Bud on to greater heights, which
is probably what Stitt had had in mind. On this same day, Powell
audaciously told Bob Weinstock, the young president of Prestige,
"Hey, Fats, go out and get us some sandwiches."

Besides *All God's Chillun,* the December session produced
Sonnyside, an *I Got Rhythm* thing, its theme perilously close to
Parker's *Dexterity; Sunset,* a thinly cloaked *These Foolish Things;*
and an unselfconsciously funky *Bud's Blues,* all credited to Stitt.
At the second date, standards like *Strike Up the Band, I Want to
Be Happy, Takin' a Chance on Love,* and *Fine and Dandy* were
cut. The clarity and swing of the latter are phenomenal, with

Powell outdoing himself on both "takes" of *Fine and Dandy*. It is not surprising that because of Powell's hornlike execution, many reedmen, including Stitt, have listed him, along with Parker, as a main influence.

Earlier in 1949, Powell made his first recordings for the Blue Note label, the start of an association that produced some of Bud's best performances. Jackie McLean believes that "if Alfred Lion and Frank Wolff [the men who run Blue Note] had been able to handle Bud from the early part of his career, he would have turned out a much different person. 'Cause, those are two very good friends of Bud. They've always treated him with the greatest respect."

The debut of his compositions *Dance of the Infidels, Bouncin' with Bud,* and *Wail* marked the August session, along with Monk's *52nd Street Theme, Ornithology,* and *You Go to My Head.* The first four titles feature Fats Navarro and Sonny Rollins with Powell. The last two are trio numbers with Tommy Potter and Roy Haynes.

Dance of the Infidels is one of Powell's most famous compositions. It is typical of the period in that the chords are the augmented blues changes introduced during this era, and the theme, as Leonard Feather says in his liner notes to *The Amazing Bud Powell,* "makes use of a favorite rhythmic device of bop: the two-bar phrase with a 'hesitation' accent [the "stops"] before the third beat of the second bar."

The fifties found Powell almost exclusively at the head of his own trios—when he was playing. He did a date for Blue Note with Roach and Russell in May, 1951, that included his rhythmic Latinesque masterpiece *Un Poco Loco*. On *The Amazing Bud Powell,* it is given in three "takes" from the same recording session, presenting a graphic illustration of the process of cutting a gem.

One of the best sets he ever recorded was done in the early fifties and is now on Verve's *The Genius of Bud Powell*. It contains five unaccompanied solos: *Parisienne Thoroughfare, Oblivion, Dusk in Sandi, Hallucinations* (recorded by Miles Davis' nonet as *Budo*), and *The Fruit*. Not only is Powell's playing superb, but all five pieces are his original compositions, with melodies that have not lost their freshness.

Powell's recordings through the fifties were made for three

companies—Verve, Victor, and Blue Note. All show a gradual deterioration of his powers, but bright spots gleam through here and there. A Blue Note set recorded in 1953 (he was under contract to Verve but received permission to do this album) presents a Powell still in command of the keyboard, although much more subdued, and includes his stark, haunting *Glass Enclosure*, which manages to convey the desolation, melancholy, and anxiety of his experiences in the asylums. His playing on the Massey Hall concert album, recorded a couple of months before the Blue Note date, is much more like the old Bud, both in his own set and in the one with Parker and Gillespie. Both these albums were reissued by Fantasy in 1962.

As the 1950's wore on, his Verve and Victor releases were very uneven. One album, *The Lonely One*, recorded for Verve in two sessions in January and April, 1955 (thereby sandwiching the Parker blowup at Birdland), is generally better than the Victors but has its share of the spotty playing typical of Powell at that time. In the notes, Nat Hentoff stated the situation clearly when he wrote: "Bud's records are, in this respect, like his live appearances. They're not consistent. Some may be distorted in various ways throughout an entire album; some may come fully alive in sections; and a few in recent years have been sustained achievements."

George Duvivier, who was often Bud's bassist in the middle fifties, was quoted by Hentoff in the same notes: "When you catch him right, he can still do some really surprising things. There have been times when Art Taylor and I would look at each other, and say, 'What?' because of some way he had conceived a tune. Those are the nights when his technique is clean and his arpeggios aren't muffled. His eyes are clear; he becomes very aware; and he seemed to be really enjoying himself. There have been times when he's been loose when he could take *Salt Peanuts,* let's say, at a fantastic tempo, equal to what Tatum might have done or Oscar Peterson can do now, and he'd sustain. Other times he might start at that tempo, but wouldn't be able to keep it up."

The version of *Salt Peanuts* in *The Lonely One* is a perfect example. At a tempo that the Powell of five years before would have eaten up, Bud's articulation suffers, and he falters in many places. Compare his *Strike Up the Band,* recorded with Stitt, with *Frantic Fancies* (based on the same Gershwin standard), which is in his Blue Note trio album entitled *Bud! Frantic Fancies* lacks the bold authority that Powell once showed, and the execution is painfully sloppy in spots. In the same album, he does *Bud on Bach*, a minor-key swinger based on C. P. E. Bach's *Solfeggietto*, which he had played as a child. Before launching into his variation, Powell plays *Solfeggietto;* and while the over-all track is more than enjoyable, the little flubs that creep into the Bach portion would not have occurred with the Powell of the forties.

Until he left the country, Bud stayed with Blue Note. *Time Waits* and *The Scene Changes* were the last two albums he did in New York. In general, these are far better than the Victors and the later Verves. For one thing, there are more Powell originals, and he was undoubtedly more relaxed with Lion and Wolff.

The Scene Changes, which is Volume 5 and the last in the Blue Note series titled *The Amazing Bud Powell,* is a strange album. The first four tracks are minor key and bear a strange resemblance to one another. The fifth track on side 1 is *Borderick,* an eight-bar nursery tune for his then three-year-old son; it is repeated, with small variations, over and over, even getting into a Fats Waller stride in the second chorus.

The other side has a Latin number of about eight minutes entitled *Comin' Up.* For the entire track, Powell plays around with rhythmic figures that smack more of a monotonous mambo pianist than of the genius who did *Un Poco Loco.* A comparison of *Comin' Up* with *Un Poco Loco* indicates the toll of the intervening eight years of Bud's life.

Although Parker and Gillespie based their style on the chords, there is more "melody" playing in their work than in Powell's. As Teddy Charles has said: "With Bud it was more an ingenious connection of scales and arpeggios, but the strength was not melodic."

This is not to say that Powell did not construct beautiful melodies—his compositions have proven this—but his up-tempo and medium-tempo work was oriented to the "changes." Here and there in his career, he has done some atypical playing. On *Some Soul,* in the *Bud!* album, he investigates the changes on this slow blues more in the crevice-seeking manner of his childhood compatriot Elmo Hope. Further away from his own idiom are the stride sections on *The Last Time I Saw Paris* (on the LP *The Genius of Bud Powell*) and *Idaho* (on *Bud!*), with echoes of Art

Tatum on the first and Teddy Wilson on the second. He also sounds like Wilson and Tatum on *Jubilee* (*Hallelujah*) in his Massey Hall trio set.

As he has been to countless pianists, Tatum was a god to Powell. On certain ballad offerings, Bud would perform in a style very close to Art's. *It Could Happen to You* and *Over the Rainbow* from the 1951 Blue Note session without Roach and Russell are examples of this approach. Yet Bud's own ballad *Dusk at Sandi,* which is also unaccompanied, has no vestiges of Tatum. *Just One of Those Things,* from the same Verve recording as *Sandi,* is an attempt at a Tatumesque tour de force: a combination of the old master and Bud's own brand of modern lines, played at an inhuman tempo without the aid of bass or drums. Not everything comes off, but there are moments of ecstasy and desperation—a man walking a tightrope over a chasm of poetic beauty and madness.

One night at Birdland in 1950, Powell told Tatum that the older pianist had made five mistakes in a Chopin prelude. Tatum saltily responded with, "You're just a right-hand piano player. You've got no left hand. Look, I've got a rhythm section in my left hand."

The next night Bud played *Sometimes I'm Happy* entirely with his left hand at a furious tempo and drew Tatum's praise. A tribute from his idol was the ultimate compliment, and Bud's jubilation knew no bounds that evening.

The public face that Bud Powell has presented through the years is one compounded of the quiet mask, the snarl, and the leer. The last named was seen most often at Birdland, where Powell appeared quite often in the mid-fifties. It might happen between numbers or after his solo. While his bassist was soloing, Bud would turn and face the "bullpen" area, a fixed stare in his eyes and an eerie grimace on his face. Sometimes he would hold this pose for minutes.

Powell's strange behavior has been the topic of conversation among all members of the jazz fraternity. Dexter Gordon remembers that "Bud was always—ever since I've known him—he was a little on the border line. Because he'd go off into things—expressions, telltale things that would let you know he was off."

When Powell and Gordon were members of the all-star band at the Clique at Christmastime, 1948, the group playing opposite was George Shearing's quartet, which featured Buddy De Franco on clarinet. "Bud used to run around behind George," Gordon remembers, "and thump him, slap him. And I'd say, 'Oh, man, what are you doing?' Bud was into his Napoleon thing then." It sounds more like the act of a mischievous boy than that of some- one motivated by active maliciousness. In any case, Powell showed an admiration for Shearing by playing his compositions *Conception* and *Consternation*.

Many people feel that Powell's strange actions were calculated, a put-on, or at least that they began that way. Gordon calls it, "Kind of double, triple cross. Elmo [Hope] told me that Bud got this from him—playing crazy."

Hope is not the only musician to claim to be Powell's teacher in this respect. Thelonious Monk has told Jules Colomby, the brother of Monk's manager, that it was he whom Bud picked it up from. Lennie Tristano related another such claim about Powell to Robert Reisner: "I was sitting with Charlie [Parker] and some musicians at a table in Birdland when Bud Powell came by and said hello, then, for no apparent reason, he said, 'You know, Bird, you ain't shit. You don't kill me. You ain't playing shit now,' and went on putting him down unmercifully. I said, 'Bud don't talk that way: Bird's your poppa.'

"Bird said, 'Lennie, don't pay any attention. I dig the way he plays.' . . . Concerning Bud, Charlie once said to me, 'You think he is crazy? I taught him to act that way.'"

Because of his essentially introverted nature, Powell was marked as the "quiet one," the "strange one" from the earliest days at Minton's. His strange behavior probably began as a com- bination defense mechanism and attention getter.

In 1945 his erratic behavior began to cause him trouble with the law. Early that year, he was arrested for the first time in his life. The charge was disorderly conduct. He had been drinking and became very noisy in Philadelphia's Broad Street Station. Some musicians believe he was beaten over the head by the po- lice. After he was fined and released, he went to his mother's house in Willow Grove, Pennsylvania, to rest up. A month later, however, he was sent to Pilgrim State Hospital, a mental institu- tion on Long Island where, according to Alan Morrison, during his ten-month stay "he talked garrulously to all who would listen and was generally over-active. 'His thoughts were flying away with him,' one psychiatrist reported."

After an active year of recording and playing on Fifty-second

Street in 1946 and early 1947, Powell's problems began multiplying. In May of 1947 he began drinking heavily again. Morrison reported: "He began to acquire a bad reputation and was abusive when drunk. He got into brawls too often and had an irrational fear of being attacked on the street."

There was apparently great anxiety within Powell concerning his race and the prejudice to which it is subjected. Once he was observed at Birdland frantically rubbing his hands, supposedly trying to remove the color. Yet another time he told Miles Davis, "I wish I was blacker. I'd like to be as black as you are, Miles."

A nervous breakdown occurred in November of 1947, and he was recommitted to Creedmore. During eleven months there, he was given electric-shock treatments, but little improvement was noted. He did some playing, and toward the end of his confinement he was allowed to come home for weekends. It was during this period that Jackie McLean met him.

McLean had started playing alto in 1946 when he was 15. His stepfather acquired a record shop on 141st Street and Eighth Avenue the following year, and Jackie used to clerk for him. "One day I was playing some Bud Powell records in the shop for a friend of mine," McLean relates, "and this fellow came in. He had on coveralls, paint all over him, and he was browsing through the records. I happened to mention Bud's name, and he turned around and said that was his brother. It was Richard." Richie Powell was Bud's younger brother and was a member of the Max Roach–Clifford Brown group until June 26, 1956, when he and Brown were killed in an automobile crash.

"I looked at him and I said, 'Yeah,' and I fluffed him off as if he was telling a fib. He told me he would prove it to me. I asked him if he played piano, and he said no, so then I really told him that I was sure he was just kidding me, 'cause if he was Bud's brother, I thought he would play the piano or at least know him when he heard him on the record, which I don't think he did. He said his brother was in the hospital but would be home for the weekend, 'cause he was coming home every weekend. He said if I came up Sunday, I would meet him."

On Sundays, McLean would open the shop at 11 A.M. and close at 2 P.M. "I had my horn with me, but I had forgotten about the meeting. Richard came around to the shop and took me around to his house.

"Bud lived on St. Nicholas Avenue between 140th and 141st

Streets," McLean remembers. "He had a beard. He was sort of quiet and seemed eccentric in his ways but friendly towards me. He saw my horn and said, 'Do you play?' I played *Buzzy* with him, and he was amused by it. That's how I began to see Bud. Richard and I got very friendly at that time."

Through McLean's prodding, Richie Powell took up the piano. Jackie had become a regular visitor at the Powell house. "I used to go down there quite a bit—Fridays after school especially. I practiced with Bud whenever he felt like it. When he'd go to the piano, I'd take my horn out. Lot of times I would just sit and listen—sometimes an hour or two straight of Bud playing. Most of the time conversation was music—actually, Bud sitting down and playing. He would sit and play, and I'd just be quiet. He'd play through some ballads and ask me if I'd heard this or that. Then he'd play something by Monk and quite a lot of tunes I'd never heard before. He started to help me to play different tunes. He was married and his daughter, Celia, had just been born."

According to Allan Morrison, Powell was released from Creedmore near the end of 1948 but went back in after ten weeks. This new breakdown supposedly took place after Bud recorded the composition dedicated to his daughter, *Celia*. This time, it was reported, Powell seemed to make a better adjustment to life in the institution. "His playing was one of the highlights of the hospital's annual minstrel show," Morrison wrote.

Powell left the hospital in April, 1949, and enjoyed several years of uninterrupted musical activity, but in the summer of 1951 his drinking became excessive again. In August he was arrested, along with four others, for illegal possession of narcotics. While Bud was in the Tombs that night, he went beserk and was doused with buckets of ammoniated water. Taken to Bellevue, he told doctors that people were trying to murder him. He was committed to Pilgrim State on September 4, 1951. His eleven months at this institution included more shock treatments. He was allowed to play the piano once a week, supervised by an attendant. Later he was transferred to Creedmore and eventually released on February 5, 1953, in the custody of Oscar Goodstein, the manager of Birdland, who became Powell's manager and legal guardian. Before Bud's release, Goodstein had arranged for two one-night passes that enabled Bud to play at Birdland in December, 1952, and to see how he would react in a nightclub atmosphere.

During the 1947–1951 period, McLean was very close to

Powell. He became friendly with Mrs. Powell ("I used to call her Momma") and spent weekends at the house. "Bud liked me to take him on his job. I used to take him to his gig on Sunday afternoons at the Roost, or up to the Audubon one afternoon when he played opposite George Shearing."

Powell was a homebody, according to McLean. "Bud stayed in a good deal. He didn't go out at all as I recall. The only time Bud went out was when he had to go somewhere and play. Very seldom he went out on his own. One afternoon he asked me to go up to visit Benny Harris. It was a strange thing to go out into the street with Bud just on a social visit. And it was sort of strange to him too, because of riding on the subway and everything. Bud was looking around like he was coming to New York for the first time."

I told McLean about the time I had walked with Bud and Red Rodney from Birdland over to the Three Deuces; Bud was really togged out, the epitome of sartorial taste, right down to a new, expensive umbrella. Jackie was not surprised by this. "When he did get *dressed*, he would always get in front of the mirror and ask me if he was sharp and how did he look and did I think he was handsome."

Another time I was with Powell at a friend's house. He didn't say more than a few words during the couple of hours we were there. He sat in a chair, occasionally laughing to himself, getting up only to play the piano or to eat. McLean confirmed Bud's quietness in the presence of strangers. "That's Bud. Even today, like in Paris, Bud wouldn't have too much to say about too many things. He would with me if we were alone, but as soon as there was another person on the scene, he would tend to clam up and just look."

Jackie feels that the many shock treatments Powell received were far more detrimental than helpful to him. They affected his memory strongly. "I think Bud got a severe treatment when he was over there. . . . Bud didn't remember too much, actually, about his life prior to going to the hospital because of the treatment they had given him. I remember there were times when I would mention names, and they would come back to him, like Sonny Stitt's name. I remember the day Bud really recalled knowing Sonny Stitt. . . . At that time, I was very wrapped up in Sonny and asking about him.

"I'd mention names to him, and he had to stop and think and ask me, 'Who?' and 'Tell me about it.' That used to be a statement he used to make to me all the time, 'Tell me about it,' or 'Did I?' or 'What did I do?'—things like that."

When Powell returned from Creedmore in 1949, McLean says, he had forgotten a lot of things that had happened just before he went in. "When I went down to see him, it was just like meeting him again. But he did know me."

It was late in 1949, right after Birdland opened, that Bud brought Jackie, then 17, to the club and had him sit in on *A Night in Tunisia*. In 1951 he arranged for Jackie to play with Miles Davis, and McLean was hired as a result. "After I started playing with Miles, I didn't see Bud much," says Jackie. "Then when he was with Oscar [Goodstein], I really didn't see Bud much unless I went down to hear him play."

Someone who did see Powell quite a bit during this time was a girl named Dede Emerson, a pianist who once worked club dates when she felt like it but is now completely out of the music business. In the summer of 1953, when she came to New York from Utah, she was an aspiring jazz pianist and much involved with the scene. As wide-eyed visitors to the big city, she and two girl friends used to frequent the "bullpen" area at Birdland every night in order to hear Powell play. Soon they got to know Goodstein, and because Bud had noticed them talking to Oscar, he asked them to have a Coke with him. As he was not allowed to drink liquor or beer, he would consume ten to twenty Cokes or ginger ales and three or four double-egg malteds during the course of a night at Birdland.

Because Goodstein liked the girls' guileless attitude and knew they liked Bud, he asked them to keep an eye on him and make sure he didn't drink. Miss Emerson recounts that during the course of a walk, "he would say, 'Do you think we can get a beer?' and almost with a complete togetherness, we would give this *no* look to him, and he would say, 'I'll just have one glass. You can have the rest of the bottle.' Of course, none of us drank, and we felt almost like Carrie Nations. It was in our minds that we were going to preserve this great musician, and if alcohol was an enemy of his, then we were going to keep him away from it. So, by and by, we would talk him into having a soda, and he did it—he was quite nice about it, accommodating us."

Later, the girls had him over to dinner and to listen to records. "He would laugh, not prompted by anything but by something he was thinking," says Dede. "By the same token, Bud was very aware of everything everyone was doing; and as silent as he could be, there were other times when he would chatter for quite an extensive period, and he would talk about his songs—whether we liked a particular rendition of something he had recorded or played that evening. He talked about brother Richie or asked about us—asked me about my progress on the piano."

One day Dede took Powell to her class at Juilliard, where he was warmly received. "It was very satisfying to him," she says, "because these were very eager people who not only appreciated Bud Powell but who themselves were trying to become pianists."

Dede Emerson's teacher was John Mehegan. He was very taken with Powell's talent and wanted to help him. Powell had respect for Mehegan as a teacher. "If he had been around John Lewis or Hall Overton, I'm sure it would have been the same," says Dede. Once she and Mehegan went to the Willow Grove house to visit Bud and his mother. Dede describes Mrs. Powell as "a small, older woman—definitely not matronly. Bud was like a panther. He couldn't wait to get back to New York."

On another occasion, Mehegan and Miss Emerson took Powell to see composer Henry Brant, one of the teachers at Juilliard. Dede was impressed with Bud's ability to arrange at the piano. "Bud would always talk about someday having his tunes played by a fifty-five-piece orchestra." This statement seems to underline a recurring wish by many jazz musicians for what they feel will give them esteem and respectability.

The visit with Brant was a success. "Bud was very articulate," Dede says. "He played *Dance of the Infidels,* and he was telling Brant how he would like to have it arranged with the trumpets and trombones. It was just amazing how he moved inner voices—not playing in a piano style but just as you could imagine it orchestrated."

They thought that giving Powell another musical interest by encouraging his writing would benefit him, but he never carried out the plan and failed to see Brant again.

In his relationship with Dede Emerson and her girl friends, "he almost liked being a child again, which is almost the way we treated him. I don't know whether it was healthy or not, but at

the time it seemed to make him a little happy. At the piano he
was mature, away from it he was a child. Everything he couldn't
say in life was in the piano."

During the time that Dede knew Bud, a new love came into his
life. It was Buttercup, who became his wife and eventually
assumed the guardianship that Goodstein had held. All did not
run smoothly, however. In 1954 or 1955, Powell was in Central
Islip, where Pilgrim State is located, and at Butter's request,
Dede went out to visit him. "He had a piano in his room," she
remembers, "and was very talkative."

Just before leaving for Paris in 1959, Powell had been released
from Kings County Hospital in Brooklyn. In Paris, according to
McLean, he drank "when he could get something to drink. But all
Paris knows Bud—when I say 'all Paris,' I mean all the jazz people and artists, and they know that it's not such a good idea to
give Bud anything to drink. And most people shy away from giving him a drink, because he goes way out when he has anything
to drink. . . . One little glass of brandy can completely flip him
around. I've never seen juice affect anyone like that."

If all Paris knew Bud, they also appreciated him. McLean said,
"He gets respect that he needs over there in Paris. He's *Bud Powell.* Over there, they give you a little personal applause for your
efforts and all the years you've been playing, besides just clapping
their hands from the audience. They seem to be always applauding you—when they see you in the street."

McLean did not think that Powell would return to the United
States to stay for any length of time. Journalist Jack Lind's report
from Copenhagen bore this out at the time: "Powell had intended
to stay only for a week, but hung around for a whole month,
bringing with him his wife Altevia [Buttercup's real name] and
their 6-year-old son John, who speaks fluent French but English
with a French accent."

Lind described Bud himself thusly: "The pianist still has the
same introspective air about him. He sits astride the piano stool,
tapping out the rhythm with a cowboy-booted foot, humming the
counterpoint, staring glass-eyed in front of him—and paying no
heed to the audience. He acknowledges the rousing Danish applause with the same grace as Miles Davis.

"Powell is under the firm, guiding hand of his wife," Lind also
wrote, "who manages his business affairs. 'He has made a marvel-

ous adjustment in Europe,' she said. 'We've had several offers from the States, but they weren't interesting enough, and Bud still has a health problem. He isn't quite ready for the States yet.'"

Buttercup was right. In the middle of 1963, Powell became ill with tuberculosis in both lungs. Ironically, in the first half of the year, before the illness put him flat on his back, Bud had done some recording that, even with its shortcomings, was remarkably close to the old Powell. Solos with Dizzy Gillespie and the Double Six of Paris on Philips and with Dexter Gordon in *Our Man in Paris* on Blue Note reveal a flowing line of improvisation, even if the old fire is not all there. When I reviewed his Reprise album *Bud Powell in Paris,* done in February, 1963, I wrote in *Down Beat:* "On *Benny (Little Benny)* . . . he is very articulate, but the old Powell would have given it more intensity. And the old Powell would not have missed notes, or flubbed the break on *Stockholm (Dear Old Stockholm)*." Nevertheless, this album stands far above the painful Victors and Verves of the 1954–1956 period and is more like early Powell than the Blue Notes of the late fifties.

In late October, 1963, many musicians gathered at Birdland to give a benefit performance for Powell. As 1964 opened, rumors began to be heard again about his coming to the United States. On August 16, he arrived at New York's Kennedy International Airport, accompanied by a friend, young French commercial artist Francis Paudras. According to the news report in *Down Beat,* Paudras was "credited by Powell's friends with nursing the pianist back to health and shielding him from undesirable influences. Oscar Goodstein, who met the two men at the airport, said: 'Without this man, Bud might not be with us today.'"

Powell, when asked what he was looking forward to most during his stay in New York, replied, "Handling my own dough."

On opening night at Birdland, the packed club gave him a standing ovation before he even played a note. If he again was not the "old Bud," he did reach heights of inspiration during the evening, especially in his own *John's Abbey* and Monk's *Epistrophy* and *Bemsha Swing.* Through September he remained at Birdland, except for one week during which he recorded an album for Roulette. His playing here is erratic, like his work at the club. Depending on to whom you spoke and when they had been to

Birdland, you might learn that Bud sounded wonderful or that he sounded really sad.

On October 10, Powell did not show up for his first set of the evening. He was missing for two days. Eventually he was found at the house of some friends in Brooklyn. With that, it was decided that he and Paudras should return to Paris, but on October 18 he disappeared again, this time from the Weehawken, New Jersey, home of Baroness Nica de Koenigswarter. While other members of the party were engaged in conversation, he slipped out and did not return until October 23. Photographer Don Schlitten, on his way to the Village Vanguard, had seen him the day before in a Greenwich Village doorway and tried to convince him to go down to the club and call Goodstein. But Bud, failing to cadge a drink, wandered off.

Powell then returned to the Baroness's home. According to attorney Bernard Stollman, he was in good spirits and "talking more volubly than usual."

Although the jazz community in New York assumed that Powell had left with Paudras for Paris on October 27, it was later surprised to find that only Paudras had departed and that Powell was living in Brooklyn, with no apparent plans to return to France.

In March, 1965, Powell appeared at a special memorial concert at Carnegie Hall on the tenth anniversary of Charlie Parker's death. He had been overweight at the time of his return; now he was bloated, and his eyes had a lost look as he slowly shuffled to the piano. Horace Silver's *No Smoking*, ordinarily taken at a brisk tempo, sounded like a 78-rpm record being played at 45; and *'Round Midnght*, although negotiated at a pace closer to what Powell seemed to be capable of on that evening, was almost equally disturbing. It was indeed difficult to look at or listen to Bud that night.

By this time, Stollman had become his manager, and he presented Bud on the same program with some "new thing," avantgarde players at Town Hall in the spring. Dan Morgenstern, reviewing the concert, wrote of Powell's solo piano: "Though in considerably better form than at his distressing appearance at Carnegie Hall in March, Powell was far from his peak. However, his final selection, *I Remember Clifford*, was extremely moving, and what had seemed to be faltering time on the faster pieces

now became a nearly Monkish deliberateness, each phrase ring-
ing out full and strong. What Powell hasn't lost is his marvelous
touch and sound, and everything he played revealed a sense of
balance and proportion not much in evidence elsewhere on the
program."

What Powell had lost was his health. During the summer, his
liver, among other things, acted up on him, and he was in critical
condition for several days. The people who had said in August,
1964, "Bud's come home to die," had almost been prophets. But
Powell rallied and began another in his long series of conva-
lescences.

Despite the deterioration suffered by Bud Powell through his
many and varied encounters with illness, his mark has been in-
eradicably stamped on the music of his native country. Pianists
quickly adopted his style in the forties, and in no time he had
founded a school.

Powell's influence has been widespread among both the pianists who were playing during the period of his first flowering and
the young players who came slightly afterward. Men like George
Wallington, Al Haig, and Elmo Hope go back to the beginning of
the bop movement and grew up, musically, with Bud. Each exerted a certain influence on some of the others, but Powell
emerged as the greatest stylist.

Around the mid-forties, the second wave of the decade's
promising players appeared. In the East, there were Argonne
Thornton and Gene Di Novi, who was Haig-like; and in the
West, Joe Albany, who showed a direct Parker influence. In
Chicago, there was Lou Levy; in New York, Hank Jones made a
switch from Wilson and Tatum to Powell and Haig. As the forties
moved along, youngsters like Walter Bishop, Jr., Kenny Drew,
Junior Mance, and Hampton Hawes were heard from, and still
others, like Horace Silver, Sonny Clark, Barry Harris, and Red
Garland, were just around the corner. Young Freddie Redd, who
was inspired to take up the piano in 1947 after having heard
Powell play a year earlier, wore his sideburns long and had a part
cut in his hair just the way Bud did.

Elmo Hope, who was very close to Powell in their youth,
studied classical piano as Bud did, and by the time he was 15 he
was winning medals for solo recitals. Later, like Bud, he showed
a fondness for the style of Thelonious Monk, an attitude most of

their piano-playing contemporaries did not share. While the new music was catching hold in New York in the mid-forties, Elmo was working with rhythm-and-blues bands like Joe Morris's and was seldom on the local scene. He was not discovered by the jazz public until he recorded for Blue Note in 1953. Through the mid-fifties, he was in obscurity, but he showed up in California at the end of the decade. He did some recording, but the Los Angeles area was not a terribly active one for jazz. In 1961 he returned to New York and did two albums for Riverside and one for Audio Fidelity. The latter is entitled *Sounds from Rikers Island*. Hope's style parallels Powell's in many ways, but it has its own highly personal harmonic twists and turns and is less charged than the Powell style of the mid-forties.

As we have mentioned earlier, George Wallington was with the Dizzy Gillespie–Oscar Pettiford group that played on Fifty-second Street in 1943. Billy Taylor, himself a former follower of Wilson and Tatum who later incorporated bop into his own style, recalls that Bud Powell was originally supposed to be the pianist with the band. Cootie Williams, then Powell's legal guardian as well as leader, wouldn't give him permission to leave his organization, and the Gillespie-Pettiford group was forced to open without a pianist. Taylor, working on The Street with Ben Webster, began filling in with Diz during his intermissions. Irving Alexander, owner of the Three Deuces, where Billy was working, finally got tired of Taylor's doubling and fired him. Wallington eventually became Dizzy's regular pianist.

In such a position, Wallington was one of the first bop pianists. Pianists in the new style were scarce. Clyde Hart, who was developing his style from swing into bop when he died of tuberculosis in March of 1945, was one of the first of the musicians from the previous era to understand and execute the harmonic demands of the new music. Oscar Pettiford has explained: "All of us were thinking about the new style, trying to get used to playing it. Clyde was the only pianist that could play those things without any trouble. In fact, he was the first to play the modern-style left hand. He told me as long as I was playing that much bass, he didn't need to play rhythm in the left hand and he could just use it to establish chord changes."

Hart was a fine accompanist to the moderns, but in his solos, which were excellent in the older style, he never made the change

to the new music. In Wallington, Gillespie had a youngster who
had naturally gravitated toward his music. Wallington's piano
was urgent and fiery and, in essence, similar to Powell's, but with
its own sense of time, touch, and phrasing. Wallington's long-
lined, skittering introduction on *Gabardine and Serge* with Serge
Chaloff on Savoy is a good example of his early general solo approach. Actually, Wallington hadn't yet heard Powell (that didn't
happen until Bud sat in at the Onyx one night when George was
working with Dizzy). But Wallington had heard of Powell
through guitarist Rector Bailey, who had told him, "This is someone who thinks along the same lines you do."

Wallington left school at 16 in 1940 and began working in
small Brooklyn and Greenwich Village clubs. He met Max Roach
and pianist Clarence Profit, who became an early influence on
him. Then came the gig with Bailey, and many of the important
modernists, including Charlie Parker, used to sit in with them.

Through the forties, Wallington was a sideman in various
groups, including Joe Marsala's and Georgie Auld's. He also
played and recorded with Allen Eager and Kai Winding, respectively. As a composer, he is best known for *Lemon Drop* and
Godchild, although he has many other fine pieces to his credit.
Except for a couple of weeks with Lionel Hampton in the early
fifties, Wallington never worked with a big band. He was the
leader of his own trios and quintets until the sixties, when he left
performing to go into the air-conditioning business with his
brothers. Wallington has lately also become an expert skeet
shooter and in 1962 began winning prizes for his marksmanship.

Al Haig, the pianist for Parker and Gillespie in their classic
quintet of 1945, was superficially like Powell but quite different in
his lighter-touch approach. His style was impeccable and quite
pianistic, reflecting a very highly developed technique. He was a
definite influence on Hank Jones and, through him, on other men,
such as Tommy Flanagan. Besides his solo abilities, Haig was an
excellent accompanist. One trademark was his "comping" two
octaves below his right hand's single solo lines. "At their best
Haig's accompaniments, like those of John Lewis, are enhancing
commentaries rather than mere backgrounds," Max Harrison wrote
in the June, 1960, issue of *The Jazz Review.*

Haig shone as both soloist and accompanist with Charlie Parker's quintet (1949–1950) and Stan Getz's quartet and quintet

HERMAN LEONARD

Broadcasting from the Royal Roost, from left, Bud Powell, Nelson Boyd, Chuck Wayne, J.J. Johnson, Budd Johnson, "Little" Benny Harris (partially obscured), Cecil Payne, and Buddy DeFranco

Dizzy Gillespie, then with his big
band at the Royal Roost, 1948–1949,
with Ernie Henry

HERMAN LEONARD

The Lennie Tristano Sextet in a rehearsal session, including,
from left, Leo Konitz, Warne Marsh, Lennie Tristano,
Billy Bauer, and Jeff Morton

HERMAN LEONARD

The founder of modern
jazz drumming,
Kenny Clarke

HERMAN LEONARD

At the piano, Bud Powell,
with Max Roach in the
background

HERMAN LEONARD

The house band at the Royal Roost,
1948, here featuring Fats Navarro,
Jimmy Ford, Tadd Dameron, Curly
Russell, Allen Eager, and Kenny Clarke

Charlie Parker and Kenny
Dorham at a recording
session

Max Roach with Charlie
Parker's group in Chicago,
1948

DON SCHLITTEN

Oscar Pettiford, listening
to a playback at a
recording session

DON SCHLITTEN
Dizzy Gillespie

(1950–1951). After that he drifted in and out of obscurity, appearing briefly with Chet Baker in 1954 and Gillespie in 1956. By the sixties, he was back in the New York area on a permanent basis, but his musical alliances were with small pop groups that catered to the dancing needs of the society set, from East Side clubs to Southampton and Bermuda.

Haig and Wallington went through a lot of the personal turmoil peculiar to their idiom and era, but when they leveled out, each in his own way, both left jazz.

The same seemed true of Dodo Marmarosa, the brilliant young pianist of the Boyd Raeburn band and the Charlie Parker recordings of the mid-forties. He was reported to be playing in his native Pittsburgh in the fifties, but he didn't record, and no one knew where he was. It wasn't until he recorded for the Argo label in Chicago in the early sixties that he was heard from again. His style had changed, however. No longer does he flash the same fluid right hand that, if it was not playing bop in the strictest sense, was very much in tune with the practitioners of the new music.

The way in which Marmarosa got to record with Parker has been explained by Ross Russell, who produced the recordings. Joe Albany was working with Parker at the Club Finale in Los Angeles, and Albany was supposed to be on the upcoming recording date. "I recall walking into the Finale early one morning during an embittered altercation between Bird and Albany over some musical detail," Russell wrote. "The Bird was no man to brook under such circumstances. Albany, who is nothing if not sensitive, did what for him has become a pattern. He walked out. Apparently he has been walking out on one opportunity after another ever since."

Anyone who has heard Albany's solos on *New Lester Leaps In* and *You're Driving Me Crazy* with Lester Young on Aladdin (since reissued on various LP's) will realize the latent talent in his grasp. All we have heard from him since the forties, however, is a now out-of-print Riverside LP entitled *The Right Combination*—a taping of a rehearsal in the living room of an engineer, involving tenor man Warne Marsh and Albany, dating from the fall of 1957. During the same period, he was working at a small club in the Los Angeles area, but little jazz activity has been attributed to him in recent years. A short visit to New York in 1963

found him appearing briefly with Charlie Mingus before returning to California.

In his comments on Albany, Russell makes an interesting point.
After mentioning Powell, Monk, and Clyde Hart, he says: "The
future seemed to depend upon a very few piano players, curiously enough all of them white, all well trained academically, who
possessed that unusual combination of qualities: technique, harmonic depth, jazz sense, and a grasp of the new idiom. One
thinks immediately of Al Haig, Dodo Marmarosa, Albany, and
after that names do not come to mind easily." Of course, leaving
out Wallington was an oversight.

In the late forties, a raft of Negro pianists, strongly influenced
by Powell, became active. Though many outgrew the disciple
role, they did not stand out immediately as individuals the way
Duke Jordan did. Jordan was heard on Fifty-second Street with
Coleman Hawkins, J.J. Johnson, Roy Eldridge's big band, and
guitarist Teddy Walters' trio. Charlie Parker heard him with the
latter group and hired him. Duke spent close to three years with
Bird and was a member of the fine 1947–1948 group. As a soloist,
Jordan shows his Teddy Wilson–Art Tatum background but in
an oblique way. Harmonically it is right with Parker's music, but
in comparison with the high-velocity attacks of the Powell-
oriented players who were aligned along similar harmonic lines, it
is spare and melodic. Jordan also shows melodic invention as a
composer. His *Jordu* has become something of a modern-jazz
standard. Like Haig, he is a brilliant accompanist who knows just
where to place his chords. His introductions are usually little
gems too. Jordan has recorded a few albums under his own name,
but generally he has been a sideman, one who has never received
the recognition equal to his talent. Again, personal problems have
hampered Jordan.

A schoolmate of Dodo Marmarosa's from Pittsburgh burst on
the Fifty-second Street scene in 1944 and in the next three years
established himself through numerous recordings for a variety of
small labels. That was Erroll Garner, who, along with Powell,
must be considered to be one of the most significant pianists to
come to light in the forties. As an influence, he nowhere approaches Powell, but, as Mimi Clar wrote, as an individual stylist
he "occupies an important position in jazz history since in his

playing, he maintains elements of traditional jazz while developing the resources of modern jazz."

Leonard Feather states in *The Book of Jazz:* "Garner's regally emphatic touch and right-hand rubato are among the most personal of his many attributes; others are the use of spread chords on ballads, and the ability to propel his right hand through a lengthy passage of eighth notes at a breakneck tempo while scattering chords like seeds."

Garner, who does not read music at all, is a persuasive performer both aurally and visually. At the keyboard, sitting on a telephone book to compensate for his short stature, he has a pixie quality. As leader of his own trio, Garner has concentrated on standards and current show material, which in part explains his great popularity among the general public. Some of his ballad performances are schmaltzy, however, and smack more of the cocktail lounge than of the jazz room. His compositions usually are as successful as they are tuneful. *Misty* is a good example, equal to the best of popular music.

There is quite a contrast between Garner, the successful concert artist, for a while booked by the famed impresario Sol Hurok, and Bud Powell, whose greatest achievements seem, unfortunately, to lie in the past. Powell had a genius that should have been cultivated. If he had received better personal handling or perhaps if there had been the kind of chemical therapy that is available today, we might know a different Powell.

Whatever "ifs" there are, one thing is certain: Bud Powell's exalted place in jazz history is secure even if he never plays another note. As John Lewis told an interviewer for the West Coast music magazine *Theme,* in the fall of 1957, "Bud is the most influential pianist of the last ten years, I think. No, I don't think that—I know that's true!"

Recommended Listening

The Bebop Boys, SAVOY SJL 2225
The Genius of Bud Powell, VERVE VE 2-2506
The Amazing Bud Powell, Volume 1 and 2, BLUE NOTE 81503, 81504
Bud Powell, QUINTESSENCE 25381
Bud in Paris, XANADU 102

(see also Stitt, Navarro)

4

J.J. JOHNSON
AND THE TROMBONISTS

As THE BOP REVOLUTION spread, solo instruments other than the trumpet, alto sax, and piano began to echo the doctrines of Parker and Gillespie. The trombone, largely a rhythm instrument in the dawn of jazz before it was granted true solo privileges, had never been played in the swift, extremely legato, eighth-note style that J.J. Johnson introduced in the mid-forties. Since that time there have been few new trombonists who haven't shown some manifestation of Johnson's style in their playing.

An innovator in areas of tone and technique, translator of bop ideas on his instrument, Johnson became the most influential and popular trombonist of the modern era. Whereas most of the giants of the forties were volatile personalities in one way or another, Johnson has always been soft-spoken, modest, and usually reserved, completely different in temperament from Gillespie, Parker, or Powell. His self-effacing attitude is pointed up in a statement he gave me for an article, "The Remarkable J.J. Johnson," that appeared in *Down Beat* (May 11, 1961): "When I was approached [about this article], it occurred to me that I had read, in this publication and others, many articles, interviews, profiles—some very witty, some very dull, some very intellectual.

"On the premise that I am not especially witty, except on rare occasions, not particularly brainy, except on even rarer occasions, and have no particular beefs or gripes, and don't want to put anyone down, I had certain misgivings about doing the story."

This self-appraisal is overmodest. In truth, J.J. is "brainy," and his wit is in evidence on more than just rare occasions. It is dry and subtle, a parallel of his playing style, as it were. A backstage conversation between Johnson and "beat" writer Jack Kerouac, reported by Dan Wakefield in *The Nation*, illustrates this beautifully. Kerouac, who was reading his works aloud at the Village Vanguard that week, is notorious for a sometimes misguided enthusiasm about jazz. "I should have been a jazz musician," he told Johnson. "I would have been a great tenor saxophonist."

J.J. thoughtfully replied, "No, I picture you more as a trumpeter."

Although he claims otherwise, Johnson is interesting in and of himself. His influence as a trombonist dates from the time of his first recordings as a combo leader. His general popularity dates from around 1955, when he began winning first place in jazz-magazine polls, something he has continued to do ever since. In the sixties, his compositional and arranging talent, previously relegated to a secondary role, really came to the fore.

Up to Johnson's emergence, the trombone favorite of the forties was Bill Harris, a Philadelphian who had earlier failed to stick with a couple of bands because of his slowness as a reader. He conquered this fault and rose to prominence in the Woody Herman Herd of 1944–46. Harris' style was in the rough-and-ready tradition and on up-tempo numbers could be directly linked to that of J. C. Higginbotham. At the same time, his more personal, wide-vibratoed ballads were far from the new trends in jazz that were being echoed around him by other players in the Herman band. *Bijou* was his tour de force with Herman, but his fervid, preaching style is also well-represented on many of Woody's up-tempo recordings and a *Sweet Georgia Brown* side done on a WNEW "Saturday Night Swing Session." A powerful individual in his own right, Harris never had an extensive influence on the young trombonists who came after him.

If you had heard J.J. Johnson at a Los Angeles Jazz at the Philharmonic concert in 1944, you might have enjoyed his playing, but you wouldn't have prophesied that it would shape the trombone style for the next twenty years. Recordings of the concert, first issued in 1946, were bought more for Illinois Jacquet's tenor saxophone shrieking and for a "tag" game between guitarist Les Paul and pianist Shorty Nadine (Nat "King" Cole). They show a swing-oriented Johnson who only in rare instances hints at the kind of phrasing he was to be using exclusively in a year's time.

There is no doubt about Johnson's roots in the swing era. Around 1938, when he was in the high-school band in his native Indianapolis, Indiana, James Louis "J.J." Johnson, born January 22, 1924, started listening to jazz. He met musicians of his own age, and together they investigated, through records, the bands of

Count Basie, Jimmie Lunceford, and Duke Ellington. Since there was no trombonist in the crowd, J.J., who had studied piano at the age of 11, was persuaded to take up the slide. "My dad began to realize that I was serious about this thing, and he saw to it that I got a trombone," relates Johnson.

His parents were not too kindly disposed, however, toward his leaving town with Snookum Russell's band in 1942. J.J. had graduated from high school the year before, and they felt that he should go on to college. But J.J. flew from the nest, and in Russell's band he met trumpeter Fats Navarro, who had an immediate influence on his musical conception. Although only four months older than Johnson, Navarro, as J.J. explains it, "was already playing so great, and I was still trying to get with it, so to speak."

Indeed, hornmen other than trombonists have been his greatest inspiration, though J.J. once wrote: "The late Fred Beckett, once with Harlan Leonard's orchestra and shortly afterwards with Lionel Hampton, was the first trombonist I ever heard play in a manner other than the usual sliding, slurring, lip-trilling or 'gutbucket' style. He had tremendous facilities for linear improvisation. In general, Beckett's playing made a very lasting impression on me."

Other of the important trombone stylists of the thirties had their effect on the aware Johnson, but he states flatly, "My original influences were Pres and Roy, then Diz and Bird."

When the Snookum Russell band ran into tough going, Johnson returned to Indianapolis. Singer Earl Coleman, at that time with King Kolax, remembers that Johnson was working as a dishwasher. "J.J. was wailing, but he didn't think so. Indianapolis was a town where bands used to lay off a lot. Benny Carter was in town, and he needed a trombone player. I told Benny about Jay and then persuaded Jay to go down and audition. He joined the band and has been knocking everyone out since."

That was 1942. Johnson spent close to three years with Carter. The band recorded for Capitol (J.J.'s first recorded solo is on *Love for Sale*) and several small labels. The shifting personnel included, at various times, drummer Max Roach, bassist Curly Russell, trumpeters Freddie Webster and Karl George, and saxophonist Porter Kilbert. "Benny Carter is one of the greatest musicians I've ever had the pleasure of working with," says J.J. "The whole time I was in Benny's band, it was one continuous education in music."

In 1945 Johnson joined Count Basie. He remembers that it was not one of Basie's most productive periods and that he was not spotlighted often. "There are only about two recordings with the Basie band where I play. There's one original tune of mine called *Rambo*. I solo on that and another thing called *The King*, which featured Illinois Jacquet primarily." Karl George was with Basie too, and J.J. recorded with him for a now defunct firm called Melodisc in 1945.

When J.J. left the band the next year, he began to appear in the clubs along Fifty-second Street. Young fans heard him when he sat in with Dizzy Gillespie's quintet at the Spotlite, and they were amazed at his extraordinary dexterity. They were beginning to get accustomed to Dizzy, but now here was someone playing *trombone* with the same kind of "chops." It was not merely his prodigious technique, for the "what" of his playing was not obscured by the "how." This has been consistently true through the years. British critic Max Harrison, after having heard him at a London concert in 1958, wrote: "It has always been one of his virtues that although gifted with a fabulous technique, he has never displayed it for its own sake but always made it the vehicle and servant of his rarely-failing inspiration. One can speak here of technique in the broadest sense for his tone is consistently full and warm and his phrasing effortlessly fluid."

Shortly thereafter, J.J. fronted his own quartet, with Bud Powell on piano, at the Spotlite. Often he would play with an old gray-felt beanie hanging on the bell of his horn to render a singularly delightful tonal effect. Adding Cecil Payne on alto saxophone, he made his first recordings as a leader (*Coppin' the Bop, Jay Jay, Jay-bird,* and *Mad Be-bop*) for Savoy in June, 1946. The first two, released as a coupling, were soon in the hands of every young trombonist in New York. People who hadn't seen him refused to believe that he was playing a slide, not a valve, trombone. He won the new-star trombone award in the *Esquire* critics' jazz poll and, as a result, recorded with other winners for Victor in December. His featured number was *Indiana Winter,* an up-tempo original based (as so many tunes of that period were) on the chord changes of *How High the Moon.*

In 1947, Jacquet, his former Basie band mate, formed a small band and hired him. By this time, collectors were searching for the Karl George Melodiscs and any other bit of Johnson they could uncover on record. (I remember feeling especially rewarded on finding Savannah Churchill's *Daddy Daddy* in a Columbia, Missouri, five-and-ten because it contained, as the label stated, a "Trombone solo by Jay Jay.")

Johnson remained with Jacquet into 1949 and then gigged around the New York area. He played at the Three Deuces on Fifty-second Street in a sextet with Stan Getz and Fats Navarro and also spent some time with the bands of Woody Herman and Dizzy Gillespie. In October, 1951, he joined Oscar Pettiford's group for a USO tour of Japan, Korea, and various Pacific islands.

J.J.'s next important job was in 1952 with Jazz, Inc., a touring unit under the aegis of disc jockey Symphony Sid. The rest of the formidable lineup included Miles Davis, Zoot Sims (later replaced by Jimmy Heath), Milt Jackson (on piano and vibes), Percy Heath, and Kenny Clarke. When this group broke up, the trombonist became discouraged with the music business. ("If that couldn't make it, well . . .")

He continued to work around New York, but jazz clubs and jobs were scarce. This was a period when what had been the rhythm section of Jazz, Inc., joined with John Lewis and tried to become a permanent unit. They were then billed as the Milt Jackson Quartet. In view of the popularity of the Modern Jazz Quartet today, it is often forgotten that they, like everyone else at the time, had a difficult time getting started.

The lack of work depressed J.J., but he was also doing some strong self-evaluation. "I felt like I was on a treadmill," he recalls. "I wanted to get off so I could look at myself more objectively."

Johnson felt that he wasn't developing as a player, and so it was a self-prescribed rehabilitation when he took a job at the Sperry Gyroscope Company as a blueprint inspector. He explained his aptitude for the mechanical and technical with the comment, "I always liked to tinker around. Now it's with hi-fi." Charles Graham, *Down Beat's* former high-fidelity editor, says, "J.J. has even more equipment in his house than I do."

Until June, 1954, Johnson remained at Sperry, making recordings and gigging only occasionally. It was a period of constant soul-searching and practice. In 1953 he played at several rehearsals for a Miles Davis record date but then was unable to do the actual recording because of his Sperry commitments.

The event that brought him out of retirement was a record date for Savoy. Savoy's A&R man at that time, Ozzie Cadena, called J.J. about doing a two-trombone session with Bennie Green. It ended up with Johnson and Kai Winding, and as a result a new group, Jay & Kai, was born.

Actually, their paths had crossed, run parallel, and even come together before. The Danish-born Winding, who came to the United States with his parents at the age of 12 in 1934, developed in the big bands of the early forties like Johnson. While J.J. was with Carter and Basie, Kai was working with Benny Goodman and Stan Kenton. He left the big-band ranks after Johnson, but by 1947 he had recorded with a small group for Savoy on both slide and valve trombones. In 1948 Winding did some of his most inspired playing at the Royal Roost in a group with Tadd Dameron, Allen Eager, and Fats Navarro. When, a year later, Davis formed his famous nonet, Kai made the first recordings and J.J. replaced him on the later sides. In 1949 they were the two trombonists in the Metronome All Star Band that recorded for Victor. In early 1950 a Chubby Jackson big-band session for Prestige found them together as a two-man section; their chorus of "conversation" on *Flying the Coop* was a definite forerunner of the Jay & Kai Quintet.

Although both played in the same general idiom, there was enough of a contrast, as well as similarity, to make their combination interesting. Winding is brash (sometimes some of Bill Harris seems to have rubbed off), Johnson drier and far more inventive. Both speak the same jazz language but in different dialects. Jay & Kai subsequently recorded for many labels and made countless club, concert, and festival appearances between August, 1954, and August, 1956, when it disbanded. The two-trombones-with-rhythm format, at first commercially repugnant to booking agents, became highly successful and helped both men entrench themselves with the general jazz public—that public which has grown suddenly and encouraged a jazz-recording boom, partly because of the popularity of quartets like Dave Brubeck's and Gerry Mulligan's.

Johnson and Winding reunited for a 1958 tour of Great Britain and the Continent and in 1961 for a record date. Otherwise they

have gone their separate ways. Winding has led a group consisting of four trombones and rhythm section in formula performances. But toward the end, the Jay & Kai Quintet had played
with similar patness.

Johnson's subsequent groups (either quintets or sextets) have
been less commercially oriented in general and, as a result, more
rewarding. Although stamped with their leader's personality, they
have been varied. "With Bobby Jaspar on tenor and flute, there
were a lot of possibilities," Johnson said. "When it changed to Nat
Adderly [cornet], there was another approach."

A Johnson group which disbanded in 1960—and which included Freddie Hubbard, trumpet; Clifford Jordan, tenor sax;
Cedar Walton, piano; Arthur Harper, bass; and Al Heath, drums
—was, to Johnson, "the best I had. I'd always wanted three
horns." They did a fine, representative record, *J.J., Inc.*, for
Columbia.

At the time of that band's demise, it was said to be the victim
of bad business. Johnson emphatically denies this. "I didn't break
up the group for economic reasons, as generally advertised," he
said. "Actually we had so much work that the guys in the band
used to say to me, 'When are we going to get some time off so we
can lay off in New York?' The reason we worked so much is because we were so reasonably priced that one club owner in the
Midwest came to me and said, 'J.J., how come you work so
cheap? I would have paid double the amount because you're
doing good business.'"

Johnson did feel his group could have commanded a better
price, but it actually disbanded for a combination of reasons. One
was, as in 1952, Johnson's personal stocktaking. "Having been on
the road extensively, traveling and touring for the last seven or
eight years," Johnson said, "it suddenly occurred to me that I
needed a change, and I even began to wonder was it possible that
a musician or artist could be much too dedicated—so much that
he lived in a very narrow world." To the suggestion that he had
been physically separated from the jazz world during his period
at Sperry, J.J. responded with, "I was still thinking about nothing
but music."

When he returned to his Teaneck, New Jersey, home in August, 1960, he began to see through new eyes. "I made a startling
discovery," he said. "It was the first time in years that I had a

chance to spend more time with Vivian and my two sons, Kevin and Billy. I discovered that both my sons had made the transition from rock and roll to jazz. Billy, fifteen, was studying tenor sax and had worn out quite a few Coltrane records. Kevin, at nine, was an avid drum enthusiast. His favorites were Philly Joe Jones, Arthur Taylor, and Al Heath. Kev is supercritical over drum performances and becomes downright bitter over what he considers a bad performance by any one of them."

Johnson found time to take his wife out to the movies, and in addition to guiding the boys musically, he taught Billy how to drive and helped Kevin with his model-plane building. Photography is something that actively interests the whole family.

The discoveries did not stop there. J.J. developed a new feeling for the daylight hours, something that had not happened during the Sperry period. "I discovered," he said, "what it is like to be up and wide awake with the world at eight o'clock in the morning and to see people in the daytime world."

But he did not neglect the night people. "I've found time to go to clubs and hear more of other musicians because I'm not listening through the supercritical ears of a jazz musician. There's a lot of good jazz being played. There's quite a few very interesting things happening in jazz."

Evidently, Johnson was in a very tranquil, happy frame of mind. He had achieved one of the objectives he sought when he left the road: "wanting to compose in a relaxed atmosphere, away from the pressures that a bandleader is subjected to."

But the usually sober-minded Johnson was not completely at ease. Writer Nat Hentoff likens him to a traditional Jewish worrier. "He's never unqualifiedly happy," said Nat. "When he opened at the Vanguard with Miles Davis, I said to him, 'Well, you don't have the worries of a leader now; and he answered, 'Yeah, but there are other worries.'"

After Johnson joined the Davis group in June of 1961, any worries he may have had did not prevent him from devoting a lot of time to his composing. He had the time for it, since Davis picks his spots and therefore the group is not constantly traveling.

Writing has been a Johnsonian occupation from high-school days. He was transcribing from big-band records then ("the first was a Basie-riff thing") but didn't start seriously on his own until he joined Benny Carter's band. One of his arrangements featured

Jean Starr, a girl trumpeter. Another was a chart behind vocalist Savannah Churchill.

For Basie he wrote only *Rambo,* and from that time until the mid-1950's, J.J. turned most of his attention to playing, occasionally writing a line for a small-group record date. His *Wee Dot,* a riffy bop blues, has been adopted by other players as a jamming tune, and *Kelo* and *Enigma,* recorded by Miles Davis in 1953, are memorable examples of Johnson's melodic invention.

Johnson has done a lot more writing than people realize. J.J. said, "Kai and I split the writing in our group. In my groups since then, I have done ninety-five percent of the writing." Johnson's ability as an arranger was greatly responsible for the success of the Jay & Kai Quintet. The limitations inherent in writing for two horns, especially horns of the same kind, can be as great a challenge as working with a more varied musical palette. *Lament,* written in fifteen minutes for the group's first Savoy date, was later done by Miles Davis and Gil Evans in the LP *Miles Ahead.* Its beautiful, haunting, melancholy air is typical of one of Johnson's compositional styles.

The aforementioned LP *J.J., Inc.* not only contains arrangements by Johnson but also is the first album in which he is represented entirely by his originals. *Aquarius* (in 12/8 meter) and *Minor Mist* are particularly expressive.

The decision to remain at home and devote himself to writing could not have been made as easily, the family magnet notwithstanding, if J.J. had not had encouragement. The convincing came from John Lewis and Dizzy Gillespie. Lewis, as musical director of the Monterey Jazz Festival, was familiar with Johnson's extended works. (Two pieces, *El Camino Real* and *Sketch for Trombone and Orchestra,* were originally commissioned for the 1959 festival. The former is included in his first Victor album, done in 1965.) Lewis asked for a piece that would feature the MJQ and a large orchestral accompaniment. The result was *Rondeau for Quartet and Orchestra,* running about twenty minutes. The orchestration calls for thirty strings and ten woodwinds.

The work for Gillespie grew out of Johnson's extended *Poem for Brass.* Dizzy heard it and put in a call from South Carolina to New York City's Village Vanguard, where J.J. was playing. "I want you to write a piece for me just like that," said Diz.

"A whole album?" J.J. asked.

"Yes!"

Johnson responded with a suite titled *Perceptions*, which runs thirty-five minutes; among other instruments, it calls for six trumpets, four French horns, and two harps. It was played at Monterey in the fall of 1961.

At the same time, Johnson's work with Davis convinced everyone that his concentration on writing had not dulled his playing at all. If anything, he played better than ever. Some nights he seemed never to miss a note, and certainly with a style that does not play it safe, this was remarkable. It was nearly perfect jazz technically—achieved without the sacrifice of emotional content.

Johnson has some definite ideas on the art of playing jazz. They are indicative of the evolution and maturation of a sensitive and perceptive musician. "There are times," he said, "when what you don't play is as important as what you do play. In other words, there are times when, during the course of a solo, I will have played something that I shouldn't have, and when this happens, it sticks out like a sore thumb. It is out of context or doesn't relate to the over-all feeling or mood—like breaking continuity with fast flourishes that don't relate."

J.J. thinks that many young musicians play too fast. "Doubling up on ballads can be effective," he said, "but it has been run into the ground." Perhaps he is especially aware of this situation because of his feelings about his own early work. "There was a time in my life—in the mid-1940's—when my aim was to play as fast as physically possible on the trombone." With older trombone players who disapproved of this approach, he "felt a draft."

He said, "In Philly, a ridiculous club owner had a sign outside which read 'Fastest Trombone Player Alive.' Inevitably, jazz and tempos became more civilized, and musicians began to play along more melodic lines."

Perhaps some of J.J.'s early flights were mere flash, but it seems certain that his conception was always true to the music being played and always "civilized." The ways he has altered his conception are the result of inevitable change—a matter of a great musician becoming greater as his experience enriched him. In common with all serious jazzmen, he is "trying to tell a story on the instrument." As a trombonist, he is "trying to make it stand up as a solo instrument, like the trumpet, saxophone, and piano."

He has been eminently successful. As alto saxophonist Cannonball Adderley has written: "J.J. . . . is a soloist who happens to use the trombone. . . . J.J. has a style, and it's the kind of style that allows men on other instruments beside the trombone to emulate it, and they wind up sounding in part like J.J."

Johnson is keenly aware of audience-musician rapport—or lack of it. "There is a phenomenon and a paradox that occurs from one night to another," he said. "There have been many occasions when I felt that I played great by my own standards—the only criterion I have for this feeling is how it feels in the doing. If it feels laborious and awkward, obviously it doesn't feel good, and consequently it doesn't sound good to me.

"There have been nights I thought I really played well, and I didn't get through to anybody, by all outward indications. On other nights, I thought it wasn't coming off, and yet people would applaud vigorously and even come up and say, 'Wow, Great!' Perhaps the reason for this is that most people would rather identify what you're doing by way of the human element. I've double-checked with other players from an observer's standpoint.

"Then, too, most of us know and realize that the audience, like any musician, can have a bad night, too." He looked enigmatic as he seemed to be conjuring up his own version of "The Lady and the Tiger" and said, "That part of jazz playing that is most important is the most elusive, the most unpredictable, and the part that most defies definition."

Although it is a matter of record that he doesn't want to put anyone down, Johnson, however, has some likes to air. He still thinks well of his work on Gillespie's *The Champ*, even though his solo was cut in half on a two-part 78 rpm. He is very happy with the Columbia discs *J.J., Inc.* and *A Touch of Satin*, the latter a date with Cannonball Adderley's rhythm section.

He stated, in very precise and positive tones, "Since Charlie Parker, the most electrifying sound that I've heard in contemporary jazz was Coltrane playing with Monk at the Five Spot a couple of years ago. It was incredible. Like Diz and Bird."

Returning to opinions of his own work, the area where the jazz musician is always at his harshest, Johnson said, "The only premise on which I really enjoy having my own band is from the standpoint of composing and arranging." Then he mused, "To me Utopia would be to compose uninterrupted for four months, rehearse the compositions for two months, and play four months in the States and one month in Europe, with one month of rest and vacation."

Johnson feels that his previous approach to leading a band was "too meticulous, too mechanical, rigid—the uniforms. . . . And I'd plan every set. It was too much like clockwork, too much so, perhaps. Now I think it can be overdone. If I ever have another band, I might call ad-lib sets and a couple of nights a week have no uniforms and let the players be individuals."

The new, relaxed Johnson is reflected again in his current practice habits. "I've been experimenting with a different concept," he said. "Practicing over the years, you adopt a set routine that covers the basic requirements of playing. Now I'm experimenting with a different approach which is freer—like playing exercises ad-lib style and even playing ad lib with the radio."

The combination of natural talent with intelligence and the ability to apply that intelligence in aiding the talent assures that J.J. Johnson will continue to be an important trombone voice and a provocative, compelling composer. And it is especially gratifying to see a good composer spring from the ranks of playing jazzmen in this day when many are approaching jazz composition more academically.

Johnson was not the only significant trombonist to emerge in the forties. Bennie Green, who played with Parker and Gillespie in the Earl Hines band, is certainly one who avoided falling completely under J.J.'s large shadow. Like J.J., he absorbed from Bird, Diz, and Lester Young. Green's work also provides a strong link to trombonists of the thirties such as Dicky Wells, Benny Morton, Vic Dickenson, and Lawrence Brown. Some of his best work in the forties was done in Charlie Ventura's group on recordings like *Euphoria* and *Birdland*.

Earl Swope is another who independently developed a modern conception of his own. Lester Young was undoubtedly a strong influence on Swope before the general impact of Parker and Gillespie hit him. In Buddy Rich's band of 1945, he demonstrated that he had come up with his own stylistic conclusions, as witness *Dateless Brown*. Even more revealing are the sides he made for Savoy with Serge Chaloff—*Gabardine and Serge* (*Tiny's Blues*) and *A Bar a Second*. Swope was featured with Woody Herman from 1947 to 1949 and can be heard in brief solos on the band's Columbia and Capitol records.

The list of men whose playing Johnson has affected, greatly or partially, is a long one. A cursory reading might include Curtis Fuller, Frank Rosolino, Jimmy Cleveland, Benny Powell, Matthew Gee, and Julian Priester—but this is only a reflection, not an explanation, of his stature.

A Johnson quote, from an interview with J. Lee Anderson (*Theme* magazine January, 1957), is indicative of Johnson the man. In talking about the adverse conditions a musician may encounter when working in the average jazz club, he said, "I mean that due to the nature of jazz, the true jazz artists, the pros, don't let things like that bother them. When they get on the stand, they leave all gripes behind, and all that matters is playing jazz. We don't let it get us down; we don't let it bug us."

Recommended Listening

Mad Bebop, SAVOY SJL 2232
First Sessions 1949/50, PRESTIGE P-24081
Early Bones, PRESTIGE P-24067
Four Trombones . . . The Debut Recordings, PRESTIGE P-24097
The Eminent Jay Jay Johnson, Volumes 1 and 2,
     BLUE NOTE 81505, 81506
J. J. Inc., COLUMBIA ODYSSEY PC-36808

5

OSCAR PETTIFORD
AND THE BASSISTS

ALTHOUGH JIMMY BLANTON did not play at Minton's as frequently as Charlie Christian—and therefore did not contribute in the same way to the modern movement—like Christian, he had an important influence on the music of the forties. Both men died in their early twenties, in 1942, but in their short lives they left indelible marks in the history books of jazz. As Leonard Feather said in *Inside Jazz* (1949), Blanton "would undoubtedly have been a key figure in bop today and is still idolized by Pettiford and all current bass men."

Pettiford, of course, was Oscar Pettiford, who himself passed on prematurely but fortunately had played with major musical organizations for a length of time almost equal to Blanton's entire life. In the seventeen years from the time in Minneapolis when he joined Charlie Barnet, in 1943, until his death, in 1960, Pettiford carried on the Blanton tradition, enriching it in some ways as Blanton might have and in others as only Pettiford could have. For O.P., as Pettiford was familiarly known, was not only a bassist but a composer, organizer, and leader. His role in the formulation of modern jazz is stated flatly by Dizzy Gillespie: "Oscar Pettiford was a driving force in that music."

Tenor man–arranger Budd Johnson, who replaced Don Byas in the Gillespie-Pettiford group in 1944, once told Frank Driggs: "When I was on 52nd Street with Dizzy we were playing those unison line things that became so famous on records later on. Oscar Pettiford and I told him to write them down, but we had to do it ourselves. They were the basis of the style then."

In the opinion of pianist Dick Katz, who worked with Pettiford's small group and his big band in the fifties, Oscar "was also a wonderful bridge to the older music. He was very influenced by his association with Duke Ellington. It stayed with him, and he expressed that music beautifully. Oscar had a beautiful back-

150

ground in jazz. He had an understanding. He listened to every-thing, and it came out in his music. This is what I really respect.

"He made references to the *whole* music. He played things you never dreamed he knew. For instance, in his solo on *Honeysuckle Rose* in *The Unique Thelonious Monk*, he quotes Bix Beider-becke's *In a Mist*. How many guys know that? Not only did he know it, but if he was going to quote something, he's going to quote something right out of the literature. He was deep in the true sense. He had an unselfconscious quality that I like. He had a real genuine urge to play, and he was going to play whether he had an audience or not."

Pettiford never suffered from lack of audience. He attracted lis-teners through sheer talent. Katz spoke for many musicians and critics when he said, "I think Oscar was the type of talent that —as great a bass player as he was—had he played another instru-ment, he'd have been even more recognized. Because the kind of talent he had was more than just the instrument. He was a musi-cal personality. Aside from playing the instrument impeccably, he had that sense of drama, of timing and pacing in what he did. The way he did what he did commanded attention without re-sorting to tricks or any extramusical things.

"Oscar had a clarity which I find sadly lacking today in most of the younger musicians. This really doesn't have to do with the materials that you use when you play—in other words, whether it's modern or avant-garde. But all the music I'm attracted to is crystal clear; there's no mumbling going on. And Oscar had an ability to express with a clarity that I've never heard before or since. He could be falling down drunk, but he'd always come up with something. He had an almost superhuman quality about him. I don't want to get too mystical, but I was around him a lot."

Katz's close observation of Pettiford led him to a theory which to some may seem a trifle strange but which has a validity that becomes apparent as one considers it: "Oscar was the closest thing to Charlie Christian that we've had. He played Charlie Christian's style on the bass and the cello. Very, very close. Same rhythmic attack. There hasn't been a guitarist since Charlie Chris-tian that played as much like Charlie Christian as Oscar did on his instrument. You listen to Oscar, particularly on the cello— you'll hear this. A good example of it would be that thing he did in 1950 with Duke—certain rhythmic phrases." (The record referred to is *Perdido*, done under Pettiford's name for Mercer, the label operated by and named for Duke Ellington's son.) "Maybe not completely Charlie Christian, but some people would call this that 'Southwestern twang.' He had all those funny little turning-the-meter-around things—even melodically he played a lot of Charlie Christian's things. And that clarity—like Bird. Every note fit in place rhythmically. There are no ends flying around."

Pettiford never mentioned Christian as a specific influence, but Bill Simon's account of their early meeting does give historical credence to Katz's theory: "Oscar Pettiford was playing with his father's band in Minneapolis in '38, when he met Charlie at a place called the 'Musician's Rest.' Here the local and visiting bandsmen would come to juice and jam. 'We had a wonderful time blowing with Charlie,' Oscar reminisced. 'I never heard anybody like that, who could play with so much *love*—that's what it was, pure *love of jazz*, and great happiness just to be a part of this thing called music.

" 'We exchanged instruments: he'd play my bass, and I'd try his electric guitar. I hadn't heard about him yet, but Charlie told me, "You'd better watch out for a guy named Jimmy Blanton." I never forgot that.' "

Pettiford didn't have to remember for too long, because the next year their paths crossed. Sometimes in listing the major figures in the development of the bass, jazz critics cite Blanton as a direct influence on Pettiford. Actually, they were developing along similar lines before they met. In 1957, Oscar, in describing their meeting, told Nat Hentoff: "I did get to hear Blanton when I was 17. When I heard him, I was in love with him right away. I was just with him one night. We had a head-cutting contest right away. Our approaches were a lot alike. We hung out from early evening to break of day. If he'd stayed alive, I'd probably still be in Minneapolis."

The latter part of Pettiford's statement is highly unlikely. Though it seems like a bit of false modesty, coming from a man who was never known for a lack of confidence, it is explained in the continuation of Oscar's story. When Jimmy Blanton died, Pettiford felt he had more reason to "keep the thing moving." Many *Down Beat* poll winners, he added, weren't making it.

The "thing" Pettiford kept "moving" was a bass style that was hornlike in design, with facile runs that went beyond the old quarter-note solo conception. But even after Blanton's death, Pettiford might not have left for New York if not for the encouragement of one of his early influences. He was impressed by Adolphus Alsbrook, a Minneapolis bassist he had known since he was about 16. Alsbrook had been with Duke Ellington for a while and went to the East Coast with Basie briefly. Milt Hinton came through Minneapolis from time to time with Cab Calloway, and he also impressed Pettiford.

On one Calloway visit in 1942, Hinton found a Pettiford who was no longer in music. Hentoff quoted Pettiford's account of this period: "I had quit bass, and was working in a war plant . . . you could have starved to death trying to play music in Minneapolis then. The family band had broken down into five pieces, and still there wasn't work. Milt came into town with Cab, and I went to see him. I hadn't played for about five months, and he wouldn't believe I'd quit playing.

"Milt talked me back into music. 'Man,' he said, 'don't let talent go down the drain. There ain't nobody here playing like you. And you could more than hold your own in New York.'

"New York had worried me. They used to tell us that if we went to New York from outside, some 15-month-old kid would blow us out of the room. Anyway, two months after I had that talk with Milt, Charlie Barnet came through Minneapolis and hired me right away. I left Barnet in May, 1943, and settled in New York.

"When I got to New York, I found Milt was right. I didn't have to worry. It wasn't like the others had told me it was going to be."

It is a long way from an Indian reservation in Okmulgee, Oklahoma, to Copenhagen, Denmark, but those were the locales of the starting and finishing points of Pettiford's life (September 30, 1922–September 8, 1960). Both geographically and musically, he traveled a great distance from his humble beginnings. Oscar was three-quarters Indian (his mother was a Choctaw; his father, half Cherokee) and very proud of his heritage. "He pounded on his chest, particularly if he had a few drinks," said Dick Katz, referring to the outward manifestations of this pride.

Oscar's father, Harry "Doc" Pettiford, was a veterinarian, but his musical inclinations led him to give it up, and in the 1920's he formed the family band referred to above. The band included Doc's wife, who also taught theory and harmony, and their eleven children. They were based in Minneapolis from the time Oscar was 3 but toured extensively in the Midwest and the South. Dizzy Gillespie says, "I remember the Doc Pettiford family. They'd come through my hometown. I was a kid."

Pettiford is quoted by Nat Hentoff as saying: "Musically, it was well in advance of most bands. We played mostly our own material; we only played some standards to please the squares." Oscar's older sister, Leontine, played piano, doubled on reeds, and did most of the arranging. She also taught Oscar theory and reading. It was the only instruction he ever had; later, he taught himself bass. Brother Ira played trumpet, guitar, and bass. As of 1957 he was back in Minneapolis. He was known for his high-note work with Earl Hines. Another brother, Harry, who played all the reeds, was reported to be in Tulsa in 1951. Alonzo, who once played trumpet with Lionel Hampton, is dead.

Pettiford told Hentoff that when he heard Parker and Gillespie, on separate occasions, before he left Minneapolis, he "liked them right away. But there, too, I'd been hearing my brother Harry, who is one of the greatest saxophonists in the world, and he'd been playing in that idiom since I could remember. He'd had offers from Duke, Cab, Hines and Fletcher [Henderson] years ago, but he wasn't that venturesome to leave home. So anyway, when I heard Parker, it wasn't that different. I'd been used to hearing them kind of sounds right in the family. Why, my sister Margie is also a real great saxophone player."

These statements are beyond recorded proof, but Dizzy Gillespie feels that they are exaggerations. "He was trying to make out that someone in the family was better than he, but he was the best in the family," said Diz.

Oscar appeared with the family organization even before he learned an instrument. He told Robert Reisner: "I got started at six, when I used to dance with my father's band. When I was seventeen, I had a bit role with Olsen and Johnson in Minneapolis. Before I settled on bass, I played piano, trombone, and trumpet (which hurt my jaws), and I studied tailoring in case the music business ever got tough."

When he was 10, Oscar was fronting the band, along with dancing, singing, and baton twirling. Sometimes he would play drums. At 14, he moved into the ensemble as a bassist. The bass horn player, presumably not a family member, got married and left, so Oscar was drafted. He figured out his own technique.

In the February, 1958, issue of *Metronome*, Pettiford was quoted as saying: "The first impression I got, years ago, was that some of the guys, for entertainment reasons I suppose, were slapping the bass and getting on it and riding it like it was a horse or something. It received lots of applause from the audience." This was not the way Pettiford wanted to get his applause, however, and he paid attention to the bassists who were serious instrumentalists. He listened to Hinton; to Billy Taylor, who preceded Blanton in the Ellington band; to Mose Allen, who was with Lunceford; and to Israel Crosby, who played with Fletcher Henderson. "Then, of course, listening to them, I began to try my own approach to the instrument, trying to get more sound, rather than those slapping noises."

From January to May, 1943, Pettiford formed a two-bass team with Chubby Jackson in the Charlie Barnet band. This being the time of the record ban, there is no evidence on wax of this association. During this period, he once carried his bass for two miles in sub-zero weather—without gloves—to make a jam session in a Chicago hotel with Charlie Parker and Dizzy Gillespie.

Upon settling in New York, Pettiford plunged right into the Minton's scene, where he worked with Thelonious Monk for four months. Then he moved downtown to the Onyx, where he played with Roy Eldridge. This was followed by the first organized modern group to play on Fifty-second Street, which Oscar co-led with Gillespie. One of Pettiford's innovations for the ensembles set the style for the many small combos of the bop era. Having the trumpet and tenor play unison lines was his idea. The older way, with one man playing the line and the other playing whole notes behind him, seemed corny to him.

Some of these lines were Pettiford compositions. One number featuring Max Roach was entitled *Max Is Making Wax;* it was recorded by Oscar and a big band, which included Gillespie, for the Manor label under the title *Something for You* in January of 1945. (It showed up as *Chance It* on a Miles Davis Blue Note recording of 1952.) His *Bass Face* was the basis of *One Bass Hit,* which Ray Brown recorded with Gillespie in 1946.

Pettiford made his first recordings in December of 1943 with a group of award winners in the *Esquire* magazine critics' poll. (Pettiford won the Gold Award in both 1944 and 1945.) Billed as Leonard Feather's All Stars, in honor of the date's producer, the personnel also included Coleman Hawkins and Art Tatum. Later in the same month, Oscar recorded with Hawkins for the Signature label. Pettiford's solo on *The Man I Love* still stands as one of his great ones. Part of its early fame stemmed from the attraction that his clearly audible breathing between phrases had for some people. While this does add to the immediacy of the solo, the musical merit is what keeps it a significant piece of improvisation today. When *The Man I Love* was reissued on a Brunswick LP, *Blues Changes,* a previously unreleased track from yet another December Hawkins session, was included in the album. Pettiford's solo here is remarkably like the recorded work by which Blanton is remembered.

Eventually, Gillespie and Pettiford parted company. "Oscar was really bullheaded," says Dizzy. "He used to quit all the time. I told him one time, 'Look, I was in New York before you got here. I'll be here when you're gone.' He was winning all the polls. I called him a prima donna. He said, 'I quit,' and I said, 'Let the doorknob hit you in the back, baby.' He said, 'I quit my father's band when he called me a prima donna.' I said, 'Prima donna, prima donna, prima donna, prima donna, prima donna.' "

After the Gillespie-Pettiford unit broke up in 1944, Oscar continued to lead groups in the Fifty-second Street clubs, such as the Onyx, Spotlite, Yacht Club, and Three Deuces, for the remainder of the year. He was with the Boyd Raeburn band long enough to record *Interlude* (*A Night in Tunisia*) and *March of the Boyds* with the group (in January, 1945). Then Pettiford went to California, where he worked and recorded with Hawkins again, recording *Stuffy* and *Hollywood Stampede*. In October, 1945, he headed his own trio in San Diego and Los Angeles. Milton Benny reported the following in his Hollywood news column of the November, 1945, *Metronome:* "Oscar Pettiford and his trio are clicking nicely at the Swanee Inn on La Brea. His recent San Diego 'engagement' was disgusting, with Jim Crow and American Facists pushing him around a la Himmler."

I do not know the full extent of the San Diego unpleasantness to which Benny referred, but if the Pettiford trio was doing well in Los Angeles, then such incidents probably did not have any bearing on his decision to join Duke Ellington's orchestra. He had originally met Duke in his youth when the band came through Minneapolis. He told Nat Hentoff: "One night Duke Ellington heard me at an after-hours jam session and asked me to join the band. This was before Blanton. But I was 14 or 15 and was breaking the law playing as it was." Pettiford remained with Ellington from November 10, 1945, until March 11, 1948, and later rejoined him briefly on several occasions. "It had always been my ambition to play with Duke, but when I joined him, some of the guys I really wanted to play with—Cootie [Williams], Rex [Stewart], Ben [Webster]—had left the band. The only real enjoyment I got from working with Duke was concerts, because then we'd get to play some new things. At dances and theaters, we'd play the same thing over and over again. There was nothing to inspire you."

This may have been one of the strongest reasons for his leaving, but during his stay with the band, Pettiford left behind some durable examples of his work. In both *Suddenly It Jumped* and *Swamp Fire*, he and Ellington engaged in some fascinating interplay, and Pettiford cuts through the large ensemble passages with great strength. A specific example of his power can be heard behind Al Sears's tenor solo on *Swamp Fire*.

The year 1948 found Pettiford as the leader of a small group again. First he had a trio at the Three Deuces with Erroll Garner, who was later replaced by George Shearing. Then he took an all-star band into the Royal Roost, with Garner, Lucky Thompson, Bill Harris, Red Rodney, and Shelly Manne. In February, 1949, he joined Woody Herman's orchestra. It was the first time in a big band he had ever been around players his own age—Stan Getz, Zoot Sims, Ernie Royal, Serge Chaloff, Terry Gibbs, Red Rodney.

A date under Chaloff's name done at this time for the Futurama label included a number called *Chasin' the Bass*, which featured Pettiford in a typically brilliant, integrated set of improvisations.

Later Gene Ammons replaced Getz in the Herman band, and Shelly Manne joined, marking a reunion for him and Oscar. All three were present on the exciting *More Moon*.

In July, disaster struck. Pettiford, the pitcher for the band's softball team, broke his arm during the course of a game, and for eighteen months he was out of action. To Oscar, the accident did not have only negative sides. "I enjoyed the rest," he told Hentoff. "Because of the injury, I had to change my approach to the bass, and I feel the change was for the better because with the new system I was able to get more tone. It did slow me down a little bit, but I don't mind sacrificing speed for sound."

Another development during the period of enforced inactivity was Pettiford's cello playing. While with Herman, he had stumbled on one by chance. The band was at the Adams Theatre in Newark, and between sets the men were invited to a music store run by Bob Gutentag, a bass player. A cello was sitting on the counter. Oscar had never touched one before. He picked it up, started fooling around, and started to play. Someone said, "You ought to play that on the show."

He did. When the time came for his solo, he put his bass down and walked offstage. Herman just stared at him. Herman's manager, who was in on the gag, handed Oscar the cello in the wings, and he played it in the solo spot. The fingering is not the same on the two instruments, and the positions are smaller. But he just played it from the beginning. Pettiford said it had been the same way with the bass—he had just picked it up and started to play.

After his recovery, Pettiford toured with a Louis Bellson–Charlie Shavers unit in 1950. In late 1951 he took his own group, which included Howard McGhee, J.J. Johnson, Rudy Williams, guitarist Skeeter Best, and drummer Charlie Rice, on a USO tour of fifteen thousand miles, through Korea, Japan, and the Pacific Islands. Ralph Gleason reported of this tour in *Down Beat:* "In Okinawa on January 7, at the conclusion of a six-day tour of that Island during which the band played two shows a day, Pettiford was relieved of his leadership of the band, confined to the Island while the rest of the unit went on to the Philippines, and ordered home to the States by Gen. Beichtler, commanding general of the Island.

"Cause of the incident was a fracas in the plane during a briefing prior to taking off for the Philippines. Clifton (Skeeter) Best slugged Pettiford in the eye when the leader told him to be quiet during the briefing. Best broke his own right hand and gave Pettiford a shiner that lasted some time.

"Best had been drinking at the time, Pettiford said. 'He's a great guitar player and a nice guy, but he had been influenced by the other guys in the group who wouldn't even set up the stands for their own mutes when we played jobs. Best told me he was sorry and he told the army authorities it was his fault.' "

Pettiford also told Gleason that his bass was pierced by sniper fire while the band was performing behind the front lines. Howard McGhee's version was different in several respects. "There was never a shot fired near us," Gleason quoted McGhee as saying. "I was right there and it wasn't like that. Maybe he shot a hole in it himself. We didn't play at the front lines but we went up there once to see what it was like and we saw one Chinese shell explode. That's all."

Gleason wrote: "As for Pettiford's story that guitarist Skeeter Best hit him, admitted his guilt but the authorities sent Pettiford home instead, McGhee said: 'Oscar told Best to shut up and when he didn't, slapped him. *Then* Best got up and split him. They both had been drinking. Oscar told the officers with us he was at fault and he was sorry.

" 'But this wasn't the first trouble. Pettiford missed 2½ shows in Northern Japan and a full report is with the USO authorities and army special services.

" 'Everything was all right until Pettiford discovered whiskey was $20 a case in Tokyo!

" 'Once Pettiford had been drinking and wouldn't get up to catch a 9 o'clock plane so we had to make a long trip by truck because he wouldn't make it. He didn't want to go to bed at night, just sit up and juice.

" 'We were a test group and it's too bad something like this happened. Oscar just drinks too much, he likes to socialize, and he has a terrible temper. It's odd that he laid over in Frisco until the day before we got here.' "

From 1952 to 1958, Pettiford was active in New York, leading his own small group and big band. It was during this period that Dick Katz met him. Katz recounted to me some of the incidents that occurred while he was working with Pettiford. The pianist's keen insight provides a clearer picture of the man and musician than does the Oriental escapade.

In 1955, Pettiford was house leader and musical director of the Café Bohemia in Greenwich Village. At that time, the Bohemia was *the* jazz club in New York, the one where musicians who weren't working would congregate to hear what was happening.

Katz, who was working with J.J. Johnson and Kai Winding, dropped in one night, and Pettiford asked him to sit in. "I'd admired him from afar with my jaw hanging down in awe," says Katz. Oscar had a kind of forbidding personality if you didn't know him. He played with real authority. That's an understatement. His was real authority, wasn't any kind of fake—I mean as music went—because underneath, you know, basically he was a gentle man. People don't see him that way.

"He was an unhappy man in lots of ways. He was a frustrated man. He had illusions of grandeur. It happened to a lot of people who came up when he did. He was trying to make his own adjustment to the inequities of the scene. He couldn't understand why he wasn't as famous as Dizzy Gillespie. He actually consciously thought about this a great deal. He was very unrealistic in his business dealings, particularly in that period.

"He was a proud man. You don't see this kind of pride any more. It wasn't cockiness—it was a different thing. It wasn't a hippie thing—like, 'I'm *it* and you're not.' It was a kind of competitiveness that comes with real authority and knowing you can do something really well. He didn't go around beating people up with this. It was kind of healthy—he put the kind of realistic pressure on a musician playing with him, like, 'Well, can you play or can't you play?' and I found it refreshing, although when I first played with him, I'll admit I was a little scared."

After this sit-in, Pettiford asked Katz to play with his group. "So I worked there for a few weeks," says Dick. "It was Kenny Clarke and Oscar, Art Farmer and Gigi Gryce." Playing in a rhythm section with two masters like Pettiford and Clarke was a revelation to Katz. In Chapter 6, he talks about Clarke's "playing" the drums rather than "beating" them. "Oscar Pettiford played the bass the same way," he said. "It was a kind of strength. Technique is not merely facility. A lot of guys mix this up. They think that the ability to play fast is technique. It's only one aspect of technique, because technique is control, the ability to control what you're doing. To play softly—strong but at a low-volume level—is exceedingly difficult.

"Sometimes Oscar and Kenny were like two old women. They'd bicker. Each would accuse the other of goofing in the music, when they'd actually sounded great."

Pettiford and Clarke played *together* with an unusual brand of finesse. Katz compared them with the rhythm teams of the late fifties who are usually described as "cooking" or "really taking care of business." "These same kind of people who play hard— Kenny and Oscar would cook most of them out of the place on the same level that they're talking about, but they would do it with some grace. There was an intensity. My God, the first time I played with those two, I felt like I'd been run over by a Mack truck or a freight train. It was powerful, but it wasn't stevedore powerful—it's the difference between a Rolls Royce and a tractor.

"They could express a variety of feelings. They would listen to the music and adjust what they did to the music. There wasn't this kind of superselfconscious, sickening, overindulgent, 'I'm an artist' routine."

Those few weeks were very instructive to Katz. "And I enjoyed it, although there was an interesting misunderstanding between Oscar and the front line. They really respected him and knew how great he was, but Oscar—all that time he spent with Ellington really rubbed off—he was very conscious of variety, pacing in music, and an over-all performance. He liked color in the music, and Art and Gigi probably were still more concerned with soloing. They went along with it, but Oscar would bear down on us, and there would be funny kinds of grumblings. I'm sure they understand what he was after now, but then I don't think they did.

"There's a funny thing used to happen. Oscar had this wonderful piece he wrote called *Bohemia After Dark*. And the bridge sounds like some American Indian-type thing—tom-tom. And this was very tricky rhythmically. And he used to keep this piece on the music stands, and naturally a lot of people would come to sit in. He used this as a theme to end every set. A lot of very important players would come down there—big stars and all that. He used to get the biggest kick—they'd sit in, and everything was fine; and at the end of the set, he'd say, 'Theme, play the theme. There it is, up there, play the theme, go on out.' And these guys would say, 'Oh, yeah, sure,' and they'd read it and do the first sixteen down fine, then they'd get to that bridge—to a man they'd mumble and stumble all over the place, couldn't play it. And Oscar used to crack up. This was his idea of a musical joke. 'Cause nobody could play it. They'd just sorta ride along and come to a big rut in the street. It was a very unorthodox phrase. If you got to look at it a little bit, you could play it, but it's not the kind of thing anybody would sight-read that well. So he used to get a tremendous kick out of stumping the experts, so to speak."

As a composer, Pettiford was capable of producing little gems. "They weren't ambitious," says Katz, "but all his little tunes were flawless, and every one had the Oscar Pettiford stamp." Such things as *Swingin' Till the Girls Come Home, The Pendulum at Falcon's Lair,* and *Now See How You Are* are good examples. His blues line *Blues in the Closet* (also known as *Collard Greens and Black-Eyed Peas*) has been widely used by musicians of the fifties and sixties.

During his tenure at the Bohemia, Pettiford kept only Clarke as a permanent fixture in his group. People like Jerome Richardson and Horace Silver were some of the replacements he used. What seemed like an ideal setup soon exploded when Oscar started running up bar bills in excess of his salary. Katz remembers, "Oscar asked him [the owner] for a hundred-dollar advance. He said no, and they had a terrible argument. Oscar could get extremely belligerent when he was drinking.

"As usual, he was his own worst enemy. He goofed one opportunity after another because he always felt he deserved more than he was getting. Maybe he did, but he just had no patience with the vagaries of the business.

"He wouldn't qualify as an alcoholic, I suppose, but he drank more than any alcoholic you ever saw—I'm sure he drank more than the people who are supposed to be alcoholics. But that's another aspect of him that kind of mystified me. I think he had a physical constitution that was extremely unusual, because he would go on these drinking binges, and he would consume more liquor and beer than anybody could dream possible, wouldn't eat very much, wouldn't sleep at all. He wore out everybody, and he'd be playing through all this. And then he would finally collapse and sleep for a couple of days, and then you'd see him in a bar, Junior's or somewhere, and he'd look like he just came from a health farm. He would be glowing, look rested, like he'd never taken a drink in his life—and then he'd take a beer and get giddy, like a high-school kid who never had a drink before. So that each drinking experience was like the first time. I mean, that's the way he would react physically. I never saw anything like that. Usually people that drink, either they become alcoholics or get sick or something. But this man, he must have had a constitution of iron.

"He wanted to get *drunk*. There's another thing I didn't know —Oscar had a slipped disc in his back. He was in great pain, probably most of the time. He wore one of those corsets. I really think a good portion of his drinking was to ease the pain in his back. I was told that. I don't know whether it was true, but it makes sense. 'Cause he was supposed to be operated on and never went through with it.

"At the Bohemia I was apprehensive—possibly overanxious for his approval. Actually, Oscar would put people who didn't know him that played with him through some kind of hazing. He would try and intimidate you. He gave me a hard time with the music at first. 'Play this, play that. It's this chord; no, not now,' and all that. If you were a little tense, you'd just get in deeper that way."

One time Pettiford became angry with Katz for asking to take time off so that he could play with Jay & Kai, the group with which Dick had been working. "He always put it on the basis of 'I'm more important, and no one else could be possibly as important,'" said Katz of Pettiford. "But he only half meant it. If you didn't know him, you'd think he was—particularly when he was drinking, which was, at night, most of the time—some kind of prima donna or egomaniac, but he really wasn't. This was a covering up; it was a genuine pride. It wasn't conceit. It was a defensive thing. It's nothing at all like Mingus or some of the other strong personalities around.

"He was very angry, but he would always forget pretty fast. What he was doing, as I learned later, was, in his funny way, trying to test you, to see if, by his peculiar code, you could stand up to him.

"Not long after that, I was working out in Sunnyside [Queens] one night. They had Monday-night jazz things. Oscar and Roy Eldridge were also there this night. Marilyn Moore came in, and Oscar asked her to sing. He was very gregarious, and he liked the way she sang. So I had had a few that night, fortunately. I say 'fortunately' because of what happened.

"He asked her, 'What do you want to sing?' She said, 'Yesterdays.' 'What key?' 'I don't know.' 'Start singing, then.'

"So she started singing, and it turned out to be A major— F-sharp minor—which is rather an unfamiliar key for that tune —understatement. Whether by luck or what, I found the chords pretty fast, and Oscar was like W. C. Fields, mumbling under his breath with his hand to his mouth, 'Drop it down a half a step,' which would have made it much simpler. A lot of times bass players think in terms of the open strings available to them in a particular key, although I don't know if that was Oscar's reason, because one of his best keys was D-flat, which to most bass players is very difficult. Flat keys are harder for a lot of bass players, but not to Oscar. But in some situations, Oscar would cop out. He wasn't infallible.

"I don't know where I got the brass, but I said, 'No, come on, play it where it is,' and from that moment on we got along. I didn't mean to call his bluff or anything, or maybe I did and didn't know it psychologically. But he was pretty sheepish. He would get a sheepish grin, like a little boy. He was really a little boy in many ways. Actually, he was a very lovable person. I know there are some musicians that would say I must be out of my mind, but I found him very lovable, kind, and gentle underneath all this bravado. I remember sometimes I would see him when he'd be completely sober, and he was actually melancholy, sad, and introspective. Very rarely did he show an introspective side."

In the 1957–1958 period, Katz played with Pettiford's combo at Small's in Harlem and Jazz City, a short-lived midtown spot. Katz related two incidents, one occuring at each place, that further add to the Pettiford lore.

"One night during a colossal heat wave, we were working at Small's Paradise—what a misnomer—during the summer of 1958. All power had failed in the city. I came to work five to ten minutes late, annoyed with myself for being late and thoroughly uncomfortable from the heat. All the lights were out, and the air conditioning was off. The band was already playing the first number, in the dark. I slid onto the piano bench and could feel Oscar's wrath. The piano keys felt unbelievably strange. To my horror I discovered many of the black keys were missing. Oscar was obviously unaware of this sad fact and blew his top when he heard me play something that would make Cecil Taylor sound like Art Hodes. 'I can't play—the black keys are missing,' I told him.

" 'So what,' he said, 'I heard guys play with no keys.'

"What happened then was the lights came on, and we all broke up—the black keys were on the floor. We got some shoe glue from across the street and glued the keys back on."

At Jazz City, the Pettiford group was appearing on the same bill with Charlie Mingus' combo. "They'd both introduce each other as 'the world's greatest player,' " explained Katz. "Pettiford had this amplifier, which he didn't need. It was tuned up so loud that it was louder than the horns. I couldn't hear what I was playing. 'I'm the leader, and I want to be heard,' he would say. I would sneak in and turn it down, and he'd turn it up. Someone else would turn it down, and he'd turn it up."

Pettiford's big band, actually a pocket-size big band of about thirteen pieces, was formed for a 1956 Town Hall concert billed as the Easter Jazz Festival. During the next few years, it recorded twice for ABC-Paramount and appeared intermittently in person, usually at Birdland. The very fine arrangements were written mainly by Pettiford, Gigi Gryce, Lucky Thompson, and Ernie Wilkins. Katz, who did not play with the first edition, joined it later and participated in Volume 2 of the recordings. "The big band was very close to his heart," said Dick. "I think that secretly he was very jealous of Duke. Not jealous—envious. He wanted very much to be in the limelight like that and have a big, symphonic-type, magnificent orchestra, very impressive. And sometimes he would be comical. He was a very complicated man.

"He had a very naive side to him. To add a harp in that context—he needed it like a hole in the head. But he wanted his harp. It was some kind of link with the classical world. And he'd stand up in front of the band and wave his arms like he was Toscanini, and a lot of the guys would be laughing, affectionately, at him. You know, like, 'Uh-oh, he's gone again.'

"I remember one night in particular, at Birdland, he raised his arms and brought them down with a tremendous flourish for this big chord, and there was nothing in the music that had anything to do with that, and there was just this big silence. And we all cracked up. A comedy writer would be hard put to think of something that funny."

Again the theme recurs of the great natural jazzman whose need for acceptance makes him feel he will get that acceptance if he can go legitimate and/or acquire "class." We have already seen Parker and Powell manifest this desire. According to Katz, it also showed up in Pettiford's bowing. "The art of bowing is a relatively primitive thing in jazz bass playing. I feel that only very, very recently are some bass players now getting into it with any skill. The improvising and the ideas were always good, but the actual playing . . . Slam Stewart was really very fine. He was probably the best until very recently.

"Symphonic bass players are weak in pizzicato. Jazz bass players can't bow. Their intonation is poor; it sounds like bees flying around. Oscar was no exception. He bowed very poorly. He didn't bow too much, 'cause he knew it. He would never admit it.

"Listen to *Tea For Two* on *The Unique Thelonious Monk*, where he bows and picks. It's like two different people.

"On the cello it was even worse. He also had this weird thing about souping up the cello with an amplifier and adding some kind of theremin-sounding tremolo to it which sounded like a soap opera. There are these funny kind of inconsistencies that were part of his personality. But when he played jazz on the cello pizzicato, he was in a class by himself. Listen to *Now See How You Are* with Mat Mathews in *The Modern Art of Jazz*.

"If I had to sum up Oscar, I would say that he should be ranked with the select group of great jazz artists, beyond merely one of the great bassists. I don't think he'd be too patient with this 'action jazz,' you might call it, that's going on now. I say 'action jazz' to make a parallel with the 'action painting.' Real freedom, to me, comes from discipline and tremendous work and ability to edit yourself. It's out of style now. You're supposed to throw out anything in this free-association business—and ninety percent of it might be garbage; but if you get ten percent, that's great, then that's fine. You weren't allowed that luxury in any art form till very recently.

"Oscar had this wonderful ability to put in so much work— artistic work, not just on the instrument—that he could control himself and his feelings well enough so that when he set up to take a solo, he had that built-in thing of knowing what not to play and what's good and what's bad. Taste, I'd guess you'd call it. That was one of the greatest qualities he had. I never in my life heard that man play a bad solo, no matter what the circumstances. Consistency. And he was a great blues artist. He could really play the blues without rolling in the mud."

In 1958, Pettiford left the United States, never to return. He left for England in September as a member of an all-star touring unit called Jazz at Carnegie Hall and decided to remain on the Continent when the tour ended. He worked France, Austria, and Germany before settling in Copenhagen in June of 1959. From the summer of 1959 until early 1960, he worked with Stan Getz at the Café Montmartre and then led his own group of Scandinavian musicians. His last recording, made with these Danes and Swedes in July, 1960, has been issued on Jazzland as Volume 2 in their *Classics of Modern Jazz* series. It demonstrates again his ability to guide and mold young musicians and serves as a document of his then undiminished powers as a bassist and cellist.

To be sure, Pettiford had not changed. He had been seriously injured in an auto accident in Austria late in 1958, but once he recovered from multiple injuries, including a skull fracture, he was the old Oscar. Stories came back about his continuing love of staying up and drinking. In the February 18, 1960, *Down Beat,* a page headed "Hassel" was devoted to pictures of Pettiford lying on his back on a stage in Berlin during the filming of a German movie. It seems that although the sound track had already been recorded, Pettiford refused to use anything but his own bass (which was not there) for the filming. Eventually, he acquiesced, as the final picture shows, but that Pettiford recalcitrance and need to boss the deal were still there. I can still remember the way he could take over a recording date at which he was supposedly a sideman, sometimes helpfully but more often to the A&R man's chagrin.

Tragedy struck Pettiford in early September, 1960. He played at an art exhibit, became ill, and was taken to Fiedfrederiksberg Hospital in Copenhagen. Four days later, on September 8, he was dead. Danish doctors attributed his death to a "poliolike virus" that began with a strep throat. Another giant talent had been lost too early. Perhaps the strange virus would have taken him anyway, but we must recognize that the hard life of the dedicated jazzman and the self-flagellation that many indulge in had more than something to do with it.

There were many bassists who contributed to the jazz of the forties in various ways. Eddie Safranski, who won many polls while he was a member of the Stan Kenton orchestra (1945–1948) and for several years after he left Kenton, was neither as great as the popularity polls deemed him to be nor as "unswingingly metronomic" as his severest critics pictured him.

Chubby Jackson may not have been the greatest bassist in jazz history, but he and his instrument were certainly lively. Leonard Feather said of him in the *Encyclopedia of Jazz:* "Most significantly, though an able bass player, he was important as the catalytic agent or cheerleader whose personality sparked the Woody Herman band at its peak." Jackson was with several of the Herds, but it was in the 1944–1946 edition that he had his greatest impact. During this time, he introduced a five-string bass, which was adopted by only a few of his colleagues. As a leader, Jackson did some exciting things in the forties. In 1947 he took the first modern group to Europe, touring Scandinavia with a sextet that included Conte Candoli, Terry Gibbs, Frankie Socolow, Lou Levy, and Denzil Best. In 1949 he put together a roaring big band that played around New York and the East for a while. It had two regular bassists, Chubby and Red Kelly. There was also one number on which Red Mitchell, who was the band's pianist, joined them in a bass trio. Tiny Kahn was the drummer, and for a time Joe Harris was on conga. Ray Turner, tenor sax; Socolow, alto sax; Red Rodney, trumpet; and Teddy Charles, vibes, were some of the soloists. Jackson's crew was an extension of the 1948–1949 Herman band. They recorded one good session for Columbia, but by the end of the decade the big-band era had really drawn to a close, and Chubby's band never really got off the ground. From the late fifties until 1963, Jackson was the host for a kiddie cartoon program on TV.

One of the most recorded bassists of the forties did not play a five-string bass, but he had some other gimmicks. Leroy "Slam" Stewart, mentioned above by Dick Katz for his bowing skill, attracted much attention by simultaneously humming, an octave away, the same solo he was bowing. Although his work took on more and more of a novelty aspect (he worked mainly with Rose Murphy, the "Chi-Chi" girl, in the late fifties and early sixties), Stewart, at his best, was a fine swing-period soloist. He first came into prominence in a duo with Slim Gaillard from 1938 to 1943. Then he was heard often along Fifty-second Street with Art Tatum and with his own trio. In 1944 and 1945 he was featured with Benny Goodman's orchestra and sextet. Perhaps he is best known for the innumerable recordings he made with Tatum, Johnny Guarnieri, and Don Byas, among others. The four sides he did with Lester Young (*Sometimes I'm Happy, I Never Knew, Just You, Just Me,* and *Afternoon of a Basie-ite*) are excellent examples of his talent, and his solo on *Groovin' High* with Parker and Gillespie is no drag on the proceedings by any means.

Ross Russell, in his essays on bebop for *The Record Changer* in 1948 and 1949, wrote: "Modern bass work demands a crisp plunging sound (Oscar Pettiford is exemplary), rapid execution, and a grasp of harmony to match the pianist and line musicians. Furthermore, it is essential that the bass and drums work as a unit. Friction, or absence of one-mindedness, is fatal to the section."

Two men who filled the bill in the classic years of bop were Curly Russell and Tommy Potter. Neither was known for his solo ability, but both were strong section men who meshed well with Bud Powell, Al Haig, Duke Jordan, Max Roach, Kenny Clarke, Art Blakey, and Roy Haynes. Russell and Roach played together in Benny Carter's band in the early forties, and later they gave Bud Powell support in some of his greatest performances. Potter, of course, was with Charlie Parker through the last part of the forties in an important role. In the late fifties, Potter was working with groups such as Tyree Glenn's and Harry Edison's. Russell, in the meantime, had sunk into the obscurity of r&b jobs; and in the summer of 1962, he worked in hotel bands on the borscht circuit in upstate New York.

Two other important contributors were Al McKibbon and Nelson Boyd, both of whom played with Dizzy Gillespie's orchestra in the 1948–1950 period. But the bass player of the forties who continues to grow in stature was their predecessor in the Gillespie band, Ray Brown (born in Pittsburgh, Pennsylvania, on October 13, 1926). Pettiford once said that his sister Leontine gave Brown lessons in 1940 and 1941. Presumably, these were on piano, for that was Ray's first instrument. "His father didn't want him to play Mozart, he wanted him to play like Fats Waller," wrote Gene Lees. "Later he wanted Ray to play like Art Tatum. 'That was asking a little too much,' Ray grins. 'But that's not the reason I gave up piano. I just couldn't find my way on it. It just didn't give me what I wanted.

" 'Besides, I was in a high school orchestra and there must have been 14 piano players in it. And 12 of them were chicks who could read anything in sight.' "

When Brown's father couldn't afford to buy him a trombone, he turned to the bass, since there was one at school on which he could practice. By the time he graduated, in 1944, he had already started playing jobs, and he went right on the road. He was with Jimmy Hinsley for eight months and then with Snookum Russell. Just before Brown joined Russell, Fats Navarro and J.J. Johnson left the band. After eight months with Russell, Brown decided it was time to explore the major leagues. The band was in Miami, Florida. "Three other guys and I began plotting to go to New York and try our luck," Ray recalled. "But the night before we were to go, everybody chickened out, leaving me with my bags all packed. So I said, 'The hell with it,' and went.

"I got to New York, took my bag to my aunt's place, and the very same night had my nephew take me down to show me where 52nd Street was.

"That night, I saw Erroll Garner, Art Tatum, Billie Holiday, Billy Daniels, Coleman Hawkins, and Hank Jones. I'd known Hank before. While we were talking, he said, 'Dizzy Gillespie just came in.' I said, 'Where? Introduce me! I want to meet him.'

"So Hank introduced us. Hank said to Dizzy, 'This is Ray Brown, a friend of mine, and a very good bass player.'

"Dizzy said, 'You want a gig?' I almost had a heart attack! Dizzy said, 'Be at my house for rehearsal at 7 o'clock tomorrow.'

"I went up there the next night and got the fright of my life. The band consisted of Dizzy, Bud Powell, Max Roach, Charlie Parker—and *me!* Two weeks later, we picked up Milt Jackson, who was my room-mate for two years. We were inseparable. They called us the twins."

This was the band that, with Al Haig and Stan Levey in place of Powell and Roach, went to California in the fall of 1945. Brown continued with Gillespie into the big band of 1946, remaining with him until 1948, when he left to form his own trio. As a soloist he was featured on both *One Bass Hit* and *Two Bass Hit;* as a composer he was distinguished for his *Ray's Idea* and the especially intriguing *That's Earl, Brother.*

Gillespie spoke of Brown in reference to young musicians of today and yesterday. He told Gene Lees: "I find nowadays that musicians are not as inquisitive as they used to be. You've got to be inquisitive. You've got to know why. If you respect a guy's playing and he does something and you don't know why, you say, 'Why did you do it?' *What* he does is easy to find, you can listen to the record. *Why* is what is important.

"Now take a guy like Ray Brown, he's always been that type of guy, very, very inquisitive. Even when he was with me. On *I'm Through With Love,* we get to one place, where the words go, *for I mean to care.* . . . Right there, that word *care.* The melody went up to an E-flat, B-natural, and G-flat, and that sounds like an A-flat minor seventh chord. *Sounds* like it. So I told Ray, 'Now Ray, you're making A-flat there. Your ears are good. Make a D there.' He say, 'But you're making A-flat minor seventh.' I say, 'No, I'm not.' He say, 'Show me.' So I take him to the piano and play D and there's the same note up there in the D. And he say, 'Ah-*ha!*' But I had to show him. He'd have done it anyway, because I'm the one playing the solo. But Ray wanted to know *why.*"

After leaving Gillespie, Brown married Ella Fitzgerald. He also became her musical partner; his trio accompanied her in all her engagements. This began his affiliation with Jazz at the Philharmonic. In 1951 he became a member of pianist Oscar Peterson's trio and continued to tour with JATP. In 1952 he and Miss Fitzgerald were divorced.

His work with Peterson soon brought him approval from the fans as well as musicians and critics. He won numerous polls in the fifties and continued to do so in the sixties. Peterson has said of him: ". . . he's the epitome of forethought. Sympathetic forethought.

"As for his solos . . . Do you know his solo on *How High the Moon* in our Stratford album? Well, that should be put in a time capsule and sealed up. Because that's it. That's *it.*"

Brown, who bakes angel food cake (Peterson claims it is "out of sight") and shoots golf in the mid-seventies when he is really on his game, is a modest man when it comes to enunciating his important role in the history of the bass. Gene Lees wrote: "After Blanton, Ray's admiration goes chiefly to his close friend, the late Oscar Pettiford. After that he is curiously silent."

One musician who has keen insight into the art of his colleagues has commented on the inevitable comparisons between Pettiford and Brown. "There's an interesting cross section of opinion, about evenly divided. They'll pick Ray because he's faster in terms of facility, a better-schooled bassist. Ray's solos are not nearly as artistic as Oscar's, although he would stand out more in a rhythm section. As great as Oscar was, he never had a great instrument, not like Ray Brown—Ray has got a fantastic instrument. He also has developed a way of playing his left hand. I don't know, it must be as strong as a . . . the way he walks in a rhythm section. I've never heard anything like that. The net result, for whatever the reason, would make Ray stand out a little more. But for over-all artistry, particularly the solos, I prefer Oscar."

In the Musicians' Musicians poll, conducted by Leonard Feather in his 1956 *Encyclopedia of Jazz Yearbook*, Pettiford preferred Brown. "My reason for not voting for Charlie Christian, Charlie Parker, Django Reinhardt, Jimmy Blanton and many other jazz immortals," he wrote, "is that I don't believe the dead can bring back the life in music; we have to think in terms of what is here, not what has been here and gone."

Before he went, however, Pettiford made sure that his name and music would live on.

He stated in the 1957 *Down Beat* interview with Hentoff: "The bass is one of the most important—if not *the* most important—instruments in any orchestra. You can take just a bass and somebody can sing to it or play to it. You don't need piano or drums. The bass can be much more of a horn, too, than it often has been in the past.

"When I finish, the bass will be right down front where it belongs."

Although he died long before his time, Pettiford's prophecy came true, helped immeasurably by his own giant contribution.

Recommended Listening

Classic Tenors (with Coleman Hawkins),
    DOCTOR JAZZ BBMI-1121
Bebop Revisited, Volume 2, XANADU 124
Dancing Sunbeam (with Lucky Thompson), IMPULSE ASH-9307-2
The Finest of Oscar Pettiford, BETHLEHEM BCP-6007
Memorial Album, PRESTIGE 7813
The Freedom Suite Plus (with Sonny Rollins), MILESTONE M-47007

The Riverside Trios, 1955-56 (with Thelonious Monk),
MILESTONE M-47052

NOTE: Pettiford's ABC-Paramount recordings of his orchestra
have long been unavailable. His work with Duke Ellington on
RCA Victor can probably be found on foreign issues.

6

KENNY CLARKE, MAX ROACH, AND THE DRUMMERS

FOR ALL THE HARMONIC CHANGES wrought by bop and the new melodies that came as a result, the greatest innovations brought about by the new music were in rhythm. Martin Williams said it well when he wrote: "The crucial thing about the bebop style is that its real basis came from the resources of jazz itself. And it came in much the same way that innovation had come in the past. That basis is rhythmic and it is based on rhythmic subdivision. . . . The rhythmic basis of ragtime is syncopated half-notes. In the New Orleans style, apparently, syncopation gradually divided the pulse until it became an even 'four' in Armstrong's work. The rhythmic basis of bebop is an eighth-note."

This brings to mind something one of the late Claude Thornhill's musicians of 1949 told me. Pianist Thornhill, although he led bands that played the music of Parker and Gillespie, could not play the style himself. "Claude is bugged," said the sideman, "because he can't play three even eighth notes in a row."

The way in which the eighth notes and sixteenth notes flowed from soloists like Bird and Dizzy, as well as the shifting accents these men employed in their lines, called for the development of a rhythm section that would be complementary. When Parker told Mike Levin and John S. Wilson, in a September, 1949, *Down Beat* interview, that bop "has no continuity of beat, no steady chug-chug," he was as seemingly mistaken as when he said in the same interview, "Bop is no love-child of jazz." (But was Parker's remark actually, "Bop is no bastard of jazz"?)

Bop maintained the 4/4 pulse that had been at the heart of the jazz that had preceded it, but transferred its keeping from the bass drum to the top cymbal. To quote Ross Russell: "The vibration of the cymbal, once set in motion, is maintained throughout the number, producing a shimmering texture of sound that supports, agitates, and inspires the line men. This is the tonal fabric of bebop jazz."

The absence of a steady four on the bass drum is obviously what Parker meant by "no steady chug-chug," but the same continuity was there, however augmented and embellished.

Just as the innovations of Lester Young, Charlie Christian, and Jimmy Blanton led to new ideas during the forties, so did the adventuresome work of Jo Jones, Count Basie's great drummer. Although he played his cymbal accents in 2/4 and maintained a steady 4/4 on his bass drum for the most part, Jones did break up the rhythm behind soloists by "dropping bombs," as these benevolent accents and explosions were termed, in the proper places to serve as a spur.

Russell, in discussing the changes that led into the new drumming, makes reference to Jones's exploring of the "tonal dynamics of his instrument, thereby improving on the dry sound and tight beat of drummers like Kaiser Marshall" and cites Cozy Cole as another forerunner of modern drumming: "Cole's superb technical facility, rapidity of execution, and dry skin sound are very much a part of Kenny Clarke's equipment, not to mention most other bebop drummers."

Kenny Clarke was a pioneer. His experimentations began much earlier than most jazz fans realize, and by the time all the tributaries of modern jazz were ready to join forces in the early forties, he was there to contribute the very important stream of his drumming.

Born in Pittsburgh, Pennsylvania, in January, 1914, Kenneth Spearman Clarke (he has been listed on some of his records with Dizzy Gillespie as K. Spearman) is from a musical family. His father played trombone, and his brothers played drums and bass. Clarke studied piano, trombone, drums, vibes, and theory while in high school. By the time he was in his teens, he was working as a professional with Leroy Bradley's band in his hometown. After five years with Bradley, he played with Roy Eldridge and his brother Joe, who had formed a band after Roy returned to Pittsburgh in 1933.

Clarke left the city in 1934 to play around the Midwest with the St. Louis-based Jeter-Pillars band Writer George Hoefer has made the observation: "It is interesting to note that both Christian and Blanton served with the Jeter-Pillars band about that time too."

In 1935, when Kenny was playing with Lonnie Simmons'

band in New York, he began using rhythmic patterns against the basic four or two, according to information he gave Burt Korall in a 1963 interview. "Freddie Green and I got something new going with Lonnie's band at a Greenwich Village club, long before the new rhythmic approach to playing drums was noticed," he said, referring to the guitarist who was later to become an institution with Count Basie. "We'd come to the job early—at least forty-five minutes before the other players—and work out patterns. The results were swinging; you could tell. Even the waitresses enjoyed what we were doing."

Clarke made his first recordings with Edgar Hayes, whose band he joined in 1937, but none of these indicates any radical departures by the drummer. After touring Europe with Hayes in early 1938 (he made some small-group recordings under his own name in Stockholm), Clarke went with the Claude Hopkins band for eight months. Then in 1939 he became part of Teddy Hill's band, in which he and Dizzy Gillespie began to integrate their ideas. In an arrangement of *Swanee River*, Clarke played off-rhythms on his bass drum, and Gillespie, taken with this, started to build on this new foundation.

When Clarke began using the bass drum for accents, he shifted the timekeeping to the top cymbal and also used his left hand to accent on the snare drum, as a complement to his right foot, or to help state the beat. Hill was not fond of these rhythmic departures. As they became more prevalent, he fired Kenny in 1940. Clark once confessed, incidentally, that in Hill's band he sometimes dropped steady timekeeping in favor of accents in order to rest when the band was playing fast tempos.

From his next leader, Roy Eldridge, Clarke received encouragement to develop his style. He wrote parts for himself that, he says, fifteen years later were termed "coordinated independence in jazz percussion."

"With Roy," Clarke has been quoted as saying, "I got everything I'd been trying to do together. This was just before Minton's. My style was just about set at this time. Roy liked it because it seemed to fit with the brass. . . . [Hill] said that I broke the tempo too much. In fact, he wasn't listening, because I was really keeping a steady beat going all the time. By my improvising with the left hand, I guess he got kind of confused."

During the summer of 1940, Clarke worked at the Log Cabin

in Fonda, New York, with soprano saxophonist Sidney Bechet's quartet. In the fall, Hill took over Minton's and brought Clarke in as leader of the house group. Teddy didn't object to Kenny's playing in this context and would talk of his accenting as "klook-mop music." Clarke picked up the nickname of Klook at this time. (The scat "lyric" to *Oop Bop Sh'Bam* follows the title phrase with "a-klook-a-mop." It is obviously a drum lick. So is *Salt Peanuts,* for which Clarke is given credit as co-composer.)

At Minton's, Clarke sometimes played vibes while Jack "The Bear" Parker or Kansas Fields sat in on drums. Max Roach has said his regard for Clarke comes from Kenny's general approach to music—"his drumming as well as his vibes, piano, and composing."

In *Inside Jazz,* Clarke tells how Charlie Christian helped him to conceive a tune during the Minton's period: "One night Charlie and I were at the Douglas Hotel on St. Nicholas Avenue visiting a friend who was a dancer and played the ukulele. I fooled around with the uke and then Charlie took it out of my hand. 'Look, Kenny,' he said, 'you can make all the chords you want to on this if you just stretch your fingers right.' He showed me, handed back the uke, and I started experimenting. I got an idea that sounded good, went upstairs to my room in the same hotel, and wrote it down. Later on Joe Guy showed the tune to Cootie Williams, and Cootie had Bob MacRae make an arrangement. I called it *Fly Right,* and Cootie used to broadcast it from the Savoy Ballroom. This was right after he'd left Benny Goodman and formed his own band. Cootie recorded it for Columbia but it was never released. Later on I recorded it for Victor with a band of my own under the new title—*Epistrophy.*" (Both versions are now available under the title *Epistrophy*—Williams' version in Columbia's *The Sound of Harlem* album, Clarke's in Victor's *The Be-Bop Era.* Somewhere along the way, Thelonious Monk collaborated with Clarke to develop the number. He is always listed as co-composer and has recorded it several times.)

Clarke remembers that he heard Tadd Dameron playing flatted fifths at Minton's in 1940. "It sounded very odd to me at first," he said. "Tadd was one of the first men I heard playing eighth-note sequences in the new legato manner too."

Although several writers have cited Clarke's playing on the 1941 jam session recorded at Minton's by Jerry Newman and later issued on discs as the only indications of the next step in jazz, there are really no strong departures. The "bombs" are there from time to time, but the pulse is kept mainly by brushwork, and the new cymbal sound is not in evidence. Certainly Marshall Stearns's claim in his *Story of Jazz* that "Clarke is playing fully matured bebop drums" on these recordings is an exaggeration.

In the sixties, Clarke denied the story often attributed to him about how the inner circle at Minton's would freeze out the undesirables. "There's no truth to the story that we purposely played weird things to keep musicians outside the clique off the stand," he was quoted as saying. "All we asked was that the musician be able to handle himself. When he got up on the stand he had to know."

Clarke continued to frequent Minton's even after he no longer fronted the group there. He was in and out of New York with a variety of bands in 1941 and 1942: a short stint with Louis Armstrong's big band; five weeks with Gillespie in Ella Fitzgerald's orchestra, from which they were simultaneously fired; Benny Carter's sextet on Fifty-second Street; and a longer period (Feather's *Encyclopedia of Jazz* calls it a year and a half, which seems questionable) with Red Allen at the Downbeat Room in Chicago.

It was in Miss Fitzgerald's band that he and Gillespie devised *Salt Peanuts*. After leaving Allen, Clarke took his own group into Kelly's Stables. There, according to Feather, he and Ike Quebec developed the theme later known as *Mop Mop*. Coleman Hawkins, who in his featured spot at Kelly's would front the group, later recorded it.

In 1943, just as he was becoming entrenched as a leader, Clarke was drafted into the Army. He went overseas and was involved in public relations in London for a while. Then, in Paris, he played trombone with a stage band and choral group that played at the Madeleine Theatre. Following this, he organized Special Service City in Seckenheim, Germany.

After his discharge in 1946, Clarke returned to New York in time to join Dizzy Gillespie's second, and more successful, big band. Kenny spent eight months with Gillespie, during which time they made such records as *Things to Come, Ray's Idea, Our Delight,* and, with the small group, *Oop Bop Sh'Bam* and *That's Earl, Brother*. The drumming on these sides is part and parcel of the new style—not flamboyant, but, as Clarke's work has always been, perfectly blended with the rest of the ensemble. The accents are there but are applied more conservatively than the drummers who came after Clarke were to do.

In September, Clarke recorded four sides with his own group for the French Swing label—*Epistrophy, Oop Bop Sh'Bam, 52nd Street Theme,* and *Royal Roost* (now included in the RCA Victor LP *The Be-Bop Era*). The group was just a recording unit, however, and in 1947, when Clarke left Gillespie, he began playing on Fifty-second Street with Tadd Dameron. He can be heard on *The Tadd Walk* and *A Bebop Carroll* with Tadd's quintet.

In December, 1947, he rejoined Gillespie in time to record *Cubana Be, Cubana Bop* with the band. At the end of a European tour (January–February, 1948), Klook remained in Paris for several months, recording and teaching. It gave him a taste of a life he would settle into permanently in 1956.

Back in New York, he rejoined Dameron and helped to spark the pianist's sextet at the Roost. His steady-rock cymbal beat can be heard rather than just felt on the Fats Navarro LP's for Blue Note. Engineering techniques had improved enough by this time to bring into focus the cymbal sound, which previously had been reduced almost to the level of surface noise. Clarke's relaxed, loose but never sloppy, and innately swinging style stands out in the Dameron sextet as a truly modern extension of the feeling that Jo Jones had achieved in the Basie band.

During the next few years, Clarke free-lanced around New York with the important modernists. In January, 1949, he recorded with his own group, one that included Milt Jackson, Kenny Dorham, Billy Mitchell, and French hornist Julius Watkins. On timbales and conga was another Pittsburgher, Joe Harris, who had been Clarke's replacement with Gillespie in 1946–1947.

In April, 1952, Clarke was instrumental in helping to found the Modern Jazz Quartet. As Ray Brown was the original bassist, all were familiar with one another's playing from the Gillespie band of 1946. Clarke had met John Lewis in the Army and persuaded him to stay with music instead of anthropology. Originally the quartet was billed under Milt Jackson's name, but by the time it recorded for Prestige in December, 1952, it was the MJQ. Clarke was featured in Lewis' *La Ronde,* a new title for what had been *Two Bass Hit* in the Gillespie band and he even played tympani in one of Lewis' reexplorations of the baroque, *The Queen's*

Fancy. As the group grew in stature and popularity, Clarke's immaculate, spirited drumming became a stylistic cornerstone. As time went on, however, he became less fond of a musical sedateness he felt that Lewis was encouraging. John was looking for a certain kind of sound and style, and Kenny was not about to give it to him. Clarke left in 1955. "As for John," he told Burt Korall, "his music is too bland and pretentious for my taste. I fell asleep the last time I heard the Modern Jazz Quartet in person."

While he was with the MJQ, Clarke recorded extensively as a free lance in New York. With MJQ bassist Percy Heath and pianist Horace Silver, he was part of the house rhythm section for Prestige Records in 1954. Particularly impressive are the sessions this trio made with Miles Davis. In December, the date that produced *Bags' Groove, Swing Spring, Bemsha Swing,* and *The Man I Love* was taped. (Monk, Clarke's old Minton's partner, replaced Silver on this one.) Some four hours after the beginning of this session, not much had been accomplished. But Clarke later said of the way the rest of it had turned out, "Miles sure is a beautiful cat," which, in telling something about Davis, also says a great deal about Clarke.

After he left the MJQ, Clarke continued to free-lance. He appeared quite often at the Café Bohemia in Greenwich Village in 1955, and he became house drummer for Savoy Records, where he also did several albums under his own name. At the Bohemia, he and Oscar Pettiford played together.

Pianist Dick Katz has as high a regard for Clarke as for Pettiford and worked with both of them at the Bohemia. He considers them the finest rhythm team he has ever heard. "It was an interesting sensation playing with Klook and Oscar," he said. "I had the feeling—mostly, I think, because of Kenny—that they were rushing. That wasn't the case at all. . . . They were so graceful in what they did—in the part of the beat that they played—it sounded like they were rushing, or it felt like they were rushing, but in reality I was dragging my behind. I learned a great lesson I've never forgotten—and this is a skill that goes past playing the instrument. It's a skill with jazz rhythm which is very rare. And it's rare today. I can name you people on my fingers that I think have it. Billy Higgins has it.

"And, you know, a lot of the hip little drummers around now —they don't play too badly sometimes—they got the word somehow, ninth hand, about Kenny Clarke with his 'tipping,' as they call it. This doesn't have much to do with what Kenny does, because they're doing it almost mechanically. It sounds good on records, strangely enough, but it doesn't really feel good if you know what it really is. I'm not blaming them, because how else are they going to get it? Kenny's been out of the country for a long time, and the pressure is around to play like this guy or that guy. But they're not really doing it. First of all, these drummers look like they're doing action painting—like whipping the cymbal. Well, you can't see that on the record anymore than you can see Philly Joe [Jones] jump up nine feet and grab the cymbal—that sound, on the beat, articulating all four beats." (This last describes the "tipping" referred to above. Drummer Roy Haynes says of this technique, "Klook would be playing single beats, but you'd get a continuity. You still got the feeling of *ding ding-da-ding*.")

Katz talked of the piece of equipment on which Clarke gets that sound. "People don't know that he had one cymbal," he said. "It wasn't very big, and we used to call it the magic cymbal, because when somebody would sit in on drums and use his set, it would sound like the top of a garbage can, but when he played it, it was like fine crystal. He kept the cymbal level, like a plate, and he played with a short, side-to-side wrist motion. He didn't get very far away from the cymbal. It was a very graceful thing to watch. As a matter of fact, he didn't hardly move at all, except that left foot. And he was coordinated in such a way that he'd make this beautiful sound.

"I don't know; I'm sure this is something that can't be verbalized—there's something that goes on about getting the feeling and emotion into beating on, striking, something. I don't know how it happens, but I've heard other people roughly get this sound. You hear dance-band drummers that'll get this four-four—*da-ding ding ding ding da-ding*—almost like a bass, but it's not the same, so that part I can't verbalize. But I'm just bringing this up because here's Kenny with this one relatively small cymbal absolutely level, with this little, short wrist motion, and here are these guys—some people today—who look like they're winding up to hit a home run to simulate the same effect. It's silly to me. To play softly—strong but at a low-volume level—is exceedingly difficult, particularly on the drums. Most drummers can't play soft because they don't have the muscular control. If he's exciting and doesn't rush or drag—that's today's standard for drummers.

"Kenny Clarke is an artist. He's a musician who plays the drums, and he plays the drums as a musical instrument—he doesn't beat the drum. I'm going to quote old Jo Jones now. He used to say this: 'You don't beat the drums—you play them.'"

In the summer of 1956, Clarke went to Paris to join the Jacques Hélian band. He has never returned to the United States. Eventually, he became leader of his own group, and he is much in demand for recording and television work. In a feature about American jazz expatriates in 1963, *Time* magazine glowingly reported: "He conceals his reasons for leaving behind a smile of well-being, and of all the Americans in Europe, Clarke is by far the most successful. He has a *pavillon* outside Paris (where he spends his Sundays gardening), a taste for *rosé d'Anjou*, a Dutch wife and an English car. . . . He tours everywhere and vacations on the *Côte d'Azur*. 'Why not stay here?' he says. 'I earn a good living —a very good living.'"

The reminder to listeners in the United States that Clarke has lost none of his power or finesse comes from records. There is a Fantasy LP entitled *Essen Jazz Festival All Stars*, done in 1960 with Coleman Hawkins, Bud Powell, and Oscar Pettiford; and, more recently, Clarke has collaborated with Belgian pianist-arranger-composer Francy Boland. The Clarke-Boland combine has produced four albums, one with an eight-piece band (for Blue Note) and the rest with big bands of varying size and personnel (for Atlantic and Columbia). The Clarke-Boland Big Band, as it is called, is made up of musicians from many countries. Sometimes, in addition to American expatriates and European jazzmen, it adds visiting Americans, such as Zoot Sims and Billy Mitchell.

Kenny Clarke is still a master, with small group or big band. Dizzy Gillespie said of him a couple of years ago, after recording with him again in Paris, "Klook plays drums just like I would play them if I played drums. He's too much."

Summer, 1956, was also the time when a conclave of musicians convened at Music Inn in Lenox, Massachusetts, to participate in a series of panel discussions concerning jazz. Among those present were Max Roach, Dizzy Gillespie, Oscar Pettiford, and John Mehegan. During the course of one round table, Roach was holding forth on the drummers who had preceded, and inspired, him. When he mentioned Clarke, Mehegan asked, "Max, do you think that Kenny is the Bud Powell of the drums?"

Roach replied, "I think that in drumming, Kenny is more akin to Thelonious Monk."

"I always thought that Blakey was closer to Monk than was Kenny," opined Mehegan.

"Not in modern jazz," said Roach. "To me, Kenny Clarke was the first to play in broken rhythms."

Gillespie chimed in with, "Yeah, I remember when Blakey didn't play that way at all."

"Yes," Roach agreed, "he did shuffle and things like that. But that was long before more modern things started, anyway."

At this point, Mehegan, who perhaps hadn't been listening too closely, asked again, "Kenny did with drums what Bud did with piano, do you think?"

To this Pettiford answered, "I would say Max Roach did. Max is too modest."

Pettiford's parallel has validity. Whereas Clarke was the link and the groundbreaker, Roach was the one who elaborated the style, bringing more complex cross-rhythms into play. He proved to be the perfect accompanist for the conception of Parker and Powell.

When Clarke was working on rhythmic patterns with Freddie Green in a Greenwich Village club, Maxwell Roach was in his eleventh year. Born in North Carolina in January, 1925, Roach moved to Brooklyn with his family when he was 4. He grew up in the Bedford-Stuyvesant section, which is to Brooklyn what Harlem is to Manhattan, except that the Harlem ghetto is perhaps more sophisticated than Bedford-Stuyvesant.

Roach's aunt gave him his first musical instruction, when he was about 8, in keyboard harmony. A year later he was playing the piano in the summer Bible school of the Concord Baptist Church. His mother is a gospel singer.

According to George Hoefer, Roach took up the drums in 1935, studying with "an elderly German teacher" for three years. However, Roach was quoted in *Metronome* as telling the panel at Lenox: "I was first introduced to my instrument in a school marching band where we played all the marches. Then I was introduced to jazz in the Dixieland style by a group of amateur musicians we heard. I guess they were playing Ragtime. That's when I was first exposed to the snare drum and the bass drum, and I became interested in the technical aspects. I guess I was really most affected by the jazz I heard on the radio; especially on Count Basie's show. It helped me to develop some sort of style up to the time when I met Mr. Gillespie. Jo Jones was the first drummer that I heard who played broken-rhythm, which, after I listened to it over and over again, really helped me most until the time when I heard Kenny Clarke.

"But, prior to that, I guess a lot of people did a lot to inspire me. Take Chick Webb, he was a tremendous soloist. And I also heard O'Neil Spencer, who impressed me quite a bit, and Kaiser Marshall. And they played snare-drum style, which I never could really master; that is, the way they handled it then, because, in my time, it wasn't too popular. Then there was Sonny Greer. I guess I was most impressed by all the paraphernalia he had on the bandstand at that particular time. Then there was Cozy Cole. I guess he brought my attention to the rudimental, military style of drumming. He was the technical man. He was with Cab Calloway then.

"So I would say that as far as I know, first there was a snare style. . . . Then there was the high-hat style, which I guess was first brought to my attention by Jo Jones, which placed more emphasis rhythmically in a jazz band on section work. Then there was Sidney Catlett, who incorporated this hi-hat style and the ride-cymbal style. But he didn't break his rhythms up in the bass drum as much as Jo Jones or Kenny Clarke did. Then I heard Kenny. He exemplified personality. He did more with the instrument—not that he ever overdid—but he seemed to get more out of it . . . it meant more . . . it affected me."

After reiterating that Clarke, Catlett, Jones, and Webb were the "important people to me," Roach added, "And Cozy Cole was the person who I guess added the classic technique to jazz drumming which today still hasn't been fully accepted because it sounds very militaristic. I really don't know what to say about it, except that it is very difficult to do. . . . O'Neil Spencer did wonderful things with the brushes which I haven't heard since."

It is obvious that young Roach was both a student and a fan of jazz. He played in teenage Brooklyn rehearsal bands that read stock arrangements from the books of bands like Glenn Miller's as well as Basie's and Jimmie Lunceford's. His friends were other young musicians, like trumpeter Leonard Hawkins, tenor man Ray Abrams and his drummer brother Lee Abrams, and saxophonist Cecil Payne. These kids would pack lunches and travel to the Apollo Theatre on 125th Street in Manhattan to hear all the bands. Later, Roach remembers going to the Savoy Ballroom, where there were two bandstands. As one band was playing its sign-off number, the other would be launching into its opening theme, and you had to be quick to get good bandstand locations in the constantly shifting scene. It was here that he first saw Chick Webb "close up."

Max tried to get into Kelly's Stables but was kept out because he was underage. He used an eyebrow pencil to draw a mustache on his upper lip, but it did not work. He was able to attend the Sunday-afternoon sessions at the Village Vanguard, however. Although he was denied entrance to clubs as a spectator, he began working in them before he was out of high school. Clark Monroe had the band at Georgie Jay's 78th Street Taproom, a Manhattan club that Roach's memory places between Broadway and Amsterdam Avenue. The band, actually led by trumpeter Vic Coulsen, worked at the Taproom in the evening and then played from four to eight in the morning at Monroe's Uptown House. Roach met Charlie Parker when Coulsen brought Bird down to the Taproom to play one night. At Minton's he met Monk and Powell. He also played uptown at Murrain's and, in the Village, at Pinto's and the Savannah. While Fifty-second Street was active, Roach remembers, there was a similar area in the Bedford-Stuyvesant section on Fulton Street and Ralph Avenue; clubs would book weekend sessions featuring whatever musicians were in town with the various big bands.

In 1942 Roach graduated with honors from Boys' High School and went full time into music. From 1943 to 1944 he was in the band at Kelly's Stables, where Coleman Hawkins was featured. Perhaps he was Kenny Clarke's replacement when Clarke went into the Army. In 1965 he told me that he was not directly influenced by Clarke and, in fact, did not hear him until Klook got out of the Army in 1946. "It was when he was married to Carmen," he said, referring to Carmen McRae, who, as Carmen Clarke, was singing with the Mercer Ellington band at the time.

Roach says that he had his own conception when he was still in his mid-teens. "When I was fifteen," he said, "I was playing at a session in Brooklyn, and Cecil Payne, who was not there, told me later that he knew I was. When I asked him how he knew, he said, 'I could hear you from outside. I could tell it was you.'"

Although Roach uses some of the same devices that Clarke does, Max's style has a different feel. But in the light of all previous statements, it seems improbable that he did not hear Kenny until 1946. When Roach got out of school, Clarke may have been in Chicago with Red Allen. However, Kenny did play at Kelly's before he was drafted. And where was Clarke when Roach was meeting Monk and Powell at Minton's?

When Gillespie and Pettiford went into the Qnyx club in January, 1944, they hired Roach. Max says the reason they couldn't get Bud Powell was not so much that Cootie Williams refused to let him go as that Powell's mother "didn't want Bud to play with Diz, because she thought Dizzy was crazy."

Through Dizzy, Max received his first chance to record. It was the February, 1944, record date with Coleman Hawkins for Apollo at which *Woody'n You* was cut. After Roach had set up his drums, the engineer came and draped a rug on his bass drum. "I was frustrated and ready to leave," says Max. "Here it was my first date, and I wanted to play. I objected to the theory that drums should be felt, not heard."

On the records, the bass drum isn't audible, and Roach doesn't seem to be playing too daringly. His beat is steady if unobtrusive. On *Bu-Dee-Daht*, he backs the theme statements with hi-hats *à la* Jo Jones, and he ends the number with a break that is anything but boppish.

When the nucleus of the group from the Onyx—Pettiford, Gillespie, and Don Byas—recorded for Manor in early 1945, Roach was not in New York. After working in the Village and at midtown strip joints, he had a chance to go with Benny Carter's band. His big-band experience had been limited to the teenage bands in Brooklyn and "two or three days with Duke Ellington at the Paramount." The latter job was during the war, when Sonny Greer became ill and there was a scarcity of adequate replacements around New York. "Clark Monroe suggested me because I could read show music," says Roach. "I had no rehearsal. The stage came up and I was sitting with Sonny's drums all about me.

I followed Duke—his conducting was so hip while he played the piano. He made it a breeze."

Roach learned a lot from playing with Carter. This big-band experience rounded him out. He met J.J. Johnson, and the two would practice like demons between theater shows. Roach says of Carter, "He's so thorough, so well versed in music."

In June, 1944, Barry Ulanov reviewed the band for *Metronome,* singling out its drummer for praise: "The big kick in this Carter band is supplied by drummer Max Roach. He is a fast drummer who pushes the band, beating it with a steadiness and a rhythmic inspiration found only in the very great drummers."

Carter recorded for Capitol at the time. In addition to making the band sides, Roach also did an all-star date with Carter, Coleman Hawkins, Nat "King" Cole, and others, under the title *The International Jazzmen,* for the same label in March, 1945.

In the spring, Roach returned to New York and the Parker-Gillespie quintet at the Three Deuces. "I didn't make the opening or the records," he says. Sid Catlett was on the Guild recordings, and Stan Levey was at the Deuces until Max replaced him.

In the fall, Max was working with Bird and Miles Davis on The Street, and they did the Savoy date that included *Now's the Time, Billie's Bounce,* and *Ko Ko.* On these the cymbal pulse is in evidence, although still not well recorded, and while the over-all feeling here is definitely in keeping with the new music, Roach's hand and foot accents are still relatively simple punctuations. His solo on *Ko Ko* begins with a bop construction but ends with a roll more typical of a swing drummer.

Next, Roach played with the ill-fated Gillespie big band that toured the South. Back in New York at the end of the year, Dizzy and Bird reunited and left for California. Max did not go, and Stan Levey made the trip in his place. Through 1946 Roach worked all over Fifty-second Street with Allen Eager, Dexter Gordon, Coleman Hawkins, and J.J. Johnson. He recorded with Hawkins for Sonora, and with each of the others for Savoy. The Johnson date in June included Roach's *Coppin' the Bop,* a *Mop Mop* type of theme in reverse, with its on-the-beat figure played first, followed by a boppish phrase. At various places in this session you can hear Roach accenting in unison with Bud Powell.

Sitting in was common on Fifty-second Street. The atmosphere

was conducive to an exchange of ideas through playing and talking. Perhaps this was most prevalent among drummers, who, by
the very nature of their instrument, seem to be more able to shop-
talk than other musicians. They tend to gravitate toward one another. In 1946 three young drummers shared an apartment near
Fifty-second Street—Stan Levey, Art Mardigan, and Roach.

Levey, from Philadelphia, had played there with Gillespie in
1942. Two years later he came to New York and met Roach. In a
1958 *Down Beat* article, Stan was quoted as saying: "First time I
heard Max play, I was petrified. He was working at the time with
Dizzy's group at the Onyx . . . hearing Max was a radically new
experience for me. Thing was, he was completely different in his
technique and musical approach. He concentrated more on
melodic playing; he split time in ways I'd never heard. After that
we worked opposite each other on 52nd St. for years and became
fast friends."

One of the relatively few left-handed drummers, Levey, besides working with most of the important musicians in the early
days, was also in George Shearing's first American group in 1944,
the bands of Georgie Auld, Charlie Ventura, Woody Herman,
and Freddie Slack. In 1952 he joined Stan Kenton, remaining
until March, 1954, when he became part of the Lighthouse All
Stars at Hermosa Beach, California. Since that time, he has been
working and living on the West Coast. Levey, a strong player,
whose dominant influence was Roach, is in fine form on his Bethlehem LP *This Time the Drum's on Me*, made in the mid-fifties.
(The title tune is really *Max Is Making Wax*.) In 1957, when
Roach was in Los Angeles, he and Levey recorded an album together titled *Drummin' the Blues*.

Since the mid-fifties, Mardigan, a native Detroiter, has worked
in his hometown for the most part. In the forties, he was in
Georgie Auld's band, and he played on The Street with Parker,
Gordon, and Eager. In the fifties, he was heard with Elliot Law-
rence, Kai Winding, Woody Herman, Pete Rugolo, and Stan
Getz. In New York his style was touched by Roach, although he
had his own sound, a relaxed and effortless echo of his attack.
Roy Haynes calls him a "natural-type drummer." He is repre-
sented on LP's with Wardell Gray (Prestige) and Fats Navarro
(Savoy).

Another Fifty-second Streeter who, like Levey, ended up in the

West is Shelly Manne, certainly one of the finest drummers in jazz. Manne is from a drumming family; two uncles were drummers, and his father, Max Manne, was a percussionist in the orchestra at Radio City Music Hall. Shelly began studying at an early age, and he turned professional when he started playing on ocean liners that made Atlantic crossings. Between ships, he frequented Fifty-second Street, where he could hear Dave Tough playing with Joe Marsala at the Hickory House. In 1940 he became Tough's replacement. Then he worked with a succession of bands before going into the Coast Guard in 1942. Since he was stationed at Manhattan Beach (which, paradoxically, is in Brooklyn) until his discharge in 1945, Manne was able to stay in close touch with The Street and the new developments. Five years older than Roach, he already had the foundations of a style going by the time he heard Max. Although he incorporated the new approach into his playing, he maintained his individuality. Roy Haynes says, "Stan Levey was playing Max Roach, but Shelly was playing different things."

In 1946, Manne, in the company of other Stan Kenton sidemen, such as Kai Winding and Eddie Safranski (Shelly had joined Kenton that year and remained into 1947), recorded with Allen Eager for Savoy in a group billed as Teddy Reig's All Stars. His wide, shimmering, top-cymbal sound on *Mr. Dues* and *Oh Kai* is a parallel of the kind of sound Dave Tough was getting in Woody Herman's Herd of 1944–1945, and bop inflections are evident. At this time, Tough, who was listening to Roach intently, had left Herman and was playing at the club of Eddie Condon, his old Chicago associate of the twenties. A distressed Condon called Tough "bludgeon foot" and "the Dizzy Gillespie of the cymbals," adding, "If anyone but Dave Tough were perpetrating that Re-Bop slop at my joint, I'd see how much my insurance would pay off and burn the club down."

In December, 1948, Tough was dead from a fall that fractured his skull. Manne meanwhile had been with Charlie Ventura, rejoined Kenton from 1947 to 1948 (he was to do this again from 1950 to 1951), toured with JATP in 1948 and 1949, and played with Woody Herman in 1949. Since his third tour of duty with Kenton, Manne has been in California, first at the Lighthouse, then with Shorty Rogers, and finally with his own group, which he formed in 1956. Now his quintet plays weekends at his own club, Shelly's Manne-Hole, in Los Angeles. Manne also works the TV and movie studios. Through the years, he has made wide use of various tonal effects without becoming gimmicky and has always applied one of the important lessons he learned on Fifty-second Street—swing.

The man who replaced Tough in the Herman band in 1945 demonstrated a great sense of swing both then and in the next edition of the Herman orchestra, the 1947–1949 Four Brothers band. That was Don Lamond, who combined Tough and the modernists in his own way. Now in the TV studios in New York, Lamond was a hard-driving big-band drummer who played exciting fills.

When Tough left Herman, the men in the band took a vote to determine whom they would like for his replacement. They wanted Shadow Wilson, but Shadow was with Basie at the time. Eventually, in 1949, he did work with Herman. An excellent big-band drummer, Wilson was equally good with smaller combos, as he proved with those of Earl Hines, Erroll Garner, Illinois Jacquet, and, for the period prior to his untimely death in 1959, Thelonious Monk. Some of his outstanding recorded work is with Basie on *Queer Street* (Columbia) and with Tadd Dameron's group on *The Fabulous Fats Navarro,* Volume 1 (Blue Note). Wilson was not a modernist in the sense that Roach was, but he fit in admirably with all the groups with which he played.

One drummer who came from the Minton's scene had not yet taken up drums when he was playing there. That was Denzil Best, a man whose entire life was stalked by tragedy, until the final one, a fall down the steps leading to a subway, killed him on May 25, 1965, in New York.

Best, who studied piano at the age of 6, later switched to trumpet, and at 23 he was playing around New York on the latter instrument. He sat in on both instruments at Minton's in 1940. Thelonious Monk has praised him as an outstanding hornman with great ideas. Unfortunately, Best contracted a lung ailment that put him out of action until 1941. He then worked jobs on piano and bass, and in 1943 he took up drums. He was with Coleman Hawkins from 1944 to 1945, went to Sweden with Chubby Jackson in 1947, and joined George Shearing in 1949. His masterful brushwork became one of the main components of the sound that the Shearing quintet popularized. Everything was going right for Best. His distinctive compositions were being recorded by many people: Hawkins did *Allen's Alley* (later it was to be known as *Wee*); Clyde Hart and Jackson each made *Dee Dee's Dance;* both Miles Davis and Fats Navarro recorded *Move;* and Shearing cut *Nothing But D. Best.* In 1952 Monk recorded *Bemsha Swing,* an earlier written collaboration with Best. It since has become, like several of Denzil's other pieces, a jazz standard.

An automobile accident left him with fractured legs, incapacitating him from 1952 to 1953. After his recovery, Best worked with Artie Shaw in 1954 and with Erroll Garner from 1956 to 1957. Then calcium deposits formed in his wrists and impaired his drumming facility. Although he worked with a variety of small groups, he was never to regain the dexterity and finesse of his injury-free days.

Perhaps the best of the modern drummers immediately to follow Roach's achievements was Roy Haynes. Born in Roxbury, Massachusetts, in March, 1926, he played around nearby Boston with Sabby Lewis, Frankie Newton, and Pete Brown while still a teenager. Then he was with Luis Russell from 1945 to 1947, when Lester Young hired him to go out on the road. It was then that he began to build a reputation. In 1949 Haynes based himself in New York, appearing with Kai Winding on Fifty-second Street and at jam sessions, like the ones at Georgie Auld's club, Tin Pan Alley. That same year he recorded with Winding and with Wardell Gray, both times for Prestige. His accents were clear, crisp, and completely in keeping with the current drumming style.

In Boston he had been listening as well as playing. He first heard Kenny Clarke at the Ken Club with Red Allen. Haynes says, "The MC didn't introduce him. He said, 'Just ask Jo Jones about him.'"

That was about 1942. Then Roy heard Art Blakey with Fletcher Henderson in 1944, Max Roach with Benny Carter and with Parker and Gillespie in 1945. "There was something I had always wanted to play," says Haynes, "a certain figure—and [Roach] played it. A lot of Max rubbed off on me."

When Haynes first heard Roach, "Max had one cymbal, bass drum, snare, no tom-tom. He had his right hand on the cymbal, his left on the snare drum. At the time, the drummers weren't playing on the two and four. The bass drum was like another hand. Maybe guys didn't have a tom-tom because they couldn't afford it, but I got rid of mine."

Haynes was admired for his particularly lively pulse and also for the way he played his fours—the four-bar exchanges with the hornmen. They were both witty and intelligently constructed. Roy says he became experienced in playing fours with Lester Young. He enjoys "sixteens and twelves better than fours now. You can paint more of a picture."

His fills behind a soloist have always been pungent. "I wouldn't practice them," he says. "I would think about them."

In the 1949–1950 period, Haynes was Charlie Parker's drummer. When asked how it was to play with Bird, he replied, "Like with Pres, the drums seemed to play themselves."

From 1953 to 1958, Haynes worked in the relative anonymity of the trio backing Sarah Vaughan. People began to say that he had become stale in this environment, but it didn't take the diminutive drummer long to prove them wrong once he left the trio. He played his way into the sixties with a variety of jobs for people like Phineas Newborn; Miles Davis; Lee Konitz; Thelonious Monk; Lambert, Hendricks, and Ross; George Shearing; Lennie Tristano; and Kenny Burrell. Since 1962 he has led his own quartets, and he has also played with John Coltrane on occasion, substituting for Elvin Jones. His style has shifted to more of the "stating of the beat all over the set" favored by some of the newer players. While he did not sound like Elvin Jones when he worked with Coltrane, his attack was in keeping with the leader's music. Among his assets, Haynes has always counted flexibility.

Haynes remembers well the help he received from Clarke and Roach in the forties. It took different forms with each. "I feel close to Max," he says, "but closer to Klook." When he played at the Roost with Young, Clarke came over to him after the evening's work was done and gave him words of encouragement. "We rode uptown together on the subway, and he told me that I was the only young drummer who was swinging. That was a great compliment."

While Haynes was with Parker, Roach lent him support at a crucial time. The way Haynes tells it, "Miles had left Bird and gotten his own group. He worked out at Soldier Meyers' in Brooklyn. I was working with him at the time. Well, after Miles left, Max wanted to leave too.

"After Soldier Meyers', we went into the Orchid Room—the old Onyx—on Fifty-second Street, first with a trio of Bud Powell, Nelson Boyd, and myself; and later on Monte Kay put in Miles, Sonny Stitt, and Wardell and made a group out of it. Now, Bird is still working across the street at the Three Deuces, and Max is coming over, and we're swingin' like crazy. So then *he* cuts out from Bird, and he gets his group, and he goes to Soldier Meyers'. He had all the cats from Jersey—Hank Mobley on tenor, Al Cotten on bass, and Walter Davis on piano. So he came over and sounded me about working with Bird. I dug Bird, but at that time I wasn't particularly enthused about working with Bird. I don't know *why*. So I gave him one of those *comme ci, comme ça* type of answers, and he said, 'All right, later for you. I'll get Kansas Fields.' And then Bird came over and hired me himself.

"So after our gig closed, I went over and worked with Bird. After we'd been there a couple of weeks, Bud Powell is going to come in with a trio, and Max Roach is going to be on drums. I said, 'Uh-oh.' I was really going to have to be at my best. So one time Bird called *Salt Peanuts,* and I had never played that with Bird before.

"You know how in the Three Deuces, right near the drums, there was an open door where the guys would come on the bandstand, and Max was standing right in the door. I didn't know that after the piano solo, there was an extended drum solo—they used to feature the drums. And Max told me, 'Drum solo.' And he helped me out *so* much that night. I guess I played my best that night, because he was gassed, and I was gassed that he helped me."

At an earlier meeting in Chicago, when Haynes was with Young and Roach with Parker, Roy had his drums stolen, and Max immediately arranged with a representative of the Ludwig Company to get Haynes a new set at a discount and on credit. Stories like these balance against the ones told by people who feel that Roach is cold and difficult to approach. Dexter Gordon has said, "Max is kind of Mephistophelian. He's got that kind of—I always get that feeling from him. I dig him, I love him. He's got a very sharp mind, very apt, but personalitywise, he's not a real warm-type cat."

If Roach is sometimes aloof off the bandstand, he is completely the opposite when on it. He does not show the preaching fervor of an Art Blakey, but he is fiery in his own way, with an underlying drive that can be overwhelming. When Charlie Parker came back to New York in 1947, Roach became his regular drummer. "Bird's approach demanded new drumming concepts," Roach has stated. "He set tempos so fast it was impossible to play a straight Cozy Cole four style, so we had to work out variations.". In this climate, Roach brought his style to its height. His playing on the Savoy and Dial recordings of the 1947–1949 period is hand in glove with Bird's. The accents never impede but always propel, creating patterns that had never been played before. His solos are economical, logical, and were a giant step toward the formation of an even more "melodic" drum style. On one "take" of *Crazeology*, his break sounds like someone kicking a trunk down a flight of stairs—but what creative kicking! His Dial recordings are even more important than the Savoys, because for the first time, his top-cymbal sound was captured with clarity. Thanks to an engineer named Doug Hawkins, who was then employed by WOR Studios, each stroke is heard. Another well-recorded example of his resilient beat can be found on the Prestige sides made with Bud Powell and Sonny Stitt in 1949–50.

When he left Parker, Roach, besides leading a combo at Soldier Meyers', took a group that included J.J. Johnson and John Lewis for an engagement in Philadelphia. He also enrolled at the Manhattan School of Music, where Lewis was teaching, to study composition. (After *Coppin' the Bop*, his only written contribution had been *Prince Albert*, a lyrical line based on *All the Things You Are* and co-authored with Kenny Dorham; they recorded it in France while there with Parker for the 1949 Paris Jazz Festival.)

In 1952 Roach toured Europe as a member of JATP. In 1953 he again led his own quartet in New York. The group recorded for Charlie Mingus' Debut label, the company that issued the famous Massey Hall concert in which Roach and Mingus participated that same year. Then, in 1954, Shelly Manne left the Lighthouse, and owner Howard Rumsey, at Manne's suggestion, called Roach and asked him whether he wanted to come out to the Coast. Roach spent six months at the Hermosa Beach club. At this point, impresario Gene Norman, a club owner and concert promoter, asked him to put a group together. Max went back to New York, gathered up Clifford Brown and Sonny Stitt, and returned to California. So was Brown-Roach Inc. born. Stitt stayed six weeks, leaving before any recording was done. (Max says he has tapes, however.) Tenor man Teddy Edwards, pianist Carl Perkins, and bassist George Bledsoe are on a Brown-Roach concert that makes up one-half of an LP issued by the Gene Norman Presents label. A second concert, which comprises the album's second side, has Harold Land, Richie Powell (Bud's brother), and George Morrow in place of Edwards, Perkins, and Bledsoe. Land and Powell had come to Los Angeles with Johnny Hodges' group and then switched over to Brown-Roach. Powell, years before, had wanted to be a drummer. He used to go to Roach's house and wait for him to wake up so that he could learn from Max. Roach says he suggested that Powell take up the piano because of all the keyboard talent in his family.

On the Norman LP, there is a thrilling version of *The Man I Love* called *Clifford's Axe* in which Brown and Roach stir up a bonfire of emotion. The group was off to a flying start and gathered momentum as they went. By the time Sonny Rollins replaced Land in January, 1956, the group was rapidly becoming one of the most prominent in jazz, with two brilliant hornmen in Brown and Rollins; Powell's bright composing and arranging talent and his improving piano; Morrow's steadiness; and Roach's continued development as a "melodic" percussionist with an exceptional beat.

In June everything came tumbling down. From a section of the Pennsylvania Turnpike made slick by rain, a car carrying Brown, Powell, and Powell's wife plunged into a culvert, killing all of them. It was a severe blow to Roach, one from which it took him a long time to recover—if one can be said ever to recover from such a soul-tearing experience. Immediately he began blaming himself—he felt if he had been there, the accident would never have occurred.

It was the group's practice to travel in tandem—in Brown's car and Roach's car. In this instance, the next job was in Chicago. The men were enjoying a short layoff. Roach was in New York, Brown and Powell were in Philadelphia. Since he had to go to a factory in Elkhart, Indiana, to pick up a new horn, Brown decided to leave earlier. He told Roach he would meet him in Chicago.

Another policy of the cooperative was to have wives fly to a job location if they wanted to spend time with their husbands on the road. "We felt we were doing well enough financially by this time to afford it," says Roach.

Some weeks earlier, when Powell had gotten married, he bought himself a car. Leaving a party, he had his wife, an inexperienced driver (with glasses "five times as thick as mine," according to Roach), get behind the wheel. Roach, on seeing this, voiced a negative opinion. An argument followed. Although Roach knew that Powell didn't like his attitude about his wife's driving, Max felt that Richie respected it. "If I had been there that night," Roach kept telling himself, "he wouldn't have let her drive."

As he continued to brood over Brown's and Powell's deaths, Max Roach became more and more miserable. He continued to lead his groups (the personnel shifted several times), and he also began to drink heavily. Alcohol had a very bad effect on him. One Monday night at Birdland in the late fifties, for example, Max Roach was abusive to everyone at the bar—friends, acquaintances, and strangers alike. Although he was not booked to play there, he kept going up on the stand, berating the customers over the public-address system, and attempting to play unaccompanied solos. Miles Davis once lifted him bodily and took him back to the bar area, but Roach went up once more, this time stepping on a bass that was lying on the floor. At this point, a note of strange humor emerged in this decidedly serious affair. As Max ascended the bandstand by climbing over a railing, a young drummer appearing on the bill, who was coming off the stand, asked quietly, "What's happening, Max?"

What was happening was that a great artist was ripping himself apart. Roach went to hospitals, took medication to make alcohol repugnant to him, and underwent psychotherapy. The man emerging from this period of torture was not left to rest easy. In October, 1961, his sideman Booker Little—like Brown, a tremendously talented trumpeter—died of uremia. Little, who had joined Roach's group in June, 1958, and stayed for a year, was still closely allied with the drummer through recording work and friendship. If Roach did not stretch his imagination to blame himself for Little's death, it certainly didn't make him feel any better.

There are other things that bother Roach. He feels acutely the position of the Negro in America and has become a dedicated fighter for a real equality. In a 1961 *Down Beat* article by Marc Crawford, he told the author that he had changed, "but only in terms of content. I will never again play anything that does not have social significance. It is my duty, the purpose of the artist to mirror his times and its effects on his fellow man. We American jazz musicians of African descent have proved beyond all doubt that we're master musicians of our instruments. Now, what we have to do is employ our skill to tell the dramatic story of our people and what we've been through. . . .

"Little Rock, New Orleans . . . sit-in demonstrations . . . courage of our . . . young people . . . how can anyone consider my music independent of what I am? . . . reflection of what I feel . . . music must be fresh but also must be vital—have meaning or it's nothing . . . new ethics needed if man is going to survive in atomic age . . . no one can stand against change . . . don't have to like me or my music so long as they understand what motivates it . . . art, real art has to come from within . . . get away from this idea of who's the best drummer . . . you can't rate feeling, soul . . . it's personal and individual; what's the standard? . . . conformity . . . decadence . . . TV westerns and Madison Avenue . . . suburbia and organization man . . . richest country in the world and begging for dimes for polio . . . couldn't accommodate myself to it anymore . . . it was choking stifling me . . . praise for the color of my music, prejudice for the color of my skin . . . funny bit . . . hah! hah! hah! . . . funny if it wasn't so tragic."

In 1960, Roach and Charlie Mingus staged a protest against the Newport Jazz Festival by running a "rebel festival" in the Rhode Island town at the same time the big show was being held. Some white musicians participated, but it was a predominantly Negro show.

In May of 1961, there was a Miles Davis concert at Carnegie Hall, a benefit to buy medical supplies for Africa. Max Roach appeared, sitting on the edge of the stage with a placard protesting against the policies of the organization sponsoring the event. And Roach and his wife, singer Abbey Lincoln, appeared at the UN during the unrest in the Congo, protesting the death of Patrice Lumumba.

Today, not everything Roach plays has social significance, but much of it does. The major example is *We Insist!: Freedom Now*

Suite, a five-part work by Roach and Oscar Brown, Jr. Roach's collaboration with Oscar Brown might never have come about if Max had not met Miss Lincoln. When Max was in California in 1954, she was a singing on the Coast, and they met at the home of mutual friends. He didn't see her again until 1956. She was a sexy supper-club singer then, but she was unhappy with what she was doing and told Roach so. At his suggestion, she began singing with jazzmen and did an album for Riverside Records in a jazz setting. In 1958 she was living in Chicago and, Roach says, "involved with Oscar Brown, Jr., Frank London Brown, and Lorraine Hansberry." Through Abbey, Max met the people in this Negro writers' circle and began writing the suite with Brown. *Driva' Man, Freedom Day,* and *All Africa* were first written as part of a large choral work to be performed in 1963 on the centennial of the Emancipation Proclamation. *Triptych: Prayer, Protest, Peace,* originally conceived as a ballet, and *Tears for Johannesburg* were added for the Candid album of the suite, done in 1960. Not all of this LP is jazz, but it is a powerful, disturbing musical document of oppression and resistance from the early days of slavery in the United States to the Sharpeville massacres in South Africa. There are solos by Coleman Hawkins, Booker Little, tenor man Walter Benton, and trombonist Julian Priester; Roach and Nigerian drummer Michael Olatunji head up a four-piece percussion section on the African sections; and Miss Lincoln, who is also an actress, does some expressive wordless crooning, screaming, and sighing in *Triptych.* Max and Abbey have made the *Freedom Now Suite* part of their nightclub presentation ever since. In 1965 some Italian film makers produced a short subject composed of still shots and used part of the suite as their sound track.

The Candid album that followed *We Insist!* was Miss Lincoln's *Straight Ahead,* in which she was backed by Roach. My own review of the album in *Down Beat,* in which I found fault with both the singing and the social propaganda, stirred up a controversy that culminated in a panel discussion published in the magazine in 1962. The subject was "Racial Prejudice in Jazz," and if it didn't solve problems, it did temporarily clear the air.

Both Max and Abbey are involved with their African heritage as well as with the civil rights struggle in the United States. Their apartment on Manhattan's West Side contains many African sculptures, paintings, and objects. Miss Lincoln is fond of African garb, and although Roach dresses in a conventional American manner, when he greeted me at the door one day, he was wearing a sweat shirt with a picture of Jomo Kenyatta on it.

Burt Korall quotes Kenny Clarke, still in Paris, as saying: "I may be put down for this . . . but I must admit that I'm not interested in allying myself with causes. I'm a Negro; I know what's happening. I don't turn my back on the realities because I'm 3,000 miles away. I do what *I* can as I move through my life. But . . . as far as I'm concerned, it's the music that's important. That's the legacy we leave behind."

Besides his social action, Roach is also making sure that he will leave a musical legacy, and much of it is from his post-Parker years. The EmArcy and Prestige albums with Brown and Rollins are peak performances. In his accompaniment and solos, Roach almost seems to be playing a melody instrument as he extracts sound from his drum kit—and without the aid of tympani. When he does use the kettle drums, as on his own *Dr. Free-zee* or on Thelonious Monk's and Denzil Best's *Bemsha Swing* in Monk's *Brilliant Corners* album, the results are both instructive and startling.

One of his greatest solos is in Rollins' *Saxophone Colossus* album on Prestige. Gunther Schuller wrote of his work on *Blue 7:* "The ingenuity with which he alternates between . . . two ideas gives not only an indication of the capacity of Max Roach as a thinking musician, but also shows again that exciting drum solos need not be an *un*thinking burst of energy—they can be interesting and meaningful compositions."

Roach's success in playing jazz in unusual time signatures is well known. He was the drummer when Monk made a jazz waltz out of *Carolina Moon* in 1952, and he used Rollins' *Valse Hot* in his own group in 1956. The following year he did an entire album called *Jazz in 3/4 Time.*

In 1958, in Pittsburgh, Roach played a 5/4 blues, *As Long As You're Living,* written by Tommy Turrentine and Julian Priester. He says that Dave Brubeck heard it and came backstage to tell him how he (Brubeck) had been thinking about doing things in different time signatures for a long time. A comparison of *As Long As You're Living,* recorded in 1960 and included in Roach's album *Quiet As It's Kept,* with Paul Desmond's *Take Five* (from the album of that name recorded, I believe, the same year) points up the ease with which Roach negotiates all times. *As Long As You're Living* avoids monotony by the use of varying dynamics and bassist Bobby Boswell's alternation of the figures he plays underneath. The same cannot be said of *Take Five*.

Roach's explorations in time and his compositional abilities are combined in his Impulse album *It's Time*. With his sextet, there is a sixteen-voice chorus under the direction of Coleridge Perkinson. He makes use of 2/4, 3/4, 4/4, 5/4, 6/4, 7/4, and 7/8. If they are not all successful, it is not because of the execution of the various rhythms. Several of Roach's numbers are well realized from all standpoints, however.

Through everything, Roach remains a giant drummer. Dick Hadlock has commented on his *Conversation:* "a solo in which Roach sustains almost four minutes of brilliant drumming with melodic imagination (one is reminded of Baby Dodds) and a finesse that no other jazz drummer (save Sid Catlett) has ever equaled."

Recommended Listening

KENNY CLARKE

The Modern Jazz Quartet, PRESTIGE P-24005
Kenny Clarke/ Francy Boland Big Band, OPEN DOOR, MUSE 5056
Clarke/Boland Big Band, Sax No End, PAUSA 7097
Kenny Clarke Meets the Detroit Jazzmen, SAVOY SJL 1111

(see also Parker, Gillespie, Dameron, Navarro)

MAX ROACH

The Quintet, Volume 1 (with Sonny Rollins), MERCURY 0798;
   Volume 2, MERCURY 0898
Saxophone Colossus and More (with Sonny Rollins),
   PRESTIGE P-24050
Conversations, MILESTONE M-47061
Freedom Now Suite, COLUMBIA JC 36390

(see also Parker, Gillespie, Powell)

7

DEXTER GORDON
AND THE TENOR SAXOPHONISTS

THE FORTIES saw Charlie Parker revive interest in the alto saxophone and draw new players to that instrument. At the same time, he caused numerous tenor saxophonists already blowing to alter their approaches. His influence, of course, was felt by musicians of all instruments, but among the tenor men, many of whom had been absorbing Lester "Pres" Young for a few years, he induced split musical personalities. When Herbie Steward, one of the purest in Presian spirit, heard Parker's music, he became confused. Members of the Woody Herman orchestra of 1947, in which Steward was playing alto saxophone (switching to tenor on *Four Brothers*), remarked, "Bird shook Herbie up. He doesn't know which way to go."

It wasn't the first time Bird had caused a schism in an already established player, and it wasn't the last. Wardell Gray, who had been strictly in a Pres groove when he recorded *Relaxin' at Camarillo* with Parker, changed over to a harder attack and sound. Gray, after a while, evolved his personal version of these influences, but at first the amalgamation caused him trouble.

One man who seemed to take various influences in stride, maintaining a personal musical equilibrium, was Dexter Gordon. In *The Book of Jazz*, Leonard Feather, in listing a group of tenor men under the general heading "extrovert moderns," said of him: "[Gordon] perhaps more than any of the others transferred the characteristics of bop to the tenor."

Although Don Byas was active along Fifty-second Street before Gordon and had played with Gillespie and Pettiford, successfully negotiating many of the demands of the new music, rhythmically his phrasing echoed Coleman Hawkins and was not really in keeping with bop. Gordon, who learned from a variety of influences, was able effectively to synthesize them and bring his own personality into full play at the same time.

201

Personality is something that Dexter Keith Gordon has in abundance. Possessing a genuinely exciting saxophone style and a sense of the dramatic, the handsome, six-foot-five-inch tenor man has always commanded an audience's attention. He started igniting crowds when he was a member of the Billy Eckstine band in 1944–1945. By the time he left Eckstine to base himself in New York, Gordon had acquired a following. He became a regular along Fifty-second Street and appeared at the numerous Sunday-afternoon sessions at such places as the Fraternal Clubhouse on West Forty-eighth Street and the Lincoln Square Center near the old St. Nicholas Arena.

Often he would make a belated entrance and attract interest merely by putting his saxophone together in view of the crowd. Once he showed up at Lincoln Square with a finger encased in a cumbersome bandage; though unable to play, he was the center of attention. On the night in 1947 that the Royal Roost was first used as a proving ground for modern jazz, some seven hundred people attended. Gordon, booked to appear, arrived late. At 2 A.M. he began to descend the long staircase leading to the club. At that moment, a throng was coming up the stairs; but on seeing Dexter, these jazz buffs reversed their course and followed him back into the club, where they sat and listened to him play for an hour and a half.

Although Gordon's music was "hot," his manner was "cool." In the fall of 1945, he and Red Rodney were playing a set together at the Fraternal Clubhouse. Dexter made his entrance by starting his solo in the wings and shuffling laconically onstage. One night at the Spotlite, a drunk dropped a handful of change into the bell of his horn during a solo. Outwardly impassive, Gordon continued his lovely ballad statement; when he finished, he calmly upended his saxophone and pocketed the coins.

Gordon's magnetism for an audience extended to his fellow musicians. His influence began in the mid-forties. It was readily apparent in Allen Eager's first Savoy recordings (*Booby Hatch, Rampage*), and Stan Getz was persuaded for a while, as witness his *Opus de Bop* and *Running Water*. Billy Smith, who recorded with Thelonious Monk for Blue Note (*Evonce, Suburban Eyes, Humph*), played in a definite Gordon groove, and there were doubtless many other players under his sway who never reached a recording studio.

Gordon's influence really flowered in the fifties, however, in John Coltrane and Sonny Rollins. Players such as Jackie McLean, Clifford Jordan, Jimmy Heath, and Bill Barron also showed the Gordon imprint in varying degrees. Coltrane and Rollins both became extremely individual musicians, but the touches of Gordon in their playing are a strong reflection of Dexter's stature.

One of the things most often said about Gordon from his earliest days on Fifty-second Street was that he had great harmonic awareness ("Dexter really knows changes," was the way it was usually put). When he took up the clarinet at the age of 13, Gordon simultaneously began to study harmony and theory, subjects that most jazzmen of that time took up much later, if at all. The teacher he speaks of with great respect is Lloyd Reese. "He plays trumpet—all brasses—piano, sax. A lot of people out there studied with him. I got a musical integrity from him that has been invaluable to me."

Gordon's studies with Reese were in Los Angeles, California, where he was born on February 27, 1923. Dexter's father was a well-known doctor; two of his patients were Duke Ellington and Lionel Hampton. At 15, while in high school, Dexter switched from clarinet to alto saxophone. Two years later, in 1940, he became a tenor man, quit school, and joined a local band called the Harlem Collegians. In December he became a member of Lionel Hampton's band. This opportunity was quite a surprise to him. "I thought Marshall Royal was kidding," he recalled, "when he called me up to offer me a job with Hamp's band. I went over to Hamp's pad, and we blew a while, and that was it. We went right on the road, without any rehearsal, cold. I was expecting to be sent home every night."

Evidently, the youthful Gordon was good enough to stay, for he didn't leave the band until 1943. Since Illinois Jacquet was the featured tenor man, Gordon was for the most part a section man. ("There was a number called *Po'k Chops* with Jacquet—it was about the only thing I had to play," said Dexter of his solo chances.) It was in the section that he learned some valuable lessons. Alto saxophonist Marshall Royal and his brother, trumpeter Ernie Royal, were in the band. Marshall, best known in the fifties and sixties as lead man of the Count Basie sax section and straw boss of the Basie band, served in a similar capacity with Hampton. Although he was only 28, Royal was much older than the rest of the musicians in the band. "There's a cat who showed me a lot—Marshall," said Gordon. "I didn't really come to appreciate it until recently—a few years ago. He used to stay on my ass all the time in that section. I'd say, 'Oh, man, won't this guy ever get off my back?' But everything he told me was right—breathing, phrasing. 'Man, tune up, tune up, man.' "

Gordon feels that the absence of big bands today has cheated the younger musicians. "A pet peeve or gripe of mine is the lack of big bands, which are so essential for young musicians," he said. "The experience you get in a big band, you don't get anywhere else. It develops your tone, your intonation. The discipline that you get in a big band, you just don't get in a small group. Slurring, attacking, phrasing—in a small group it's at a minimum."

The sound that Gordon produces is strong proof of the validity of his preachment. Separated from his attack, which itself is quite varied and a formidable tool, it serves as a powerful means of communication. British writer Michael James has called Gordon's lower-register sound "cavernous"—and, to be sure, there are some beautiful formations in that cavern. His middle range can be lighter, toward Lester Young; or harder, toward Charlie Parker; the upper reaches contain that eerily beautiful wail that almost seems to emanate from his throat. Dizzy Gillespie's *Blue 'N Boogie,* recorded in early 1945, was Gordon's first small-group recording after he hit Fifty-second Street. His solo contains the "scream" that ten years later showed up in John Coltrane's work with the Miles Davis Quintet.

Some think that more than Gordon's sound was affected by his Hampton days. Michael James, in referring to the Savoy records Dexter made in 1945–1946 (*Dexter's Deck, Long, Tall Dexter,* etc.), wrote: "It is tempting to see in the early part of Gordon's career, especially his spell with Hampton, influences that helped to shape his style. The forthright, even-noted swing and square-cut turn of phrase to be heard on his 1945 and 1946 sessions for Savoy recall the regular melodic outlines of Hampton's improvisation rather than the shifting accents of Lester Young, or even the comparatively symmetrical patterns of a Chu Berry. It seems likely that he took Illinois Jacquet as an exemplar. Besides the strong tonal resemblance, Gordon was very ready to indulge in the repeated-note motifs that were part of Jacquet's stock-in-trade. Whether these similarities were coincidental or not, Gordon's achievement was to present, as early as 1946, a taste of Parker's harmonic richness in a framework that was no less than conservative in its attachment to the beat, and to do this in a way logical enough to make for a style that was individual, integrated and unfailingly cogent."

Actually, although Gordon retained many of his Lester Young effects in the 1945–1946 Savoys (some of the riffs are right out of Pres's Basie performances), the height of his allegiance to Lester came a couple of years before, when he recorded *Rosetta* and *I Found a New Baby* for Mercury with trumpeter Harry "Sweets" Edison. (This twelve-inch 78-rpm has never been reissued.) *Rosetta* displays a Gordon extremely close to the tender, flowing Pres, while *I Found a New Baby* finds him in a trigger-fast Young-directed style.

The similarities to Jacquet are there, as James states. Certain Jacquet-type squeals, over and above the high-register "screams," are still in evidence today, but Dexter uses these judiciously, never descending to Jacquet's poor taste.

Ross Russell, in his brilliant essay "The Parent Style and Lester Young," wrote: "As Dexter Gordon describes it: 'Hawk was the master of the horn, a musician who did everything possible with it, the right way. But when Pres appeared, we all started listening to him alone. Pres had an entirely new sound, one that we seemed to be waiting for. Pres was the first to tell a story on the horn.'"

Dexter says of his formative high-school years, "I hadn't been exposed to Hawk as much as Lester." His first influences were the two Basie tenor men of that period—Young and Herschel Evans. (Evans played in a style closer to that of Hawkins; and Herschel, in turn, seems to have been Jacquet's principal mover.) With Gordon, Young was definitely number one. "I got a chance to hear Lester with the Basie band in Los Angeles. They came out there in 1939. All the cats cut school that day—the opening day at the Paramount Theatre. Herschel had just died, so I didn't get a chance to hear him. Lester was really in his thing then—very exciting, very dynamic."

Dexter had heard Evans on record, even if he was never to hear him in person. He also admired the work of another tenor man who died prematurely—Dick Wilson of the Andy Kirk band. Records enabled him to hear Ben Webster with Duke Ellington and Hawkins' *Body and Soul.* But until he came to New York and heard Hawkins and Don Byas in person, Gordon didn't receive the full impact of their style. "I said, 'Wow!' because they were really into it."

He also went outside the tenor sax category for inspiration. "I dug Roy Eldridge—I still do," said Dexter. "I used to get almost the same thing listening to Roy as I did listening to Lester—the same 'story' feeling."

Gordon first came to New York with Hampton in 1941. "I heard a couple of young alto players who were nice—Bird and Rudy Williams," he said, laughing. The band played at the Savoy Ballroom and the Apollo Theatre. "When we came into town, we didn't have any money, so most of the cats stayed at the YMCA —that was wild. Benny Harris was ribbing us about that."

After leaving Hampton in 1943, Gordon returned to Los Angeles and worked with Lee Young and Jesse Price. Then, for six months in 1944, he played with Louis Armstrong's big band. "I had more to play than with Hamp, but the band wasn't saying too much. Pops was using all those old, thirtyish arrangements— Teddy McCrae was the straw [boss]—*Sleepy Time,* all those funny things."

Besides the corny arrangements, Gordon found an age gulf. "Most of the cats were older cats, and there wasn't much fire." The few guys he could relate to included alto man John Brown, later with Gillespie's big band; trumpeter Fats Ford; and trombonist Taswell Baird, later with Eckstine and Gillespie. Despite his discomforts, he found Armstrong a very good man to work for. "He's beautiful, a wonderful cat, real warm. I remember coming out of Louis Armstrong's band into Eckstine's band, which was like night and day—because there was nothing but happenings, excitement, and enthusiasm in Eckstine's band; whereas in Pops's band, everything was just blah. You played a job, and that was the whole thing. Of course, Pops sounded very beautiful at that time—I loved the way he sounded. He used to play some things that really gassed me."

Gordon joined Eckstine at the Howard Theatre in Washington, D.C., in 1944, without benefit of a rehearsal. "I just went onstage and made it with them. I didn't know what was going on. And they had an opener they used to use called *Blitz*—it was a Jerry Valentine thing, up-tempo—short for *Blitzkrieg.* I don't think I made a right note in the whole thing, 'cause it was *flyin'!* Buhaina [Art Blakey] was dropping all those bombs back there. I just kept comin' up out of the seat."

It didn't take Dexter long to acclimate himself to the band, and soon he was one of the stars in its veritable galaxy. Unfortunately, the band never was able to imprint its in-person dynamism on record. "Those labels—what was it?—National and DeLuxe—they were horrible," said Gordon. "It was wartime, and they just made them for the minute, not thinking to make them last. Maybe they couldn't get the necessary materials." The poor engineering and bad surfaces couldn't completely nullify the forcefulness of the band and its soloists.

On the other hand, mechanical drawbacks considered, it was still not a polished crew. "The band was still a little rough. It had a lot of individualized individuals," Gordon said as he grinned knowingly. "I personally thought that the reed section was the best section in the band—the most cohesive, most together. Sonny Stitt was on the band and sounding like a whirlwind then. Part of the sax section was called the Unholy Four —Stitt, myself, John Jackson, and Leo Parker. We liked to rehearse, so we'd get our parts first from Jerry Valentine. We'd room together, hang out together. We were so full of tempestuous youth that things didn't always go too smoothly," he said referring to the quartet's extramusical activities.

Of Jackson, the same alto man who had been with Parker in the McShann band, Gordon said, "He played beautiful lead— first; he had a marvelous conception for playing lead—real warm, very butterish. Somehow or other he got lost, or he hasn't been heard of lately anyway. And he really didn't get his recognition then." Jackson's one recorded solo with Eckstine, on *Opus X*, shows a mixture of Benny Carter and Charlie Parker.

Later, Gene Ammons joined the band on tenor. The Gordon-Ammons duet on *Blowin' the Blues Away* was not the first tenor saxophone tandem in jazz, but its success triggered a new and lasting interest in this type of combination. Gordon was also featured on *Lonesome Lover Blues,* which, like *Blowin' the Blues Away,* had an Eckstine vocal.

In 1945, after eighteen months with Eckstine, Dexter left the band (it was in St. Louis) and came directly to New York. "What happened was that the Unholy Four left the band," he said.

Ammons stayed. "Gene was a loner. He's got a thing going now where he's an Unholy One."

Gordon explained, "We had been fuckin' up, really—'specially me—and wanted more bread. And he [Eckstine] didn't want to come up. . . . I don't know whether he didn't want to or couldn't. I don't know what it was, but anyway he didn't. In fact, for a couple of months before I left the band, he had been bringing tenor players up on the stand to try the book.

"It was a very together reed section, so all the cats split. Of course, since that time—since I've mellowed a little bit—I feel kind of bad about that. Because actually B. was and is a great guy, and it was nothing he had done to me. It was just me, just youth."

When he had been in New York with Hampton, Gordon had done no extracurricular playing. By the time he joined Eckstine, it was a different story. "Prior to this time, I didn't come out to play too much," he said. "I mean to jam. I was just struggling to play those parts in the band. I didn't feel I *should* come out and play. But in 1944, I went down to Minton's one night and got on the stand and sat in between Lester and Ben, so that was a hell of an experience for me. It was a gas. I say 'sat' because at that time everybody was sitting down playing. There was no standing up."

Dexter was standing up on the bandstands along Fifty-second Street and at the various Sunday-afternoon sessions after leaving Eckstine. In 1945 he played in a group that included Charlie Parker, Miles Davis, Bud Powell (or sometimes Sir Charles Thompson), Curly Russell, and Max Roach (or sometimes Stan Levey), plus tap dancer Baby Lawrence "taking fours and eights with the band. Baby was the floor show," remembers Dexter. "Bird would leave Miles and me with our mouths open every night."

Of The Street, he says, "Unquestionably, it was the most exciting half a block in the world. Everything was going on—music, chicks, connections . . . so many musicians working down there, side by side."

Connections were important to Gordon because he had become enmeshed in the heroin habit. He commented in an interview with Brooks Johnson: "Basically I think what happened was that although I was on the verge of really getting off the ground, psychologically I wasn't ready. Musically, I didn't feel I was ready. Personally, I didn't feel I was ready. I joined Hamp at a very early age. I was seventeen at the time. I got along well with the cats, the guys dug me. This was during the war years. A lot of the older cats had gone to the service. This gave me more leeway. It gave me more opportunities. But I never felt right within myself, honest, justified, in getting this acclaim, the spotlight. So in order to bolster my confidence, to immune me, I had to resort to artificial means. So consequently, after a while, I just got off on the wrong track."

During his Fifty-second Street days, there were many stories told about Dexter's escapades, some true, some exaggerated, some false. Gordon tells of playing a solo for his connection on the corner of 111th Street and Fifth Avenue. "He had just gotten me high, so when he asked me to play, I unpacked my horn and blew right on the street corner." This incident was not typical, of course, but it certainly is symbolic of the era.

Before he returned to the West Coast in the summer of 1946, Gordon had made quite a number of recordings. In addition to *Blue 'N Boogie* with Gillespie, he did a session on the Apollo label with Sir Charles Thompson as leader, Charlie Parker, and Buck Clayton. Then there were his many sides for Savoy as sideman and leader. The latter may well be remembered for the inclusion of his first name, or part of it, in almost every title—*Dexter's Cuttin' Out, Dexter's Minor Mad,* and so on. About these influential sides, Gordon says, "I dig 'em," but noting their titles, he adds, "I'm a little embarrassed by 'em too." (Actually, Savoy, not Gordon, was responsible for those titles.)

After playing in Hawaii with Cee Pee Johnson, Gordon settled in Los Angeles again. It was here that he and the late Wardell Gray became a team. It started at an after-hours place called Jack's Basket and at other weekly sessions. "There'd be a lot of cats on the stand, but by the end of the session, it would wind up with Wardell and myself," Gordon recalled. "*The Chase* grew out of this. Wardell was a very good saxophonist who knew his instrument very well. His playing was very fluid, very clean. Although his sound wasn't overwhelming, he always managed to make everything very interesting, very musical. I always enjoyed playing with him. He had a lot of drive and a profusion of ideas. He was stimulating to me."

Trumpeter Art Farmer has told me that at these sessions, Gordon and Gray would generate such excitement as they exchanged musical ideas that people would wind up standing on tables and chairs.

The Chase was originally cut for Dial, the company that Gordon had affiliated himself with on the Coast. Also recordèd were *The Duel*, with Teddy Edwards; a session with trombonist Melba Liston; and a marvelous piece of minor-key blues playing called *Bikini*. These recordings date from 1947.

When he returned to New York in that same year, he again recorded for Savoy with Leo Parker and with Fats Navarro. He played at the Roost with Tadd Dameron; at the Clique in December, 1948, first with the all-star band that included Bud Powell and then in front of Machito's Afro-Cubans; and at the Roost in January, 1949, with a ten-piece Dameron band. The latter band recorded for Capitol that same month, and Gordon took a fine solo on *Sid's Delight*.

The association with Gray, discontinued in 1947, was not resumed until 1950, for when Gordon returned to California in 1949, Gray was in New York. A Prestige LP (*The Wardell Gray Memorial Album*, Volume 2) captures their reunion, at the Hulu Hut on Sunset Boulevard, in a spirited version of *Move*. The two also made sides for the obscure Swingtime label that never found their way to LP, to the best of my knowledge; and the results of a concert held at the Pasadena Civic Auditorium in February, 1952, were issued on a Decca LP called *The Chase and Steeplechase*.

"Cool," or "West Coast," jazz was in the ascendancy at that time, and soon the hard-swinging music of Dexter Gordon was out of favor. Even if it had not been, Gordon would not have been around to play it. In 1953 and 1954 he was an inmate of Chino— the famed prison without bars. Gray was hung up with a heroin habit; but he recorded occasionally and was working with Benny Carter's band in Las Vegas when he died under mysterious circumstances in 1955. Gordon had just gotten out of Chino. He went to visit Gray and found that Wardell had left for Las Vegas. Three days later, he heard the news. The truth was never unraveled, but an overdose of heroin seems to have figured strongly in Gray's death.

In 1955, Gordon recorded again for the first time in three years. Two LP's were done for Bethlehem, one with Stan Levey and the other under his own name, called *Daddy Plays the Horn*. The third album, *Dexter Blows Hot and Cool,* was for Dootone. In a 1961 *Jazz Monthly* article, Michael James commented on some of the performances on these 1950's LP's: "All four demonstrate Gordon's quicksilver swing, his audacity in the upper register, his tonal power and the apt use he makes of inflection whenever he contrasts a sustained note with those complex, elbowing phrases he manages with so expert a sense of time."

At the time the records were released in the United States, no such lavish praise or serious appraisal was given them. But to those of us who had held him in high esteem in the forties, Dexter served notice that he had not lost his power and that he had been keeping his ears open.

During his stay at Chino, Hollywood made a movie about the prison called *Unchained.* It starred former football star Elroy "Crazylegs" Hirsch and included many of the Chino inmates in the cast. It was the beginning of Gordon's acting career. "I had a few lines, but when I was seen playing tenor, the sound track wasn't me," said Dexter.

In 1960, Gordon was leading a group at the Zebra Lounge in Los Angeles when playwright Carl Thaler asked him to read for his play *The Dying of the Light.* "The play had a musical background," said Gordon, but nothing happened with the proposed production. However, later in the year, through Thaler, Gordon became part of the Los Angeles company of *The Connection,* the Jack Gelber play about heroin addicts. His duties included writing the score, leading the onstage quartet, and handling an important speaking role that called for a lot of ad libbing.

Gordon was very happy with the way he handled the assignment. "The play was startling from an audience standpoint," he said. "I got very involved in it. The score I wrote was sympathetic and identifiable with the theme of the play. [Three of the numbers from the score were later recorded by Gordon in the Blue Note album *Dexter Calling.*] Basically, I think it was an honest approach. It did a lot for me. It gave me confidence. I had to do the score in three weeks and fit everything in. It gave me exposure and publicity. I had several good write-ups.

"The daily papers liked it. No papers mentioned any racial angle. Only John Tynan commented and intimated that this was what the producers wanted. It's not so. These were the guys I wanted." (In the October 13, 1960, *Down Beat,* West Coast editor Tynan, in a general condemnation of the play, had written: "One supposes the fact that the musicians onstage are all Negro is also symbolic.")

The Connection, ironically enough, seemed to open a new era for Gordon. Cannonball Adderley, acting as emissary from the East, recorded him for Jazzland Records in October of 1960. The resultant album, his first appearance on record in five years, was properly called *The Resurgence of Dexter Gordon.* Then Blue Note became interested, and in May of 1961, Gordon flew to New York to record for the company. At this time, he was still on parole and therefore could only spend a limited period away from Los Angeles.

He did two albums for Blue Note during his short stay and sat in with Kenny Dorham's group at the Jazz Gallery. At that time, he expressed a strong desire to "get back in touch—to find myself musically again. Technically I've improved," he said. "I have more of a mastery of the instrument—not that it's anywhere near perfection. I've been studying quite a bit. Harmonically my whole musical grasp has broadened." Coming from a man who had always been harmonically aware, this was quite a statement.

Gordon's long solo on the blues *Stanley the Steamer,* from the 1955 Stan Levey session, shows that he had been listening to the Sonny Rollins of that time. The later Jazzland album includes passages that indicate he had picked up on the Coltrane of the late fifties. In both cases, it was like receiving interest on something he had banked a long time before. In neither instance was he slavishly imitating—Gordon is much too powerful an individual for that. "Trane has opened things up quite a bit on the instrument—technically and from the standpoint of conception," said Dexter. "For myself, I like a more rhythmic approach." His two Blue Note albums, *Doin' Allright* and *Dexter Calling,* bear this out. As Kenny Dorham has said, "He's a swing master. He has a method. It sounds like a natural, but it's a method. He can get outside on the chords."

Once his parole period ended, Gordon was free to travel again. In October, 1961, he went to Chicago, where he was reunited with Gene Ammons. The kind of response he elicited from the people who hadn't forgotten him was shown when some of them hung a sign in the window of the club where he was working: "Dexter We Love You." He told Brooks Johnson: "Since I've been here, nearly everyone I talk to tells me how much they've missed me. It's a very good feeling, knowing that you have been missed. It's inspiring. It touches you where people like to get touched."

He also talked of his addiction. In response to Johnson's questions, "Does it affect your ability? Does it impair your facility on your instrument?" he answered: "Technically speaking, I don't think it helps you any. It in itself doesn't impair your facility any. Getting hung up in the pursuit of it, getting so involved so that you don't have the drive and interest to constantly search, this is what it did to me. It affects different people different ways. All in all, it's a very bad, ridiculous scene. But evidently it was one I had to go through with."

Gordon came to New York again in the spring of 1962. He did not have a cabaret card, that piece of paper that New York's license bureau issues to all employees of clubs where liquor is served. Under this system, a man may have paid his debt to society by serving time, but still cannot get a card and therefore cannot work more than once a week in any of these alcohol dispensaries—many of which are owned, off the record, by ex-bootleggers and presently practicing racketeers. I do not refer here to jazz clubs specifically but rather to all New York nightclubs.

Because he was formerly a member of the New York local of the musicians' union, the customary three-month waiting period was waived and he was able to get his union card. He was philosophical about his cabaret card. "If I don't get it this year, I'll get it next year," he said. (No doubt his failure to get a card was one of the factors contributing to his subsequent migration to Europe.)

He continued to record for Blue Note and played a variety of one-night appearances at clubs in the Metropolitan area. He was also featured in concert at Town Hall. Everywhere he played, the reaction was the same—high enthusiasm. He never failed to draw applause beyond mere politeness. At the Jazz Gallery, I observed this from an audience that contained many young people—kids who were too young to have applauded him when he was *the* Dexter Gordon. He got through to them with the emotion in his playing, something that has been lacking in the sixties. Gordon himself put it very well in describing his reaction to the New York scene. "The feeling I've had since I've been in New York—

partly due to the reception I've received—is that cats here are bored. They don't seem happy or enthusiastic—this type of personality doesn't seem to be in. Everyone is on an introverted, odd-type thing where they don't express happiness or love or anything like that. I get that feeling from listening to them play—with the exception of a few. But I'm speaking of the over-all feeling. There seems to be a sickness prevalent that excludes any type of warmth or love. I just don't hear that any more. Everyone seems to be playing schizophrenic—like they're sick, really.

"Vitality is something that's lacking today," he went on. "Watching cats on the stand—different groups—very seldom I get the impression that they're really enjoying what they're doing. Everybody looks drug [colloquial past participle of "drag"—nothing to do with narcotics] and bored.

"Funny thing, Don DeMicheal [editor of Down Beat] said to me in Chicago, 'Man, I sure wish you and Jug [Gene Ammons] would go stay around New York for a while. They need you there.' I didn't understand what he meant. I didn't get to discuss it with him at all. He just said it and left it hanging. But I retained it, and since I've been here I understood what he meant." Gordon summed up by saying, "And the majority of the cats can play too, but there is no enthusiasm, no fire."

Jazz has always reflected the times, and Gordon agrees that "these are very unstable times"; but because of this, "perhaps people have got to make a more decided effort to help them get stabilized rather than just say, 'Fuck it,' and let it go. And especially with youth. They have a big tendency to discount the things that have gone before them."

Gordon has his own experience to draw on in this instance. He said, when he was explaining how he came to appreciate other musicians besides Lester Young, "Such is typical of youth. They get one idea in mind that they think is very hip before their minds open up and they mature. You've got to appreciate the things that went before."

He says of the forties, "It was a very exciting era—the war and all that bit going on too. But it was the new era in music, so things really were exciting." When I asked him why he thought today's young musicians didn't get together and jam, he said, "I've got the feeling that people aren't that happy any more.

Seems there are more—in a sense—cliquishly different schools of thought of playing. They don't mingle, they don't integrate."

Though far from a dewy-eyed optimist, Dexter Gordon has the love and warmth and vitality in his playing that he finds lacking in the performances of others. When he starts stretching out on a number and those firmly-anchored, long legs began vibrating rapidly from side to side as he swings intensely through his solo, you don't have to ask yourself whether you've been moved. As a friend of mine, not given to overstatements, said after hearing Dexter at the Jazz Gallery, "That was thrilling."

His ballads are equally moving in their way. Warmth and melancholy replace excitement, and the range of expression is wide. On *You've Changed* in Gordon's Blue Note *Doin' Allright* album, some of the low-register tones remind one of ballad master Don Byas. This is logical, for Gordon heard Byas extensively on Fifty-second Street—and once both had horizontal white stripes bleached in their goatees. Gordon relates that "one night at the Deuces I played his horn, and I dug his mouthpiece so much I asked him about it. It was a Linck, metal, an eight; had a short facing, and it blew so easy. So next day I went down to Linck and told them I wanted a 'Don Byas Special.'" Although Gordon eventually lost the mouthpiece, he retained some of the Byas spirit.

In 1962, Dexter made his first trip to Europe. When he returned to the United States two years later, in December of 1964, he told *Down Beat's* New York editor, Dan Morgenstern: "It's funny, when I left for Europe, Paris was the place I really had in mind. I hadn't thought too much about Scandinavia, and the first time I went to Copenhàgen I wasn't too taken with it. But now I just love the place."

The jazz fans of the Danish capital feel the same way about Gordon, and although he has played all over the Continent, Copenhagen—the Club Montmartre in particular—has become his main base of operations. He returned there in June, 1965, after having played engagements on both coasts and Chicago, as well as recording two albums for Blue Note.

The LP's he had recorded for Blue Note just before leaving for Europe in 1962—*Go* and *A Swingin' Affair*—were highly praised by the critics, and for good reason. He also did two albums for the company during the 1962–1964 European period. *Our Man in Paris,* particularly, features some extremely exciting extended performances.

Gordon also got a chance to play with Byas again one night at the Montmartre. "I was working there," he told Leonard Feather, ". . . and the boss hired Paul [Gonsalves] and Don Byas to work with me. Oh, it was fantastic. It was in the summer, it was hot, the joint was just packed; you couldn't move. After the first set Don took off his shirt and undershirt; he was just playing in his pants; you know, playing nude tenor!"

This is the way it was in the forties: young saxophonists followed Lester Young, Coleman Hawkins, or Charlie Parker— directly or through one of their close disciples. Frequently these sax players showed a mixture of two, or perhaps all three, of these stylistic elements.

Of the Young men, there were, of course, Gordon, Ammons, Gray, and Eager. Each one was also affected by the music of Charlie Parker to different degrees.

Ammons, when he came on the Eckstine band in 1944, was a typically pure-toned Pres disciple who could drive, but just as often would lay behind the beat. A record of *St. Louis Blues* made with Ammons' father, pianist Albert Ammons, for Mercury in 1947 is an example of the Lester Young style as played by a young modern of that time. With his own small group on Mercury, Gene exhibited a harder sound and a more boppish approach; and in Woody Herman's orchestra in 1949, this was in evidence on *More Moon* and *Not Really the Blues.* After the "tenor battle" group he co-led with Sonny Stitt in 1950–1952, Ammons played a single, performing in front of various rhythm sections. His sound, as big as a house, has thickened with the passage of time. Jug, as he is called, is a huge, bearlike man whose playing can be aptly described as soulful.

Dexter Gordon heard Wardell Gray for the first time in the early forties with the Earl Hines band. "He was playing note-for-note Pres solos," says Dexter. If Gray's solo on a Hines record of *Straight Life* on the ARA label is not note-for-note Pres, it does reveal Young's influence. When Gray first came to prominence in 1947, a result of numerous concert appearances on the West Coast for promoter Gene Norman, he was developing his own light, mellow sound and personal ideas on melody. His solos on

Blue Lou, Groovin' High, Hot House, and *One O'Clock Jump*
from the recordings of the Coast concerts are outstanding for
their effortless swing and lyrical idea patterns, and his "battle"
with Vido Musso on *Sweet Georgia Brown* is an apt demonstra-
tion of subtlety versus crudeness.

After his records with Gordon and Parker for Dial in 1947,
Gray came to New York in 1948 and joined Benny Goodman's
sextet. He had recorded with Goodman in California in December, 1947, on *Stealin' Apples* (Capitol), but his performances on
Bedlam (the piece is called *Stoned* on his own recording for the
label called Sittin' In With) and *Blue Lou* with the Goodman sextet in 1949 are graphic illustrations of how his style had changed.
He was then briefly with Tadd Dameron's sextet. The Blue Note
recordings, now on LP under Fats Navarro's name, contain five
solos by Wardell that show a slightly heavier tone and a leaning
toward Parker. By 1950, when he played at the Orchid (the old
Onyx) on Fifty-second Street with Sonny Stitt, the changeover to
the harder sound and crisper attack had been completed. His
Prestige records from this period bear this out. Yet *Little Pony*
(Columbia), done with Count Basie the next year, while essentially in his new style, contains more than a few remnants from
the past.

Gray, slightly built, was given to wearing suit coats with a lot
of shoulder padding. Dexter remembers him as a "nice, warm
cat." Primarily he was a swinger. Art Farmer says that even in an
up-tempo number, he would exhort the rhythm section to "bear
down." Wardell Gray's swing had its own grace and beauty.

The other tenor man on the Dameron-Navarro Blue Note
records was Allen Eager, one of the first of the Lester Young disciples around New York in the forties. In a 1948 *Blindford Test*
with Leonard Feather, he commented on Lester: "He was the
first giant to put down the harshness of jazz and instead just express pure beauty." Eager was good at doing the same. His sound
on *Lady Bird* and *Jahbero* from the Blue Notes has a beauty that
defies Roget. Another solo, perhaps even more gorgeous, is on
Deedle (on Sittin' In With; it was later issued—and most inap-
propriately retitled *Static*—on Jax) with Dave Lambert and
Bennie Green. Particularly breathtaking are his four-bar statements toward the close of the record. Eager, like Gray, was a
master at making a meaningful statement in a short period. Also,

like Gray, he was a swinger, and some of his best recorded work was captured in performances before an audience. His choruses on *Sweet Georgia Brown* from a WNEW "Saturday Night Swing Session" (issued on Esoteric) are exceptionally exciting, and his work on the broadcasts from the Royal Roost (issued on the Jazzland LP *Fats Navarro Featured with the Tadd Dameron Band*) is typically fine Eager of the 1948 period. In the liner notes for the latter album I wrote: "His inspiration was clearly Lester Young. This is evident throughout but most apparent in the similarity between phrases in his *Lady Be Good* solo and ideas Lester played on *Lady Be Good* with Jones-Smith Inc. in 1936. Eager was not merely an imitator, however. He had his own interpretation of Pres's style, and already other elements, like Charlie Parker, were changing it more. Whatever he played swung with a happy, light-footed quality and pure-toned beauty. His interior time was equal to his fine overall swing. Many a night in the Roost, he had us ready to get up and start dancing along the bar."

In the 1948 *Blindfold Test* by Eager, Leonard Feather described him as a Jekyll and Hyde: ". . . his Dr. Jekyll is an amusing, well-read and highly articulate guy, while the Hyde side is a typical gloomy product of the frustrations and neuroses of 52nd Street, with ornithological overtones."

The pattern that Eager followed as the forties ended was definitely Jekyll and Hyde. When he was skiing or horseback riding and completely away from music, he was healthy, but every time he returned to his tenor, the demon that pursued Bird found him again. He grew further away from his saxophone and eventually retired from music. In 1960 he made a comeback on alto, which he had been playing in France, but it was short-lived. The years away from his horn had made him rusty; moreover, the old fire and fine timing were heard only in fleeting moments—it was a case of his losing something along the way that was difficult to find again. In 1961, Eager won first prize in the touring-car class at Sebring's sports car races.

There was a record session on April 8, 1949, for Prestige that included Eager and four other tenor players—Stan Getz, Zoot Sims, Al Cohn, and Brew Moore. Each had his own interpretation of Lester Young but, with the exception of Moore, were also affected by Parker's music if not directly by Parker. Moore is reputed to have said, "Anyone who doesn't play like Lester Young is wrong!" The others, while far from being so single-minded, had their own fixed beliefs. I witnessed an incident illustrative of this at a private session held at a studio in mid-Manhattan called Don José's. The regulars there used to be Gerry Mulligan, Zoot Sims, Red Mitchell, Jerry Lloyd, and George Wallington, with Getz, Cohn, Kenny Drew, Lee Konitz, and Warne Marsh also dropping in occasionally. One night, a tenor player came in to blow but was given an obvious freeze-out. After he had departed, someone said, "It's cool for an alto to sound like Bird, but I don't like to hear a tenor played that way."

Sims and Cohn have since gone on public record as to their admiration for Sonny Stitt and Sonny Rollins, although they have not altered their basic styles because of this. In the forties, both were big-band tenor men, developing their skills as well as their musical personalities. Cohn, who since the mid-fifties has concentrated more on arranging than playing, was known for his ability to play compositional ideas. His solos, highly lyrical and behind the beat, would invariably lead his band mates to turn toward him and listen intently, a common occurrence in the Buddy Rich band of 1947. In Woody Herman's band of 1948–1949, he got little solo space—most of the tenor solos went to Getz and Sims— and he never recorded a solo with the band. His short but gemlike bits on things like *Tacos, Enchiladas, and Beans* with Buddy Rich (MGM), *I Get a Kick Out of You* with Artie Shaw (Decca), and *What Can I Say, Dear* with Mary Ann McCall (Roost) are indicative of his playing in this period if not wholly representative. *The Most,* his own composition, which he recorded with Oscar Pettiford for the Futurama label, gave him more room to display his particular sensitivity. In the late fifties and early sixties, in tandem with his old Herman band mate Sims, the lyricism was still there, but the years had added a heavier tone and a more on-the-beat attack.

Sims, whose sonority was close to Getz's when they were with Herman, played fewer notes than Stan but displayed a strong, natural swing. On his first recording, made at the age of 19 with Joe Bushkin (on Commodore), he sounds like Hawkins and Webster on *Fade Out* and like Young on *Lady Be Good.* Parker's music affected him, but he didn't seek to copy Bird. "A lot of people, when they heard Bird, they dissected him," he said. "They took his records, learned his solos, copied. But I never did that, even with Pres. . . . I must admit he did influence me, because if you love somebody's music that much, it's bound to do something." What it did was give him a new harmonic base. In the fifties, songs like Gillespie's *Woody'n You*, Davis' *Donna Lee*, Monk's *Bye-ya*, and Pettiford's *Bohemia After Dark* were part of his repertoire—far from standard for the players of his general school. Today he is one of the warmest, swingingest players in jazz, and one of the most widely admired.

Getz didn't begin winning popularity polls until the fifties, but he was already important as the forties closed. His short solos on *Rattle and Roll* and *Swing Angel* in 1945 and 1946 with Benny Goodman showed him to be a Pres disciple, and the records with Kai Winding for Savoy (*Grab Your Axe, Max; Always; Loaded; Sweet Miss*) reiterated this even more strongly. On *A Night at the Deuces*, recorded with the Randy Brooks orchestra, however, he displayed a rougher tone, sounding in places like Georgie Auld. Then there were the sides mentioned earlier, wherein he seemed to come under the influence of Dexter Gordon. When he moved to California in 1947, there was a definite return to Pres, spurred no doubt by his association with Herbie Steward. Getz's solo on *How High the Moon* from a Gene Norman Just Jazz concert recorded that year shows a resemblance to Steward. During 1947, Getz and Steward played together in Butch Stone's little band and in the original Four Brothers at Pontrelli's Ballroom in Los Angeles. Together they joined Woody Herman in the fall. Getz said of Steward ten years later: "If he only wouldn't bury himself in dance and show bands. Herbie's got such beautiful soul. Even playing lead chair. His lead alto is the nearest thing to a human voice I've ever heard."

Once, in the fifties, Getz was leading his own big band for a week at New York's Apollo Theatre. During a rendition of *Four Brothers*, he was the only soloist. When he came to the bridge of his first chorus, he played Steward's eight-bar solo from the original Herman recording. It was quite a tribute.

It was Herman's recording of *Early Autumn*, interpreted with the Four Brothers sound, that launched Getz toward great popularity. His ballad style was exquisitely beautiful, and he was not dubbed the Sound for naught. Perhaps his classic records are the ones made for the Roost label at Storyville in Boston—a performance before an audience—with Jimmy Raney on guitar, Al Haig, Teddy Kotick, and Tiny Kahn.

Getz's involvement with narcotics eventually led to his arrest for trying to hold up a drugstore in Seattle, Washington, in the mid-fifties. In 1955, while playing in Stockholm, he became seriously ill and was forced into idleness for six months. He returned to the United States and toured with a quartet and as a member of Jazz at the Philharmonic, but in 1958 he settled in Copenhagen. The sixties found him back in the States. His sometimes obvious way of getting "hot" with a brace of "funky" blue notes played with a distorted tone was one of the few negative aspects of his playing. He does not use it on *Focus*, his tour de force, recorded for Verve in 1961. Here he invents, integrating his saxophone with string music written by Eddie Sauter, showing that one of the truly individual styles developed in the forties is still fresh in the sixties. One thing Getz has in common with Gordon is that Coltrane cites both of them as early favorites.

Brew Moore, a wanderer from Indianola, Mississippi, who with his crew cut looked like Popeye the Sailor, did some of his best playing in Kai Winding's sextet at the Roost and Bop City in the late forties. He recorded with this group and also with Howard McGhee on Blue Note and was featured with Machito's orchestra in *Cubop City* on Roost. Although he did not alter his basic Pres style, he was capable of working with Parker-oriented players, including Bird himself. In the mid-fifties he migrated to San Francisco, remaining there until he moved to Europe in 1961.

Tenor players Phil Urso and Buddy Wise played in a style that was a cross between Pres's and Bird's. And there was John Andrews, one of the best Pres-styled tenor men I have ever heard. He played with Claude Thornhill, but unfortunately he was never recorded.

The Coleman Hawkins school of tenor men was far-reaching in the 1940's; there were already many branches and offshoots through the players he had affected in the thirties. In 1941 Don Byas came from the Basie band to Fifty-second Street, where he played with Hawkins at the Yacht Club. His big, creamy version of the Hawkins sound was delivered with long, melodic lines. The records he made with Gillespie in 1945 and 1946 for Manor and Victor show that he could play the new music; that even though his solos were not typical, they fit in with what was going on. His ballads were warm but never overdone. Harvey Pekar, reviewing some of Byas' Savoy sides, wrote: "His technique was flawless and he managed to achieve a lovely, pure vibrato on even the fastest tempos. . . . His melodic vocabulary was considerably enriched by the influence of Charlie Parker, but he generally was not so modern rhythmically then as he was on the *Dizzy in Paris* album cut several years later."

Byas went to Europe with a Don Redman orchestra in 1946 and has lived there ever since. His most recent recordings, *Jazz at the Philharmonic in Europe* on Verve and *Americans in Europe* on Impulse, show that he is playing better than ever.

Lucky Thompson, who followed Byas to Europe some ten years later, was following him stylistically in the forties. This was especially true of his up-tempo performances. On ballads, such as *Just One More Chance* (on Victor), he leaned more toward Webster and Hawkins, his other models. Some of his most memorable work from the forties includes his solos on the records he made with Dodo Marmarosa for the Atomic and Downbeat labels. Thompson, who had played with Redman, Hampton, Eckstine, Basie, and Kenton, before leaving for Europe, returned to New York in December of 1962. The man who had recorded so impressively with Dizzy Gillespie in 1946 and Miles Davis in 1954 had added soprano saxophone playing to his accomplishments in 1958 but showed no diminution in his tenor saxophone prowess. David Himmelstein in the notes for Thompson's Prestige album *Lucky Strikes,* issued in December, 1964, refers to the survival of his early influences and adds: ". . . but now one hears more Pres and more Bird. Can a man remind of so much and still be authentically himself? The answer is yes, and one has only to play a few bars to rest assured that the sum is distinct from its parts."

In the forties, Ike Quebec was playing with Cab Calloway and making sides like *Blue Harlem* and *She's Funny That Way* for Blue Note and *Jim Dawgs* for Savoy. Eddie "Lockjaw" Davis was heard with Cootie Williams on the Hit label, with Fats Navarro on Savoy, and on his own for Haven and Apollo. Both men came from Hawkins and Webster, but each had his own version of the style, especially the unorthodox Davis, who rose to prominence with Count Basie in the fifties. Quebec, after some years of obscurity, died of cancer in 1963, but not before he recorded a number of good LP's, one of which, *It Might As Well Be Spring*, contains an extraordinarily passionate version of *Ol' Man River*.

There were many other players who had their own way of saying something in the Hawkins or Webster style. Georgie Auld could sound very much like Webster. On the records made by the Auld-Hawkins-Webster Saxtet for Apollo in 1944, this is apparent, especially when Auld follows Webster on *Pick Up Boys*. In the mid-forties, Auld formed a group with Red Rodney and Serge Chaloff and altered his style. His tone became somewhat lighter, the phrasing more boppish. By the fifties, he became more florid, occasionally reminding one of Gene Ammons.

Charlie Ventura was first influenced by Chu Berry, one of the celebrated branches of the Hawkins tree in the thirties, but he had a Ben Webster rasp that showed in his features with Gene Krupa. Ventura would play well for a chorus or so, then his taste would be thrown to the winds. Chubby Jackson once told me, after working with Ventura in a small group around 1947, "Charlie's fine until one of those hippies comes up to him and says, 'When are you gonna play *the Moon*, man?'" In Ventura's Bop for the People group during the late forties, the material was popularized, with scat singing by Jackie Cain and Roy Kral. Again, Ventura, who had assimilated many of the bop characteristics, would start well but degenerate after a chorus or two. The best I have ever heard him play was at a rehearsal of his big band in the early fifties. The guys were jamming on *Cherokee* just for kicks, and Ventura took an alto solo that gave in to no outside pressures.

Flip Phillips was a latter-day member of the Hawkins school who played with taste and drive in Woody Herman's orchestra of 1944–1946, but both elements disappeared when he joined the Jazz at the Philharmonic troupe. His solo on *Perdido* recorded with JATP is infamous.

The man who popularized the screaming, squeaking, squealing tenor style was Illinois Jacquet, beginning with his solo on *Flying Home* with Hampton, continuing through his own *Flying Home* for the Philo label, and reaching a new "high" in his dog whistling on *How High the Moon* in the first Jazz at the Philharmonic album. But Jacquet had more to offer than did the freak-note performers who followed him. He is a Texas tenor man who was influenced by Herschel Evans, as were Arnett Cobb, Buddy Tate.

and a host of others. He also dug Pres, and touches show through here and there. After a few choruses of solid playing, Jacquet would invariably begin pandering to the lower tastes of his audience. His ballad playing, on the other hand, has always been warm and genuine. Today, he is a solid mainstream player, not given to the stylistic excesses of his JATP days.

There were other players with a heavy tone, but not necessarily Hawkins men, who were shaped by the new music of the forties. Billy Mitchell of Detroit was Gene Ammons' replacement in the Woody Herman band of 1949. His solos on the Milt Jackson Savoy recordings *Junior* and *Bubu* sound very Wardell Gray-ish, but earlier associates such as Sonny Stitt and Lucky Thompson also exerted an influence. Mitchell, who was prominently featured with both the Gillespie and Basie bands in the fifties, later co-led a group with trombonist Al Grey.

James Moody, whose driving attack was highlighted in Gillespie's band from late 1946 into 1948 (he left briefly to play in a group with Howard McGhee and Milt Jackson in late 1947), combined the ideas of Dizzy and Bird with elements from the swing tenor men. Some of his most exciting flights can be heard on Gillespie's recordings of *Emanon* (Moody's first record date) and *Oopapada*. On the band's concert recording (on a record label with a cumbersome name, Gene Norman Presents), Moody quotes from his original solo in a second version of *Emanon* and then proceeds to a fresh variation.

When Moody returned from several years in Europe, in 1951, he had reactivated his first instrument, the alto saxophone and had begun leading his own group. Later he became one of the really authentic jazz flutists. In 1963 he re-joined Gillespie and continued to record as a leader in his own right, playing in both situations with the old fervor and a new depth.

Jimmy Forrest, who played with McShann during Parker's time with the band and later worked with Duke Ellington, was playing material like *Little Willie Leaps* and *Our Delight* when I heard him in St. Louis with his own small group in 1947, and his solos showed a complete grasp of the new idiom. Later, in the fifties, came his rhythm-and-blues hit *Night Train*. In the sixties, with Harry Edison's combo, Forrest played in a vigorous, mainstream-modern vein that included a combination of the many tenor men who had descended from the dual lineage of Young-Parker—Ammons, Gray, and Gordon.

Whether or not he was given credit, Dexter Gordon is the man who wove an important piece into the great tapestry of the modern tenor saxophone style. Time, which has given proof of his importance, happily has not robbed him of his talents. His most recent work only enhances his position as a jazz master.

Recommended Listening

Long Tall Dexter, Savoy *SJL* 2211
The Hunt (with Wardell Gray), Savoy SJL 2222
Central Avenue (with Wardell Gray), Prestige P-24062
Go, Blue Note 84112
Power, Prestige P-24087

8

LENNIE TRISTANO
AND LEE KONITZ

IN THE LATE FORTIES, Lennie Tristano was mentor, teacher, nurse-maid, and confidant of a small cell of young musicians. Those outside this tight little clique were apt to name the hypnotist Svengali when describing Tristano, although he has been totally blind since the age of 10.

During the course of a 1949 date that Tristano's students—saxophonists Lee Konitz and Wayne Marsh, pianist Sal Mosca—were recording for Bob Weinstock's New Jazz label, several difficulties arose. It was the first time the "group" had been in the studios away from their leader. Only two tunes—*Marshmallow* and *Fishin' Around*—were cut, and in a final effort to get a relaxed groove on the latter, all the lights in the studio had been extinguished. Then came the painstaking deliberation of which version, which "take," to pick. Al Haig, who made frequent use of the spare pianos at the Apex Studios on West Fifty-seventh Street where the date was being held, was there for one of his practice sessions. He poked his head into the studio long enough to view the situation and sarcastically suggested, "Why don't you call the witch doctor?" Although they were obviously rankled by the remark, this is what Konitz and Marsh eventually did, playing the different versions over the phone for Tristano.

Many stories have grown up around Tristano. Some of them imply that he imposed his will, or tried to, on all his students, even to the point of advising them to enter analysis with his brother Mickey. One ex-associate has called him a "smotherer." When Mosca, now a teacher in his own right, was asked about these negative comments, he replied, "I was in analysis with his brother for six years, but not because Lennie imposed that view on me. I needed analysis; and when I found out that his brother was an analyst, since I dug Lennie I figured I'd try his brother, and I ended up digging his brother for his *own* scene. Because they both seemed very sincere about what they were trying to do, which was to help people. To my knowledge, Lennie has never imposed his will on anybody. I know a lot of people come away from him saying that. He never does that. Unless what they mean by that is that they adopt his will. Because to him it's strong and has got a lot of conviction to it, and they adopt it for their own.

"He's one of the strongest people I've ever met," says Mosca, who was introduced to Tristano in 1947 by trumpeter Don Ferrara. "I was dependent on him for a lot of things in a lot of ways. But not because of his imposing his will on me, but because I was weak. But in turn other people have done this with me too. I think it is natural in people's exchanges. If you dig Lennie—and he's strong in a lot of ways—you're going to adopt his attitudes. But then to go around and say he was imposing his will on you is sort of copping out of your own scene, and I feel that's what a lot of these people have done who studied with him."

During the time Mosca spent as one of Tristano's students, his playing was in a style very close to that of his mentor. "That was by choice, because I dug him," explains Sal. "Lennie told me something years ago. He feels that one of the ways for a person to become independent is to go through a stage where you are dependent. . . . For instance, if you are studying with a teacher, just be completely, as much as possible, dependent on his direction, without getting the feeling that you're being rooked or taken in or losing your own personality. And through this almost total dependence, you will find your own independence. I tried it, and it worked out that way."

Mosca's last recording, a nine-minute version of *Love Me or Leave Me* (issued as part of an LP entitled *Looking Out* in the early sixties by bassist Peter Ind on Ind's own Wave label), bears this out. Vestiges of Lennie's influence remain, quite naturally, but essentially Mosca is his own man. The same could once be said for pianist Ronnie Ball, who also has a featured track on the same album. But an observer reported that in 1965, Ball was again studying with Tristano and was sounding more and more like him. Ball and Ind, who met while playing in the band on the British ocean liner *Queen Mary* in the late forties, studied with Tristano during their stops in New York and eventually emigrated from England in the early fifties, later playing in Lennie's group and with Konitz.

Lennie, like Thelonious Monk (for different reasons), does not come to you—you must go to him. Tristano lives in a two-family frame house in Hollis, Long Island, that, while it is not situated in the wilderness—on the contrary, it is surrounded by many other like dwellings—is fairly inaccessible for the average Manhattanite. It is actually Tristano who keeps himself from the outside world, except for advising and teaching the many new students who seek him out. Guitarist Billy Bauer once asked Lennie, "Why don't you get out in the world sometime?" and the pianist answered, "But this is how I learn to play." Through this constant involvement with his art, he has a great fund of knowledge and a particular kind of insight to offer his students. On the other hand, perhaps it is this very isolation that prevents him from investing his music with the qualities that would bring it across to more people.

Tristano wants to be as independent as someone who can see is supposed to be. When I visited his home, he entertained me in his kitchen. He was preparing his breakfast when I came in and soon had made eggs, toast, and coffee with the ease of a person who can see his ingredients and implements. Unfortunately, this kind of achievement does not necessarily extend to other areas, and this is perhaps a source of frustration to him.

George Shearing, who came on the New York jazz scene shortly after Tristano, seems to have made his adjustment to a life of sightlessness in an easier manner. Being contemporaneous blind jazz pianists is where their similarities end. The difference in their personalities is quite evident in each man's approach to his music. As Shearing has said, "Lennie would never be happy compromising as I'm doing."

Tristano never has compromised. There have been long stretches when he did not play in public because he felt the conditions were not right. Through these periods, his teaching has sustained him. "You know," he told Bill Coss, "my ambition is to find someone to invest in a real jazz club. Maybe a place that could seat 125 to 150 people, that was comfortable, where the acoustics were right, with a good piano, and all the employees— even the girl in the coat room—really interested in music. It shouldn't be a quiet place. I don't like the concert hall sterility. I would like informality—people talking quietly without disturbing others."

Tristano was not always so choosy about the backdrop for his playing. His first job, when he was 11, was in an Illinois whore-house, "downstairs in the bar." Lennie began listening to and fooling around with a player piano when he was 2 ("I just don't remember not playing the piano," he says), and he was prac-tically a veteran by the time of his professional debut.

Tristano was born in Chicago on March 19, 1919, during an in-fluenza epidemic, and the disease weakened his eyes. Tristano says that imitating the player piano "gave me the clue." He con-tinued playing on his own until he was 7 and then studied privately for two or three years. This was the beginning of his classical training. Through elementary and high school, he played clarinet, alto and tenor saxophones, four-string guitar, trumpet, and drums, although he played no jobs with the latter. His first experience as a leader was while he was still in grade school. He was then playing C-melody saxophone.

When Tristano went to the American Conservatory of Music, the faculty tried to convince him to become a lawyer or politi-cian. He whippped through his music studies at a rapid pace. "I took two-year harmony courses in six weeks—counterpoint—it was so easy," he says. "Until I was in my middle twenties, I never worked hard at anything."

By getting his BM in three years and his master's degree in composition in a year, Lennie claims he "bugged everyone" at the school. They informed him that he would have to pay for the full time that the course normally takes. This came to $500, and since he was making only $4 or $5 a night working around Chicago, he could not pay that much and did not get a diploma. For his mas-ter's, he had written "a string quartet, a modified string quartet, and a lot of things for the piano."

In 1943, Tristano began teaching at the Christiansen School of Popular Music. They told him, "You don't have to teach our methods. Any advanced students we'll send to you."

"I learned how to teach through my students," Lennie frankly admits.

During the war, he played at servicemen's centers. As a clari-netist, he had his own Dixieland band. He worked with an ac-cordion player in a group where he alternated between blowing two saxophones or three clarinets at once. "We sounded like a big band," says Tristano from a position between Wilbur Sweatman and Roland Kirk.

Although he also played tenor saxophone and clarinet in rhumba bands, Tristano soon turned his full attention to the piano. In 1945 he was working in what he describes as "good cocktail lounges. Never did I concern myself with the idea of becoming a great jazz musician. I just dug playing."

Tristano's early listening included recordings by vaudevillians Gallagher and Shean and by Al Jolson. "At nine or ten," he says, "I stumbled on some records of Bix, Louis, Ted Lewis . . . previous to this, aside from playing tunes, I'd improvise."

As he grew older, he listened to everyone. In the forties, he "hung out on the South Side, just to listen—Roy Eldridge, Stuff Smith."

When, in 1964, he was asked what musicians had influenced him, he answered: "Oh, Roy Eldridge, Lester Young, Teddy Wilson, Charlie Christian, Billy Kyle, I guess."

There is also strong evidence that Earl Hines exerted an influence on the young Tristano, because even today you can hear Fatha's style in the way Lennie negotiates certain passages, however different the time feeling may be. In a 1946 article coauthored by Barry Ulanov (one of Tristano's first and most loyal champions) and Ruth Hamalainen (who later became Mrs. Lee Konitz), Tristano's style was described: "At first hearing his playing sounds like an amalgam of the locked-hands, block-chords of Milt Buckner, and the flashy arpeggios of Art Tatum. But this is something of a false impression, for though these two great styles are facets of his music, they are only one small part of it. When building his solos, he only increases his volume with the Buckner and Tatum techniques, he not only demonstrates his virtuoso technique, but also adds a large variety of his own harmonic and melodic ideas."

"In 1944, I had reached a point where I could rifle off anything of Tatum's," Tristano told Bill Coss, "and with scandalous efficiency."

Tristano's prodigious technique gives credence to this boast, but I was nevertheless curious enough to ask both Mosca and Konitz about it. Mosca related, "He told me that he could play *Elegie*, which is one of Tatum's fastest records, and finish ahead of Tatum. Sammy Demaro, a pianist, heard him in Chicago. He was walking along the street, and he heard Art Tatum playing and ran downstairs to hear him, and it was Lennie."

Konitz' reaction was less specific but more expansive. "He's a blowhard," he said with affection. "I know he can do all those things. I never heard him do that particular thing, but I did hear him play the tenor like Lester Young once. And I heard him play the piano, in Chicago once, like Jess Stacy. And I know from his music that he's heard all these people thoroughly."

As he continued to play around Chicago, Tristano began to attract some disciples. Phil Featheringill, writing in the November, 1945, *Metronome* reported: "Lennie is the young blind pianist who is the leader and 'father-confessor' of all the progresssive musicians in town." Featheringill's statement was too encompassing. Negro beboppers were not drawn to Tristano, although some of the young white disciples of Parker and Gilllespie did come into contact with his teaching. But he definitely did have a following that included pianist Lloyd Lifton, trombonist-composer Bill Russo, and Konitz.

In 1946, through Chubby Jackson and others in Woody Herman's band, Tristano wrote some arrangements for Herman, but they were never used. Then he was supposed to take a trio (with guitarist Billy Bauer and bassist Arnold Fishkin) on tour with Jazz at the Philharmonic, but "it didn't get off the ground," according to Lennie. Things were not going well generally for him in Chicago. His brand of experimentation was not particularly popular with the nightclub proprietors. "One manager just got out on the middle of the floor, pulled some hair out, and screamed when he heard us play some things in three keys at once," is a Tristano story that Ulanov used to take delight in, according to Bill Coss. "But," added Coss, "Tristano now says such reactions, and the stories describing them, do not altogether indicate what he was doing, 'because we weren't playing jazz clubs at the time, and the managers had no way to judge us.'"

The fact remained that Tristano had not been working that much. So when Jackson urged him to come to New York, Lennie and his first wife, Judy, left Chicago behind them. He played in Chubby's hometown of Freeport, Long Island, and on Fifty-second Street, where, he says, "I bombed."

I remember wandering into the Three Deuces on New Year's Eve, 1946. The club was completely devoid of patrons. Lennie was accompanying tenor man Ray Turner's duplication of Lester Young's choruses from the Keynote record of *Just You, Just Me*.

As he had done in Chicago, Tristano again turned to teaching for survival. In October, 1946, he also did his first recording. With Bauer and bassist Clyde Lombardi, he cut *I Can't Get Started, I Surrender, Dear,* and his own *Out on a Limb* for Keynote. The first and third were issued as a single, and in 1947 all three were included in an album that was filled out by three other sides— Tristano's *Atonement* and *Coolin' Off with Ulanov;* and Bauer's line on *Fine and Dandy, Blue Boy*—cut on May 23, 1947, with Bob Leininger in place of Lombardi. *Metronome,* with Tristano's chief supporter, Ulanov, reviewed the album in the August, 1947, issue. Four sides were given A ratings, while *Blue Boy* received A minus and *Atonement* A plus. The review stated: "Throughout the album, there is Lennie's marked attachment to linear construction, to a strong beat without a swing bass, to the development of each new phrase from the preceding phrase uninhibited by monotonously reiterated figures in the riff tradition."

In retrospect, some of what seemed daring, startling departures, now seems trite and stiff. Time has a way of bringing about such things, although Charlie Parker's *Relaxin' at Camarillo* and *Donna Lee,* which received C and B ratings, respectively, in that same August, 1947, *Metronome,* have held up considerably better over the years. Tristano wasn't to make his really definitive recorded statements until the Capitol sides of 1949, but there is still much to be heard on the Keynotes even with their flaws. *Atonement* is a moving statement despite some moments when the counterpoint with Bauer becomes precious, and *Coolin' Off with Ulanov* is a striking original with contrasting double-time runs and chordal sequences. The ballads are carefully built, piano and guitar interweaving their lines in a manner that had not been done in jazz before. Bauer was not then sufficiently sophisticated a player to cope with Tristano's ideas entirely; on the other hand, Lennie's chording behind Billy is often heavy-handed. A solo performance by Tristano on *I Don't Stand a Ghost of a Chance with You,* recorded on September 23, 1947, is much in the style of *I Can't Get Started* and *I Surrender, Dear,* but is more fully realized because the pianist is by himself. It is part of a twelve-inch LP, *Modern Jazz Piano: Four Views,* on the Camden label. Two other solo selections, *Spontaneous Combustion* and *Just Judy,* were also done at that session, but only the latter was issued, on a short-lived ten-inch Victor LP.

It has often been said that Tristano should play alone because of his general dissatisfaction with rhythm sections, especially drummers. Some of his most important and successful recordings are unaccompanied: *Requiem*, a blues for Charlie Parker, in Lennie's first Atlantic LP; and the entire second Atlantic album, *The New Tristano*. He told Bill Coss: "You know, contrary to the general belief, I love to play for people. If I could get a reasonable facsimile of a rhythm section. . . . If other pianists were as candid as I am, they would tell you about what they think about rhythm sections. My experience is that if you talk to a bass player, the only good drummer is a dead one. They all talk about Sid Catlett or Dave Tough. And the drummers are the same way. My problem has always been to find a bassist and drummer who can play *together*. See, that's the word—together. But nowadays there are no sidemen left. Everyone is a soloist."

He's not too wild about bass players either. "I have trouble with bass players and chord progressions," he has said. "I've pointed out to them that instead of trying to find out where I'm going, they'd do a lot better and get a better sound by playing the foundation chord instead of trying to get where I am at the moment. If they're on the fundamental chord, they'll get to relate to what I'm doing and eventually get to where I am sometimes."

Lee Konitz, who also has his quirks when it comes to finding compatible accompanists, told me, "Lennie's trouble with rhythm sections is different from mine. I think that a great part of Lennie's trouble, besides the obvious part of his being a very subtle player—and most rhythm sections not being subtle and just not hearing what he's doing—is that Lennie doesn't go to them. So that's *his* trouble."

When I suggested that Tristano should be a solo pianist, Konitz said, "Yeah, I don't understand why he doesn't. He's been bitching about these rhythm sections as long as I've known him, and he's never—at least that I can hear it—made too big an effort to find out where they're at, to get with *them*."

In 1949, everyone was "getting with" everyone else in Tristano's group, or so recorded evidence would lead us to believe. With Konitz, Marsh, Bauer, and Fishkin, he played opposite Charlie Barnet's band at the Clique in January, 1949. That same month part of the group recorded for New Jazz Records. It was that company's first session and, in effect, was the beginning of what became the Prestige label. "It was supposed to be Tony Fruscella's date," Konitz remembers, "and Bob Weinstock suggested that Tony and I get together, and we didn't get together. Tony didn't want to do it, so Bob asked me if I would.

"I asked Lennie to take the date. I just wanted to do it as a sideman." The 78's came out under Tristano's name, but later they were included on a Konitz Prestige LP. All four selections are based on standards, as is much of Tristano's work. I might add, the *same* standards keep reappearing. Here, Konitz' *Subconscious-Lee* is *What Is This Thing Called Love?*; Tristano's *Judy, Progression* (called *Reiteration* in some foreign releases), and *Retrospection* are *Don't Blame Me, Idaho,* and *These Foolish Things,* respectively.

The Capitol sides, *Crosscurrent, Wow, Marionette, Sax of a Kind, Yesterdays,* and *Intuition,* represent a body of work that definitely pointed to some of the developments of the fifties. Gerry Mulligan, who played with Konitz in the Miles Davis band of the same period, has said: ". . . as far as the birth of the cool is concerned, I think Lennie is much more responsible than the Miles dates. It's hard to say unemotional, because it's not exactly that, but there was a coolness about his whole approach in terms of the dynamic level: Lennie always had his own thing going; he never came out in the big world."

Besides their influence—and that was as a tributary rather than a prime mover of the jazz mainstream—these records are important in themselves. They represent a discipline in form and execution, and as performances they stand up remarkably well after more than fifteen years. *Crosscurrent,* a swift minor-key piece, has impeccable unison playing by the saxophones, and Tristano plays some of his even, descending runs. *Wow* is a lazy, lyrical theme that is contrasted by double-timing in the bridge by Konitz and Marsh with their particular kind of light sound. Konitz, in his solo, accents much like Tristano, and Lennie uses acceleration and deceleration in his extremely personal way during his own improvisation. Both numbers are Tristano compositions.

Sax of a Kind, by the two saxophonists, is, like Bauer's earlier *Blue Boy,* based on *Fine and Dandy,* but it is more fully realized. Tristano, for instance, is in much firmer control of his material. There are solos by Konitz and Marsh that fly through the air.

Then they exchange thoughts and finally fuse in a logical but exciting close.

Bauer's *Marionette* is a lovely piece, constructed in the unconventional ABCD pattern. Tristano has a beautiful solo here, one that alone should dispel the notion of "wholly cerebral" that many have held about him.

Yesterdays, on which the horns are not heard, is credited to Tristano because he never states Jerome Kern's melody and uses his own progressions, but it is obviously based on Kern's song.

Then there is *Intuition,* a track that was far ahead of its time —and a much more coherent form of "free" improvisation than in any of the attempts of the adherents of the so-called "new thing" in the sixties. "During the series of dates we made, we recorded regular tunes that we were playing," Konitz explained, "and we had had some experience in playing intuitively. At that date, Barry Ulanov was in the studio, functioning in some capacity—I don't remember what it was officially—and Pete Rugolo was in the booth. After we had played a couple of tunes, Lennie said, 'Just let the tapes roll for three minutes,' and we played this intuitive thing. Barry was to signal one of us at the end of two minutes approximately. We did four takes, and in each one we stopped at approximately about three minutes. I don't know *what* it means, except we did do that kind of playing, and it was a great feeling. We did it once at a concert in Boston, and it was very exciting. It was difficult for us to do it in a club, as it was even to just play tunes, so that we didn't play together any more for quite a few years. We really goofed. We had a lot of things going. . . .

"No one in all this talk," he said, referring to the avant-garde of the sixties, "hardly ever mentions that. And you know damn well that these cats have heard that record somewhere along the line. It just doesn't come from no place."

Tristano has said of the group, "Instead of consolidating our positions, it was always in a state of development, and that's no way to sell something."

One of the group's innovations was the use of counterpoint. Of course, early New Orleans ensemble playing is a form of counterpoint; there are a few examples from the swing era, often featuring Lester Young; and the contrapuntal theme statements of Charlie Parker and Miles Davis on *Chasin' the Bird* and *Ah-Leu-*

Cha also preceded the Tristano group's efforts. But the way in which Lennie's men handled this approach in their improvisations was unique in jazz. "It was one of the things that we did very well together," says Konitz, "one of the things I used to enjoy doing the most with that group. I don't know what kind of an effect it had. The only immediate effect that I know about was on Dave Brubeck, who watered it down enough to make it acceptable at the right time."

In January, 1949, Tristano recorded with the *Metronome* All Stars for Victor. One of the tunes, *Victory Ball*, is his, based on the chords of *S'wonderful*. Charlie Parker plays the devil out of Tristano's line, and both men's solos show that despite the differences in their music, their styles were compatible.

Tristano says of Bird, "The finest person I knew, extremely hip. I met him for the first time at the Three Deuces in 1947. The bandstand was all mixed up. He came up and helped me off the stand. We always talked music together when we'd meet."

The all-star drummer was Shelly Manne, who is also on the New Jazz–Prestige sides. Harold Granowsky is on one of the Capitols, Denzil Best on the other. All had one task in common: Tristano required them to play brushes on snare drums with a completely even attack throughout. Harvey Pekar commented in *The Jazz Review:* ". . . most frequently his drummers don't play an afterbeat, or any other kind of rhythmic decoration. Jeff Morton, who often played with Tristano during these years, is very much this kind of drummer; a model timekeeper who is not required to offer any inspiration to the soloist or to contribute color to the performance as a whole."

Morton is the drummer on Konitz' Prestige sessions: *Tautology* and *Sound-Lee;* and *Palo Alto* and *Ice Cream Konitz.* He plays brushes on all, but even when he uses sticks on cymbals, as in *Line Up* and *East Thirty-Second* with Tristano on Atlantic, the same even 4/4 pulse is maintained.

In November, 1951, Tristano recorded two sides for his own label, Jazz Records, with Peter Ind and Roy Haynes. In his quest for the perfect drummer, Lennie used men associated with be-bop, known for their accenting "bombs," and had them play the conservative-timekeeping role. (In addition to Haynes, Arthur Taylor and Philly Joe Jones later played for Tristano.)

Time has long been one of Tristano's favorite subjects. He told a *Down Beat* interviewer in 1958: "I've been playing 25 years, and I never heard anyone's foot keep steady time. If it approximates it for a couple of choruses, that's all. There's always a point where the beat slows down or moves.

"It got so bad a few years ago, I used to challenge drummers and offer to put a mike near the bass drum. Then let me hear how long they can keep a steady beat.

"Now my idea is to use a bass drum for accents, and use the sock cymbal for effect. The cymbal beat is an intrinsic part of jazz. You just cannot do without it. It adds a sound of liveness to a soloist. It seems to make a soloist sound better.

"The creative line in drumming is with the left hand. That gives him much less to do and eliminates my having to put all my subdivisions against his left foot. It's become a hideous thing. Everything has gotten tighter. Drums are tyrannical."

The two November, 1951, Tristano recordings were the fast *Ju-Ju*, which is *Indiana*, and the slow *Pastime*, or *You Go to My Head*. Tristano had Ind and Haynes back him in the unadorned style he prefers and then, listening to the playbacks, added additional piano tracks, some of which were speeded up by engineer Rudy Van Gelder in the mastering.

No one seemed to notice, but when *Line Up, East Thirty-Second*, and *Turkish Mambo* appeared on an Atlantic LP in 1956, a furore ensued. People were stimulated by the music, but many questioned the multiple taping and suggested that the piano tape had been accelerated. One man even wrote an "exposé." In an interview with Nat Hentoff, Tristano defended himself. "I remember," said Lennie, "that around 1952, when that last record came out—*Ju-Ju* and *Pass-Time* [*sic*]—there wasn't one review out of the five or so that the record received that mentioned that those two sides could possibly have been a result of multiple track recording. It was only six months or a year later that somebody got the idea it might be, and then the talk started. I never really told anybody whether it was or not.

"One of the people who got so hung up on the subject," Lennie continued with amused calm, "was Leonard Bernstein. He and Willie Kapell were over here one night, and Bernstein finally decided it *was* a multiple track recording. He couldn't stand to believe it wasn't. And then Kapell sat down at the piano and started playing Mozart 16 times faster than normal. Lee Konitz tried to save the situation earlier by telling them it *was* multi-track. But he didn't know for sure either."

Tristano related this story to the fact that musicians were always competing with the music rather than listening to it and, to illustrate his point, told of a young pianist, standing at the bar at Birdland, who became paralyzed in his right hand while listening to Tristano, through what Lennie called "kinesthetic competition."

On the actual subject of multitaping, he told Hentoff: "If I do multiple tape, I don't feel I'm a phony thereby. Take the *Turkish Mambo*. There is no other way I could do it so that I could get the rhythms to go together the way I feel them. And as for playing on top of a tape of the rhythm section, that is only second best admittedly. I'd rather do it 'live,' but this was the best substitute for what I wanted.

"If people want to think I speeded up the piano on *East Thirty-Second* and *Line Up*, I don't care. What I care about is that the result sounded good to me. I can't otherwise get that kind of balance on my piano, because the section of the piano that I was playing on is too similar to the bass sound. That's especially so on the piano I use, because it's a big piano and the bass sound is very heavy. But again, my point is that it's the music that matters."

Bassist Ind explained overdubbing and speeding up tapes on the back of his *Looking Out* LP. "I accomplished this by making a rhythm tape or bass line tape first," he wrote, "then slowing the tape to half speed and playing slow improvisation with the slowed down tape. By re-recording the resultant two tracks at the slow speed and then playing them back at the fast speed, the original rhythm tracks return to normal and the improvised track becomes twice as fast and is raised one octave into the cello range.

"In playing the overdubbed tapes for a number of persons, several expressed the opinion that the speeding up of music creates a false impression of technique. I have heard the same criticism of *Line Up* and *East Thirty-Second* on Lennie Tristano's Atlantic album, from which, incidentally, I first had the idea to record bass that way. My answer to the criticism is best given with an analogy. Many painters use a negative or condensing lens with which to study their pictures. By condensing the image of a picture, it is far easier to detect both the flaws and the strong points. To return to music—speeding up an improvised line does not improve a bad line, nor does it cover bad notes, rather it accentuates both of these."

The last thought is true enough, but one of the essential parts of a jazz performance is the tempo and what it elicits from the performer, and it should reflect the feeling of the moment. Jazz, good or bad, is supposed to be a natural expression.

Tristano stated in the course of the Hentoff interview: "I understand some people say that making a record like the one I made isn't fair because I couldn't play the numbers that fast in a club. Well, I'll learn the record so I *can* play it at that tempo 'live.'" This defensive alternative would vitiate spontaneity—a quality that Tristano has always been so concerned with in other players.

The tracks themselves, judged on their merit as music and not on how they were built, vary in degree of achievement. *Line Up* is an intense improvisation. Jack Maher, reviewing it in the May, 1956, *Metronome*, wrote: "It is *All of Me*, improvised until the stuffings fall out." It does seem as if Tristano is actually pummeling the piano in his urgent journey. Harvey Pekar commented on *Line Up* and *East Thirty-Second:* "Both are full of drive and fascinating ideas. I'd like to hear the original piano lines; I bet they would compare favorably. The tempos would be slower, but the dynamics would be more varied. All that pounding in the bass gets to be a drag after a while."

Actually, the real problem on these tracks is the mechanistic quality of the relentless attack—the sound of exercises rather than of jazz performances. *Turkish Mambo*—which consists of three lines (one moves from 7/8 to 7/4, another from 5/8 to 5/4, and the third from 3/8 to 4/4)—does not have a particularly arresting main theme. Its fascination lies in the rhythmic counterpoint; but, again, this seems to be academic rather than human.

Requiem, the blues for Charlie Parker, makes use of overdubbing in that Tristano accompanies himself in places, but there is no speeding up of the tape. It is an extremely moving performance, using the blues language in a way that is obviously familiar to Tristano but one that he rarely chooses to use. Many people seized this opportunity to say that *Requiem* proved that Tristano was not cold and unemotional. However, the speeded-up tapes aside, he had made this evident long before, to those who really cared to listen.

In 1962, some six years after his first Atlantic LP, Tristano recorded *The New Tristano,* seven unaccompanied tracks on which he accomplishes his objectives without the aid of tape doctoring, a fact that Atlantic makes sure to state in the liner notes. In lieu of a rhythm section, Lennie uses his left hand to state the bass line and builds on that with his right, punctuating with short chordal sections. In *Scene and Variations,* made up of three segments, he departs from this. *Carol,* the first section, is played out of tempo for the most part; and *Bud,* the third portion, is a hard, up-tempo linear excursion in which he does not use the walking bass. There is a tinge of the feeling of exercises that marred the first Atlantic experiments, but otherwise the album is a remarkable tour de force. As usual, much of the material is based on standards: *Becoming* (*What Is This Thing Called Love?*), *Deliberation* (*Indiana*), *Scene and Variations* (*My Melancholy Baby*), *Love Lines* (*Foolin' Myself*), and *G Minor Complex* (*You'd Be So Nice to Come Home To*).

Sal Mosca feels that *The New Tristano* is tangible evidence of Lennie's growth. "Playing these nine-eight figures or thirteen-eight figures, or being aware of them," he said, "enables you to keep your line going much longer, to extend your melodic line so you're not limited to short phrases.

"So Lennie can play all different kinds of figures that sound as if they are going out of time, but he never gets lost once. He knows where everything is all the time. That he's gotten by getting the feeling for these long things—like thirteen eighth notes and then another group of thirteen eighth notes and then maybe a group of nine eighth notes. Different-length melodic ideas coming one after another and yet keeping everything intact—the tune, the harmony, and knowing where you are all the time. I think he's gone the furthest with that, emotionally. A lot of guys experiment with it, but they don't feel it like he feels all that."

Ulanov's notes for the album explain: "Lennie calls what he does here 'stretching out in the forms.' Within the jazz forms, simple as they are, he has sought the utmost limits of spontaneity of the improvising imagination. He is never enslaved to any sequence of notes or chords. He is almost completely free—but not completely. That is part of the joy in it, he explains: 'to see how far you can stretch out in a given frame of reference.' The possibilities, he says, are 'practically infinite, endless even in the most simple forms. You are constantly creating form on form, a multiplicity of lines, a great complex of forms.' "

Tristano says, "The single-song form is my link with the people," and one of his main objectives is "that rhythmic friction that results with being able to feel the different times at the same time. It's not intellectualized," he told me, "it's felt." Ulanov quotes him in a complementary statement: "I can never think and play at the same time. It's emotionally impossible."

Tristano, who says he realized by the end of the forties that "I wasn't going to be able to make a living playing what I really wanted to play," formally opened his teaching studio in June, 1951. It was located on East Thirty-second Street in Manhattan, and it became his main base of operations. From there he tried to launch his record company, and he often talked about getting his own club. But the main concern was teaching, and many students came to study with him for varying lengths of time. One, a girl who plays piano, but not professionally (she never advanced that far), told me of her year with Tristano. "In addition to finger exercises," she said, "he had you scat along with records and play rhythm patterns with your hands on the table. He told me to practice this two hours a day.

"He had me memorize solos by Pres, Bird, and Miles, be able to sing them. Then another thing was to pick a tune I liked, take the chords and plan the changes so that the chords themselves were melodically meaningful and did not repeat.

"Fifteen to twenty minutes was all anyone got. He was interested in my problems, but if I ever volunteered an opinion about music, he would scorn it. One time he really startled me when he said, 'Why are you smiling?'—and I was."

Mosca also talked about Lennie's teaching methods. "He pinned you down more," Sal said. "If he gave you some scales to work on—like the major scales—he wouldn't do anything until you learned them. Or if he gave you some chords to work on, say, for your left hand—some formations—he would hear them in all the keys, and he wouldn't move until you played them.

"He was thorough but not to the point where he was a strict disciplinarian. You never got that feeling. Yet the discipline was there as an integral part of it. It was a more natural discipline."

Of Tristano's reputation for strictness, Mosca says, "I could see where people could take him that way, because a lot of people take me that way. But I don't feel myself to be strict.

"He never played records for students, but he would suggest that they sing with Charlie Parker or Lester Young or Roy Eldridge or Louis Armstrong. I do that in my teaching. And I do that myself. That's one of the ways you learn to play. The main thing it does is open your ears. In order to sing every note someone is playing, you have to listen to it a lot closer than if you were, say, just listening to it for enjoyment. The main good in it is that you can hear everything better, including yourself. You can hear the teacher better, others better.

"I got a very personal feeling from Lennie without really getting personal—without going into too much detail about my life. I just felt he could include me in his aura—whatever his general life thing was—because he had been through what I was starting."

Tristano has had students from other schools of jazz. Mainstream saxophonist Bob Wilber studied with him in the fifties, Bud Freeman in the forties. That a veteran of Chicago's famed Austin High Gang of the twenties was studying with the far-out modernist startled many people at the time. Saxophonist Freeman explained it to me in the sixties: "After I came back from Chile, I had lost confidence in my playing, and I liked what Tristano was doing. I heard a couple of his records and thought he was a brilliant musician. I spent about three months with him. Actually, we just reviewed what I had known as a kid—scales and intervals. Of course, he did give me terrific confidence. He seemed to like what I was doing, and I felt he was the new approach to jazz. Although I respect him highly, I was not influenced by him in any way. I had to do what is me, what I honestly can say was my own playing."

Writer Jack Maher, who studied drums at the Tristano school, set down some of Lennie's teaching principles in a *Metronome* article in the mid-fifties: "Lennie's main objective is to have the musician play emotionally. Unfortunately, emotion is too often confused with hysteria and bombastics, which in themselves are wrought up mechanically rather than emotionally. It is Lennie's sincere belief that the serious jazz musician should move away from the mechanical and stereotyped, and toward the subtler shadings of really emotional music.

"Feeling is the basic aspect of Lennie's teaching. The technical exercises he gives are to be taken with the same thought in mind. They must be practiced emotionally and with the view that they will be incorporated into improvised solos, not as rehearsed 'licks' but as living, moving parts of an entire musical idea. As Lennie would say, 'The amount of notes played, or the speed at which they are played, are of no importance unless the musician feels and plays each note to its fullest.'"

In 1964, when asked what he thought of Coltrane, Rollins, and Davis, Tristano answered, "All emotion, no feeling." He replied to "How do you distinguish the two?" with: "Well, say I believe that there is no real hysteria or hostility in Jazz. Their stuff is an expression of the ego. I want Jazz to flow out of the id. Putting it another way, real Jazz is what you can play before you're all screwed up; the other is what happens after you're screwed up."

When the interviewer followed up with: "Do you believe there is any progress in Jazz?" Tristano replied: "None at all."

Remarks like these give fuel to the arguments of those who insist that Tristano is a bitter man. Mosca is one who feels otherwise. "I might not see him for three months or six months," says Sal, "but whenever I do see him, he's never been bitter. A little dragged perhaps, but I wouldn't say bitter. I would say he loves music more now than he ever did and plays better than he ever did. And he keeps growing all the time. A bitter man doesn't do that. A bitter man stops and acts bitter."

In the early 1960's, I asked Lennie about bitterness, and he said, "I've seen them come and go. I'm happier now than I've ever been. There's nothing I'd rather do than play and teach." Then he spoke lovingly of his children and his second wife, Carol. (He and Judy split up in the fifties, and she went to San Francisco, from where reports of her tenor saxophone playing filtered back to the East for a while.) But in 1964, the Tristanos parted company.

From 1955, when he played at the Confucius Restaurant on Fifty-second Street (some of the tracks on the first Atlantic LP were recorded there), Tristano went into self-imposed exile from the clubs. "Birdland always asked me to work," he told me, but obviously he didn't choose to play there. Then in the summer of 1958, two young jazz fans, Mike and Sonny Canterino, began a frontal attack on the Tristano hermitage. They had opened their Half Note in September of 1957 and in the course of the year had employed Konitz and Marsh at their club. Through them, they got the idea of persuading Lennie to play in public again. The assault began on Tristano's stomach. "I'd cook up a big mess of ravioli, and the sauce—you know, I wouldn't, like, put the sauce on, so I'd put it separate like, and give the kids instructions how to heat it up before they're ready to eat it," Frank Canterino, the boys' father, explained to Ralph Berton. "They kept taking things like that out to Lennie's house, and, you know, got to know him that way."

"At first," Sonny said, "Lennie wouldn't even talk about playing anywhere. He didn't appreciate the way he'd been pushed around by nightclub owners. I don't want to mention no names. But he really felt the whole thing of playing in clubs was no good for the musicians."

Slowly Tristano warmed up. He came to the club for dinner and to listen. "He never would sit in, even with his boys," wrote Ralph Berton. "But he did remark—it was the first sign of thaw —that the atmosphere was unusually cozy and homelike. And the first real crack in the ice appeared when Tristano decided one afternoon (there was no one in the place but the owners) to try 'a few songs' on the piano. They helped him up on the stand. Lennie played a little, then complained that the action was very stiff. He suggested they get a different piano (this was only a $1,300 Steinway grand). They suggested he come with them and help pick one.

"Together they went to the showroom. Tristano tried one piano after another and, according to Sonny, 'he knew what every single piano was—he'd name it right off even though he had no sight, you know—like he'd play a few chords on one and tell you, 'That's a Knabe,' or a Mason or whatever. Finally the Bechstein was discovered. 'The price was two grand—but he was really satisfied.' "

In August, 1958, Tristano made his return to public playing. Since that time, practically every appearance has been at the Half Note. He has used trumpeter Don Ferrara and Warne Marsh at different times. The rhythm section was most often Sonny Dallas on bass and Nick Stabulas on drums. In February of 1959, ten years after his Capitol recordings, Tristano was reunited with Marsh and Konitz at the club. Then, in 1964, when Konitz returned from California, the quintet had another Half Note reunion. This time a show was video-taped at the club for CBS-TV's "Look Up and Live," and the group played an engagement in Toronto. "We really thought that maybe we'd come full circle," says Konitz, "and it didn't work again. All I can say is that—and I'm not trying to make any comparisons in the worth of the music necessarily—Bud [Powell] and Bird and Dizzy couldn't play together. I don't know of any group that was really trying to improvise that has been able to do it. They've all had to organize it in some way, so that it didn't get too close to what was really going on. . . . Cats were really being threatened in front of everybody and whatever goes on when people are really playing and getting castrated and getting whatever they get when something real is happening. It's tough.

"I have the feeling sometimes, playing with Lennie and Warne —whom I admire a great deal, my favorite players in a lot of respects—where I just knew I couldn't play after what I had just heard. I felt cool enough in some way to not have to play.

"This would mean in a healthy playing situation that if a cat is saying it, at any given moment, you're not obliged to say more—or anything. He can have it. If a band could function in that way, it would be a real band, where everyone respected each other's playing that much. And I can't see now, as far as I'm concerned, playing with Lennie any more. Just for all the complexities that are in this."

Anyone who has seen tenor men Al Cohn and Zoot Sims for any great length of time in a club may observe that if one is really stretching out in inspired fashion, the other will not try to follow him with a lengthy solo, unless he feels that way at that particular time. This is what Konitz is talking about. But there is always *some* statement from the restrained party. That is part of the public performer's obligation to his audience. Sims and Cohn and the Tristano quintet are quite different when it comes to music and interpersonal relationships.

Off the bandstand, away from his teaching, there are two things that consume Tristano's time. As Mosca says, sometimes he reads as much as he plays, and in one period he was playing between "six or eight hours a day." Tristano can read braille but does most of his "reading" by listening to recordings for the blind. He told the editors of *Literary Times* that he reads "Proust, Dostoevsky. Emily Dickinson is one of my favorites. She's probably our only poet in the nineteenth century." When asked what works he had read of the new novelists and poets, he answered: "No, none. You see I have to wait till their works are put on tape before I can dig them. But when they come out, I'll be listening."

One of his practice methods has been described by Ulanov: "There are, for example, the exercises for the left hand, one finger at a time, in which the single hand is divided up into lines. He will practice improvising with, say, two fingers assigned the bass line and three the melody, then with three on the bass and two on the melody, and so on and on until the fingers drop off from exhaustion or he has negotiated twelve choruses. For what it may be worth to those who want to try this out for themselves, it should be added that so far Lennie has lost no fingers; his hands are intact—and so are his twelve-chorus exercises." When he is practicing exercises, Tristano simultaneously "reads" with the aid of earphones.

Tristano's comments on other musicians can be very harsh, but there are some he looks up to. His reverence for Parker is well exemplified by his now classic, oft-repeated remark: "If Charlie Parker wanted to invoke plagiarism laws, he could sue almost everybody who's made a record in the last ten years." In the sixties, he said to me, "Pres and Charlie Christian were the only musicians to make records equal to their real power."

Lennie has always liked the work of Bud Powell. "The prevailing playing attitude was made up of seventy-five percent Bird and twenty-five percent Pres—the underlying feeling is Pres," he says. "Bud worked in this frame of reference but added his own personality to rise above it."

It was interesting to hear Powell approximating Tristano's rhythmic inflections and intervals for three sets one night at Birdland in the mid-fifties. A recording that hints at this is Powell's solo on *Buttercup* in *Bud Powell's Moods*, a Verve LP made in 1954. Of course, this was but a fleeting phase in Powell's career. Tristano has not been a discernible influence on many pianists. Perhaps the most important has been Bill Evans, who did not study with him and who says he was more influenced by

Konitz than by Tristano himself. Roger Williams, who did, apparently was not moved in the least by the experience.

The youths who gathered around Tristano in the late forties and early fifties all showed the stamp of his music. There was Willie Dennis, the trombonist who was killed tragically in July, 1965, when a car in which he was riding ran out of control in Central Park. Dennis had distinguished himself with an anxious, burry style with Tristano, Charlie Mingus, and Gerry Mulligan's Concert Jazz Band, among others.

Don Ferrara has played with Mulligan, as well as with Tristano and Konitz, in the course of bringing some of Lennie's lines to the trumpet.

There also was tenor man Ted Brown, who has not been heard in jazz circles since around 1958. At about that time, he did an album called *Free Wheeling* for Vanguard. Warne Marsh, his colleague on this LP, was also with him on an Imperial LP entitled *Jazz of Two Cities,* released a year earlier. Tristano says of the latter that it is "one of the best records made in recent years, from the standpoint of originality, swing, drive, improvising, and charts."

Lennie feels that Marsh is "one of the greatest," but he expressed the fear that Warne wasn't getting the opportunity to play in public often enough. "If you don't have this experience, it's going to hurt you," he said. Coming from someone who has shut himself off from the public for long periods, this statement is significant. It was uttered before Marsh, Konitz, and Tristano played together at the Half Note in 1964. During their time at the club, Marsh showed a self-confidence that he had often been lacking in the past. In 1965, however, he and Tristano returned to seclusion.

Marsh, born in Los Angeles, California, in 1927, studied accordion, bass clarinet, alto saxophone, and tenor saxophone, all with private teachers. His first job was with the Hollywood Canteen Kids in 1944. Then he worked with Hoagy Carmichael's Teenagers for a year and a half. While in the Army during 1946–1947, Warne was stationed in New Jersey. It was at this time that he met Tristano and began studying with him. When he was discharged from the Army, Marsh returned to California and toured with Buddy Rich for four months. In October, 1948, he came back to New York and became part of the Tristano group.

Several times he has gone back to California, but he always seems to gravitate to Tristano again. There have been long stretches when he has supported himself by working outside the music business.

Marsh is stylistically descended from Lester Young and, of course, has been influenced by Tristano. In the early fifties, there were parallels with Stan Getz in his sound, but even then Marsh's tone was much drier, more ascetic, and rhythmically and harmonically, he and Stan were quite different.

In addition to the records already mentioned, Marsh recorded with Konitz for Atlantic and did his own album for that label, both in the mid-fifties. Tristano cites the sixteen bars that Marsh plays on the 1953 Metronome All Star record of *How High the Moon* as something special—but, then, he considers Marsh himself as something special. "Warne is the only sax man today," he said in 1958, and in 1962 he added, "Warne had and has the fantastic ability to thrill me the way Pres or Roy, Christian or Bird, maybe a few others had."

Marsh's sometime associate Konitz says, "As far as I'm concerned, I've heard him improvise better than anybody I've ever heard. He's got a brilliant ability to play."

The Marsh of the sixties *is* a brilliant improviser, but not many, outside of musicians at jam sessions, have had the opportunity to hear him.

Of all the people to come out of Tristano's sphere of influence, Konitz has made the biggest mark. His experience has been more diverse, and this has been beneficial to both his music and his reputation. "One of the differences that Lee has always had," says Tristano, in comparing him with Marsh, "is that he's had to do many different things, like playing with Kenton, for instance." Lennie then mentioned a Kenton recording of Bill Holman's *In a Lighter Vein,* on which Konitz solos. "The band is bad, the rhythm section rotten," said Tristano. "Lee plays great, beautiful. But he always seems to work better when someone else is responsible for the band. His own records have never been too good." He then cited Konitz' work with Miles Davis, Gerry Mulligan, and himself.

In criticizing Konitz' own recordings, Tristano sounds like the disapproving father whose son has gone out on his own. Certainly, Konitz has made good records as a leader. The very fact that he broke away from Tristano and opened up other areas for himself has enabled him to make more personal what had been a highly individual style from the start.

Born in Chicago on October 13, 1927, into a family that wasn't particularly musical ("There were no instrumentalists, but my two older brothers sang things like *Eli, Eli, Sonny Boy*"), Konitz got interested in jazz through listening to the bands on the radio before he was 11. "I heard Benny Goodman," he relates. "I think Benny was the one responsible for me wanting to get a clarinet, and I spent from eleven until I was fifteen—when I went out on the road for the first time—I spent those years studying with teachers around Chicago. They had nothing to do with jazz, just fundamentals."

Soon Konitz began listening to records by Coleman Hawkins and Benny Carter. He was discovering the world of jazz by himself. "Until I met Lennie, when I was fifteen, I didn't have too many friends that were involved with jazz or knew too much about it."

It was while he was working one of his first jobs, on tenor saxophone and clarinet, with Emil Flint's ballroom band, that he met Tristano. "I was already a hipster in some ways," says Lee. "I was wearing yellow socks and brown-suede shoes with my tuxedo. We played clarinets into big megaphones. I don't know what my listening experience was, but I was already improvising. I was considered a young hippie or something. But I'm sure I had records at that time of Benny Carter and Johnny Hodges.

"Lennie was working on the Southwest Side, across the street from the ballroom, at a place called the Winkin' Pup, with some Mexican musicians, playing rhumbas. I went in to see a friend of mine who was working there—a pianist named Joe Lipuma—and I didn't even know Lennie was there. When I walked in, I heard him playing, and it got to me immediately. I was fascinated by it. I studied with him for a couple of years on and off, and I was going out on the road with different bands. One was Joe Lipuma's."

At one point, Konitz did three weeks with Gay Claridge, whose group was the house band at the Chez Paree. Guitarist Mary Osborne was also in the band. Then he went out of town for a month with Teddy Powell, but "he got busted for draft evasion. It was just after a whole band had quit on him. Charlie Ventura was part of that band."

Back in Chicago, Lee played at a club for a few weeks. It was then that he switched to alto, because the job called for it. Following this, Jerry Wald needed an alto player, and Konitz went with his band for a couple of months, divided between Chicago and the road. When he left Wald, he began working around Chicago with Lloyd Lifton. He was also singing, something he has kept a secret ever since. In the October, 1945, *Metronome*, Phil Feather-ingill wrote that Konitz "has promise of becoming one of the great white altos . . . has one of the finest voices for ballads or blues we have ever heard." When I asked Konitz what he was singing in those days, he answered: *"Around the Clock Blues."*

In 1947, Konitz joined Claude Thornhill's orchestra. "I wanted to be in the band," he says, "but my goal was to get to New York. I was with them for ten months and got to New York in 1948— January or February, I think.

"It was a beautiful ballad band," he says. "That was the thrill I got out of that band. Gil Evans wrote the better arrangements in the book, and it was a good group of musicians. Gil tried to teach them, as you know, how to play bebop. He was bringing in Bird's lines and teaching these cats—and a lot of them were older—how to inflect the lines, and that was interesting.

"I was just remembering," he mused, "on one of the record dates, the band was playing one of these ballads in three-part harmony, with the mutes tightly in the brass, everything in the middle register, and very slow—and it was excruciating. I was playing the clarinet, and Danny Polo, the other clarinetist, was standing next to me, and he turned to me and started mugging. I broke up, and they had to stop the date. And that happened a second time, and finally they asked me to leave the room until they finished that tune. It seemed that every place I can think of that we played, I did that. Danny was always carrying on. He was a funny man."

Konitz did not spend all his time with Thornhill laughing. He played solos on *Anthropology* and *Yardbird Suite*, two of the Parker lines that Evans arranged for the band. His pure, vi-bratoless sound was quite thin, but his personal approach imme-diately attracted attention. Of *Anthropology*, he now says, with a deprecating laugh, "That was quite a solo," but admits that the band provided "really the first chance I had to play."

His trip to New York with Thornhill gave him an opportunity to see what was happening on Fifty-second Street. "I remember not having too much money when I walked into those clubs, and that was an uncomfortable feeling," says Lee. "It was very exciting. I heard Bird, Hawk, Roy, Dizzy's big band." Young Konitz also was thrilled when people like Flip Phillips and Herbie Fields invited him to sit in.

As a result of his association with Gil Evans and Gerry Mulligan through the Thornhill band, Lee was included in the Miles Davis "cool" nonet of 1948. They played short engagements at the Roost then and at the Clique in 1949, recording for Capitol in 1949 and 1950. His sound was important in the ensemble, as a moving voice in lead parts, and in solos (*Israel, Rouge, Moon Dreams, Move,* and *Budo*). "All I can remember specifically about my reaction to the music," he says, "was, again, in some way a result of my lack of a broader kind of playing experience, because a lot of it sounded less adventurous than what I was used to hearing in a certain way, and a lot of it was due to my limited ability to really hear. As much as I enjoyed sitting there and playing with the band and as lucky as I was to get a couple of good licks on the records, I felt I wasn't as completely involved as I would liked to have been. If it existed again, I would enjoy it that much more because I would know what musical a potential there was; but it was never recognized—for a lack of enough playing. The biggest part was that I had had this particular musical experience with Lennie, and it was just different, as it is today when I listen around to the way people play. I just haven't played that way. I haven't gotten into Miles's bag, et cetera. I'm pretty much playing tunes."

I asked him whether he thought this was necessary, and he replied, "If you can play with those people, it is. I feel quite a lot of the time that I would like to play with different people, because after all the economic intentions and all of the other motivating forces—the extracurricular, extramusical forces at work in trying to get a successful band together—it still is a group of cats that would basically just like to play some music. And I would like to have that contact with these people.

"When Miles was in California, I went down to hear him at

the Workshop [the Jazz Workshop, a San Francisco club] one night," said Konitz, referring to a time in 1963, "and he asked me to play. He really wanted me to play. I had my horn in the car. Frank Strozier was playing with him at the time. The first thing I thought of was, 'I don't know those tunes,' and my fast-tempo experience might have been limited, because I generally try to play at a tempo where I can really improvise rather than just be a virtuoso—I have never gone in that direction. I've tried not to.

"Then I didn't think it was cool to go up there when Frank was there—because he was working with the band and because he sounded good too, incidentally," Lee said, chuckling. "It wasn't like a session kind of thing. It would have been me sitting in with Miles's band, which Frank was a part of and I wasn't. It just didn't seem fair in some way."

A similar incident took place at the Half Note in 1965. Art Blakey asked him to sit in. He wanted to, and he went as far as to assemble his horn; but they were playing an original, and Lee felt uncomfortable. He reasons that if someone invites you to play, he should let you name the tune. The fact that each group has its own set book is one of the things that inhibit today's jazzman from getting up and musically exchanging thoughts with performers with whom he ordinarily does not work.

Konitz' quest for new playing experience led him, in 1965, to play with a segment of today's avant-garde, of which he says, "Over-all my impression has been that this is an experimental stage. I'm interested in hearing these people as long as it stays within a certain area, but I can't take too much of it. Behind all of these people—whenever I hear them playing more conventionally—I feel that they've missed a step or two in the process.

"I've always enjoyed playing completely free off a tune. I recently spent some time with Paul Bley because I liked what I heard—some of what he was doing. He invited me to come up and play at that place above the Vanguard, the Contemporary Art Center, one night, and I didn't like that feeling at all. I just cut out. I stood there, mostly, while everyone else was playing. It was weird. Some kid was playing bass, another kid was playing drums, and another kid who had been playing saxophone since the September before, and Mike Mantler was the trumpet player. My feeling was that maybe it would be a new experience in playing together, and there was none of that. Paul sat there and played for twenty minutes or so straight, and I don't know where the bass and drums were. And I didn't dig that. I tried to rehearse with Carla Bley's band. I thought that might be an interesting experience. That's really what I'm interested in—to get different musical situations. I don't know how long that's going to last, but that's the way I feel right now. And I didn't like that feeling either," he said, referring to Mrs. Bley's ensemble again.

"I would love to play with Roy Eldridge. I would like to play with Louis Armstrong. I was really thinking of trying to find out if he would be interested."

After working with Tristano and Davis, Konitz started recording and playing on his own. He recorded for New Jazz–Prestige under his own name, with Davis as a sideman, in March, 1951; two of the compositions were George Russell's *Ezz-thetic* and *Odjenar*. Later that year, he played in Scandinavia with local groups. In August, 1952, he joined Stan Kenton, a move that was a surprise, because Konitz had a history of being very selective about his work situations, and a choice like Kenton seemed, to some of the extremists, a sellout to commercialism. "Stan called me and said he was getting Zoot Sims, et cetera," explains Lee. "It knocked me out that he called me. I'd had a childhood thing from seeing him in the theaters. I never cared for the music too much, but it always was an exciting kind of presentation. Also, it meant a steady job."

Konitz was with Kenton for fifteen months. "It was a difficult band to play with," he says. "It's a brass band, essentially, a trumpet-trombone brass band. The saxophones' function on the band is just to soften the sound in some way. I did enjoy a lot of it. I got some strength from the experience, because you just had to lay it down or they'd lay you out. I was fortunate to get a couple of records I liked, Bill Holman's *In a Lighter Vein*, for one."

There were other features for Konitz, showing him off in a variety of moods: the hard swinging on Bill Russo's *23°N–82°W* and Gerry Mulligan's *Young Blood*, the introspection with guts on Russo's *Improvisation*, and the unsentimental warmth and sensitivity on the latter composer's ballad *My Lady*. If anything, Konitz' playing still had its purity, but it had acquired a biting edge not evident in the forties. This quality was even apparent, although less obviously so, with the string-woodwind backing on *Lileth, Vignette at Verney's, Places Please*, and *Someday, Some-*

where in Ralph Burns's *Free Forms* album, recorded around 1951.

Kenton's group was Lee's last extended big-band experience. He had rehearsed with Benny Goodman in the late forties, when Goodman was first preparing his so-called bop venture with Wardell Gray, Doug Mettome, and Eddie Bert. Konitz' first reaction of elation turned sour, however. "Benny wasn't too cool," he says. "In fact, he was outright corny to me." Fats Navarro, who also rehearsed but never appeared with the band, has been quoted along similar lines.

Today, Konitz, who once avoided anything but a combo context, says, "I would still love to play with a hip big band for a while."

The Kenton period brought him to the attention of a wider audience. During this time, he also recorded with Gerry Mulligan and Chet Baker for Pacific Jazz early in February, 1953. While these studio recordings are models of restrained, sometimes swinging, sometimes dull West Coast jazz, *All the Things You Are,* one of the numbers recorded before an audience at the Haig, a Los Angeles nightclub, on January 25 of the same year, contains a lovely Konitz improvisation that grooves along in liquid fashion. Throughout the recordings with Mulligan, however, Konitz' tone and attack seem to have reverted toward softness; perhaps the brush background by Larry Bunker, akin to the Tristano sound, had something to do with it.

In 1954, Konitz formed his own quartet and played quite often at Storyville in Boston. He also recorded for the Storyville label, showing more of a vigorous attack than he had on the West Coast. His last Storyville LP was taped in 1955, the same year he recorded with Marsh for Atlantic; and during the summer, he worked at the Sing Song room of the Confucius Restaurant with Tristano. Five of the tracks in Lennie's first Atlantic LP include Lee. As in the Mulligan set, his best work is on *All the Things You Are.*

During the last half of the fifties, Konitz remained in New York. After he finished out his Atlantic contract, he recorded for five years with Verve Records. It was a subsidylike arrangement whereby he received a certain amount of money from the company each month whether he recorded or not.

Before he left Atlantic, Konitz did two interesting albums. One, entitled *The Real Lee Konitz* because he edited out everything he felt was bad or uninspired (a Tristano-type gambit), came from some performances at the Midway Lounge in Pittsburgh in March, 1957. In the notes to this LP, Konitz explains why he has played the same songs so many times: "I feel that in improvisation, the tune should serve as a vehicle for musical variations and that the ultimate goal is to have as much freedom from the harmonic, melodic and rhythmical restrictions of the tune as possible—but the tune must serve to hold the chords and variations together. For this reason, I have never been concerned with finding new tunes to play. I often feel that I could play the same tunes over and over and still come up with fresh variations."

The other Atlantic album, *Lee Konitz Inside Hi-Fi*, contains four tracks by Konitz on tenor saxophone. He does not sound like Marsh but, rather, as if his own alto lines have been transferred to the tenor. It is not quite so simple as this, because the unfamiliarity of the instrument brings out a rougher, deeper-voiced Konitz than one might expect. "I enjoy the tenor," he is quoted in the album's notes, "but if I played it a while I think I might enjoy it too much. I think a lot of the neurotic relationship I have with my alto would start coming out on the tenor. What I mean is, on alto I've come to expect that certain things are going to happen automatically, that certain notes are going to sound certain ways. The emotional and the mechanical get all intertwined. The same thing might start happening on tenor, but right now it's all new and unexpected."

Konitz has not played the tenor since, at least not on records, but the range of his alto playing has widened to encompass a usage of the lower register that sometimes imparts a tenorlike quality.

In 1961, Konitz moved from New York to California. He first lived in San Geronimo, thirty miles above San Francisco, "overlooking a farm. There wasn't a lot for me to do there," explains Lee. "I played by myself. I tried to get people to play, but they were all doing something. It seems I was still not in that fashionable groove. That was a big part of it."

The isolated Konitz lived there for a year and then moved to Carmel Valley. "That was purely because I wanted to live there, because I knew there would be no opportunity to work. So that was the best year out there." At this spot, fifteen miles inland from Monterey, he "did odd jobs, like digging gardens and painting bathrooms. Then I got some teaching in San Jose—eighty miles north. The last few months, I played weekends in San Jose and a third day in Burlingame, a little further up. The others were Cecil Gregory, a guitarist who once studied with Lennie, and Peter Ind, who was living in Big Sur."

When Lee left California, he went to Chicago to go into the real-estate business with his family. "I wanted to work outside of music," he says, "but it didn't work out. Then I talked to Lennie, who was going into the Half Note, so I came to New York."

After the jobs with Tristano came to an end, Konitz played a few nights in the band at the Copacabana, and then he did two weeks there. There were rumors that Tristano had disapproved of his taking a commercial gig and that their falling-out had something to do with it. "No," was Konitz' answer. Then he added, "It was much more meaningful than that." He enjoyed the two weeks at the Copa because it was "a certain view of professionalism. They augmented the band for Eydie Gormé, and that was pretty good music, so it was fun to do."

Lee also had his own quartet at the Half Note for a short time. He is acutely aware of his problems in leading a group. "There is always some kind of conflict that I can't understand," he said. "It takes a great sense of humor—which I think is a prerequisite to doing any of this—or some kind of great compassion to be able to get past all these things that prevent it from happening."

When I told him how much I had enjoyed his playing at the club, he acknowledged, "There were highlights that I remember." I suggested that he expects too much all the time, and he agreed. "Yeah, in some way, I do. Because of my very limited working experience I guess. I don't know how to pace myself—or the things that you learn from working all the time. I would love to have a band or be a part of a band and entertain people.

"I have to develop along these lines," he added. "I know in my heart that I have no ax to grind and all of that extramusical thing. If I end up not being an individual, or whatever the result of absorbing all of this is, then that's the way it will be. Because a lot of my individuality was a result of studying with a very strong individual, who had his effect, and a lack of my own listening and living experience. I'm enjoying listening and playing more than I was that many years ago. I'm beginning to feel a way I can work.

I hope it doesn't end up being by myself, because I prefer not to work that way, but that's the most familiar thing to me. . . .

"I have started playing with Attila Zoller recently." Konitz has often teamed up with guitarists to form duos for records or clubs —Billy Bauer, Jimmy Raney, and Jim Hall, to name three. "I always preferred that sound," he says, "and the harmonic effect of the guitar chord to the piano chord quite a bit of the time, the weight of the sound. I can play spontaneously with Zoller."

On two occasions in 1965, Konitz did play completely alone. At the Newport Jazz Festival, he had members of the audience sing long notes of their choosing, and he improvised on top of this, supplying his own beat. In March, at Carnegie Hall, during a memorial concert for Charlie Parker, he played *Blues for Bird* in a remarkable display of unaccompanied improvisation. Lee, always self-demanding, says, "If I felt the complete artist, you can believe me that I would be out there making it in some way. I don't claim to have this kind of attitude, which people want to believe. When I went out and played at Carnegie Hall that night, I didn't really know what I was going to do, specifically, but I had imagined what could be done. The most important thing to me was to do something for those few minutes that I was out there. And the only way I could conceive of doing it was in the way that was most familiar to me, because I have trouble playing with rhythm sections. It's a constant thing of adjustment. They're trying to adjust to my level of intensity or I'm trying to adjust to theirs. It sometimes happens, but usually it's that very demanding kind of strength that I just don't know if I have or not."

Konitz was always considered a member of the "cool" school because of his tonality and inflection. "The connotation was always a negative one," he says, "and that was always a drag to hear about. I can see now a lot of what they meant."

Today, his attack is more incisive; the accents and cadences are more Bird-like without imitating Parker. "This is a particular period in my life, and it's going pretty much in a straight line for me. I just have to take all this time to absorb this, because this is pretty much what I live for. And how it compares to before— well, when I hear people talking about it, I get hung up. *Before* was a result of a certain thing that is no longer the case, and I don't like to hear about that comparison. I make such a comparison myself when I listen to Lester Young—his Count Basie period was just one period, and then, later on, it was like someone else; it was a result of his failing health, mostly. I feel I am physically stronger now than I was fifteen years ago in a lot of respects. I can hear qualities in my earlier playing that are naive to me now."

Konitz first liked Benny Carter's playing. When I asked him how he reacted to Parker's early records, such as *Hot House* and *Groovin' High,* he replied by talking about his listening experience. "It took me a little while to get to appreciate that; I realized after that I was pretty far removed from a real jazz environment. I didn't hear Lester Young until I was with Jerry Wald. There was a tenor player named Stan Kosow—a very nice player." Kosow, one of the numerous Jewish Lester Young disciples from the Bronx, died in the fifties. "We were playing in Florida, and he had the Lester records, and that got to me immediately. But for the most part, I was doing more playing than I was listening, I would say. I was just involved with Lennie and his approach; and it's curious, but I didn't have that thorough a listening experience during that time.

"I'm doing Louis Armstrong listening now that I didn't do then," he said, referring to the vintage recordings of Armstrong. "That's strange, but I'm glad I finally got to it. I had a very weird kind of precious attitude about music at that time because I thought I was involved in something that was contemporary. Whatever I listened to, I listened to in comparison to that, and somehow, in some ways, it fell short to me. It just didn't seem as pure or whatever as what I was hearing around me. Now, of course, I realize it was more a case of not having listened that closely to it—the best parts of those different people."

In Chicago, when Konitz was first coming up, he came in contact with the young beboppers of that city, such as guitarist Jimmy Raney and pianist Lou Levy, but because of his involvement with Tristano, he didn't share many musical experiences with them. He remembers talking about Parker and Gillespie with Lennie but doesn't recall having gotten too enmeshed in their recordings. "I avoided getting that familiar with Bird, because already there were all the Bird imitators, and I think Lennie detected whatever was unique in my approach to the line. Maybe—I don't know this for sure—he encouraged me *not* to listen to him or get that close. I can't imagine he would have done that—but I didn't, as a matter of fact. I know that in some way I avoided doing it, because the music at this time already sounded very familiar to me, just superficially, without having to be able to play his solos or get that intimate with it, which I've since done. But that was a big hang-up—trying to sidestep this obvious and necessary influence."

Does he feel that his playing is closer to Parker's today? "I hope so. I think so," he says, "I feel now that I've been playing so long that the most important thing to me is to really enjoy the people who can play and who have played and let whatever that enjoyment of the music does to me happen. I'm not at all interested in proving anything."

At one point in the early fifties, Konitz was proving himself, in one way, by the number of players he was influencing. Art Pepper had some of Lee rub off on him, and Paul Desmond is another who was affected, but Lee has "never felt, as much as other people have led me to believe, that Paul was that influenced by me. I think he *heard* me, and he was affected in some way by me, and that part knocks me out. But I don't know that he played anything that I *played* except a suggestion of a phrase. I thought it was a healthy influence, because it wasn't one of vocabulary, but more of a sound."

Konitz' sound, though it has toughened up some, is still close to the highly identifiable tone that has long been his trademark. It once leaned more toward what is called a "legitimate" saxophone sound, but it never really came very close to that of the classically trained players like Mulé and Rascher. Konitz says that this kind of tone puts him off but admits that his own sound "must have stemmed from my original clarinet training. I studied with a man from the Chicago Symphony Orchestra who had me playing that literature, and I probably formed my saxophone embouchure from playing legitimate clarinet. In fact, I did. That was the extent of it. My classical study from a compositional standpoint or analytic standpoint wasn't really that developed."

Konitz' interests extend to "theater, books, the ballet, going to museums." He hasn't owned a television set for four years. "I'd like to see certain things, but I don't miss it," is the way he sums it up.

His instrument and his music are what concerns Lee. "I think people fail to realize what a full-time thing one subject can be. Till today, I'm still just working on the saxophone. That's a full-time thing for me—until I get to the point where I feel I have that much control over the improvising.

"It's just a feeling of being that familiar with my musicality away from the instrument enough of the time so that when I do play the instrument I can make that contact as immediately as possible. I can still feel the gap—I can still feel the effects of my early training, so that I'll allow myself, much too frequently, to just let my fingers take over and not really play what I'm hearing. Apparently, at those times, I'm not hearing anything strong enough to play."

This sounds like the idealism of a perfectionist who believes that a point of constant creativity can be reached. "Yes, I think that's possible," says Konitz. "This is the direction I'm trying to go into. I think a lot of musicians stop themselves with their vocabulary from going that far, but I think that if we can realize approximately where we're at, at any certain playing moment, we could play something spontaneous according to that feeling, as low as it is. So that if I really felt down, I would play a series of whole notes, maybe, or something that would express that particular energy."

Tristano is like a John McGraw of jazz in that many of his pupils go on to be teachers. Konitz has been teaching since the late forties. Now he uses an exchange of recorded tapes by mail as a teaching medium and finds it to be rewarding. In the spring of 1964, when he returned to New York, Konitz took out a classified ad in *Down Beat* announcing his teaching, and received a nice response. "There are people all over that need help in getting a direction," he explains. " I realized that I might be able to do this in a very concentrated way. I'm having a lot of success with a few people now."

Lee has students in Canada, Scotland, and Italy. "I've had people that I haven't heard from the second time—from Jamaica, the Fiji Islands. The whole world is open for this. It's a difficult subject, and because of the way I function, I can't print a Berklee-type method."

He is compiling a book based on transcriptions of his tape-recorded lessons. "Rather than get into a whole bunch of different approaches to playing," Konitz says, "the book is going to be one approach—realizing how much you can do with a note and then putting it into context."

In late 1965, Konitz undertook a European tour, including several festivals. His former mentor, Tristano, made a rare overseas trip to appear at one of the same festivals, but they did not play together. Lee refused to talk more about his rift with Lennie. "It would sound as if I had an ax to grind, which I don't," he emphasized. "I know that what he's done in music, as much as I *know*, is the next logical step after Bird. And it's not getting its due acknowledgment. It's too bad it isn't performed more."

Recommended Listening

LENNIE TRISTANO

First Sessions 1949/50, PRESTIGE P-24081
Requiem, ATLANTIC SP 2-7003
Quartet at Birdland 1949, JAZZ JR-1
The Lennie Tristano Quartet, ATLANTIC SD 2-7006

LEE KONITZ

First three of the above Tristano LPs

Ezz-thetic, PRESTIGE 7827
Motion, VERVE UMV 2563
Revelation (with Gerry Mulligan), BLUE NOTE LWB-532

9

TADD DAMERON
AND THE ARRANGERS

ON APRIL 12, 1958, Tadd Dameron entered the Federal Narcotics Hospital at Lexington, Kentucky. On June 28, 1961, he was released and came to New York to resume his career. However, Dameron considered himself "the most misplaced musician in the business." Known as an arranger, composer, and pianist, he disparaged his ability at the piano, disliked arranging even his own pieces, and preferred only to compose. Yet this urbane, soft-spoken man was *the* arranger of the forties, the man who translated the music called bop into the language of the big band. In the process, he created music that has thus far endured for fifteen to twenty years, a relatively long time as jazz goes. He was not someone who merely drifted into the movement that Parker, Gillespie, and Monk had actuated. Dameron's own thinking, before he had ever heard these men, was moving along the same lines. Compositions like *Good Bait, Lady Bird,* and *Stay on It,* all among his best known, were written in 1939. Dameron was then 22 years old.

Tadley Ewing Dameron was born in Cleveland, Ohio, on February 21, 1917. His family name was Peake, but when his mother remarried, both Tadd and his brother Caesar legally took their stepfather's name. Tadd's parents, Ruth and Isaiah, both played piano, but "they didn't teach me. They didn't want me to play." His mother bought Caesar, his older brother, an instrument. "She bought *him* a *saxophone,* but she didn't want me to play piano because I was too much like him," Dameron once said.

Nevertheless, Tadd was musically inclined, and a minor deterrent such as this was not enough to hold him back. "She wanted me to be a doctor, but when she'd go out, I'd get at the piano and teach myself."

Dameron did learn the rudiments of jazz from Caesar. Actually

2

he had no formal teachers. "There's a lot of things you have to learn by looking in books," he said. Tadd looked.

He must have looked long and hard, because by the time he reached his high-school courses in theory and harmony, he failed them because of boredom. "Everything they were teaching me, I knew already." In 1932 and 1933, Louis Bolden, a local pianist who co-led an orchestra, the Gutbucket Barons, with Caesar, helped him with harmony and writing for a large ensemble.

Dameron went to Oberlin College, well known for its music department, but he was there for premedical studies, in accordance with his family's wishes. His temperament was not right for medicine, however, and he soon returned to his real love, music. He had seen a severed arm dangling from a body, and it had sickened him. "There's enough ugliness in the world," he decided. "I'm interested in beauty."

Standing in front of his band while rehearsing for a recording date in 1953, he told his men, "Make those phrases flow. When I write something it's with beauty in mind. It has to swing, sure, but it has to be beautiful." In 1961 he told me, "I'm trying to stress melody, with flowing chords, chords that make the melody interesting. I'm trying to build a bridge between popular music and the so-called modern music. I think there is too wide a gap. You can tell that from the way they sell."

His active playing career began back in Cleveland during high school, when, as a singer with trumpeter Freddie Webster's band, he was suddenly drafted to replace the regular pianist, who had quit. "So I started playing—chording," said Tadd. "I could only chord—I couldn't solo. The first I soloed was when I came to New York."

Dameron reached New York's Fifty-second Street in 1944. In 1937 he started on the road that got him there. In his second year at Oberlin, vocalist Blanche Calloway, Cab Calloway's sister, came to the college town with her band for a dance date. "Clyde Hart was the pianist," remembered Tadd, "but he was sick, so they asked me to play. So I played the prom, and I left with them—quit school. My family was—whew!—they went up!"

Dameron next joined Zack Whyte's band. It was then that he started arranging professionally. "Sy Oliver had just left the band, and I heard all these arrangements," said Tadd. "I was writing just like Sy."

Dameron mentioned Oliver and Duke Ellington as his early influences. But other music predated his jazz experience. The classical influence? "Maybe subconsciously. I didn't listen to them
much. I was always listening to radio, records, way back in Louis
Armstrong's day, when he first was real great."

Dameron was a movie bug as a youth, and he had his special
favorites. "I used to go and see the musicals—when the talkies
came in. And my mother used to have to come and get me out of
the theater. Even Eddie Cantor's *Whoopee*. I used to stay there
all day. There were some interesting things that were happening.
I remember I went to see Lawrence Tibbett in *The Dove Song*.
She had to come get me out of there."

To Tadd's ear, the pictures featuring Ginger Rogers and Fred
Astaire contained "wonderful music," and one composer in particular really appealed to him. "When I heard George Gershwin,
then I said, 'This is really it.' Gershwin was beautiful. Gershwin
and Duke Ellington—always Duke Ellington."

Dameron's next band was a sixteen-piecer led by Vido Musso,
the big-toned tenor man who would occasionally leave the ranks
of the big-band sidemen to try fronting his own group. "It was in
Chicago," remembered Tadd. "I made arrangements for him, and
he liked them. Then we came to Roseland in Brooklyn, and he
fired me. I don't know why. I went back to Cleveland and formed
my group with my brother."

This was the period at home that gave birth to *Good Bait*,
Lady Bird, and *Stay on It*; they were played by the Dameron
band. In the mid-forties, they were recorded. Both *Good Bait* and
Stay on It were arranged for Count Basie, but he never recorded
either one. They really have more in common with the swing era
than with bop, as their melody figures attest, even though the
Dameron harmonic stamp is present. It was Dizzy Gillespie who
recorded both songs. Tadd said *Stay on It* didn't fit the Gillespie
style, but there wasn't much he could do about it. "I'm walkin'
down the street, the score under my arm, and Dizzy comes and
snatches it out, and he says, 'Oh, I got another arrangement.'"

In 1940, Tadd moved to Kansas City and began writing for
Harlan Leonard's Rockets. This band of fourteen pieces recorded
for the Bluebird label (an RCA Victor subsidiary), but these
sides, originally issued on 78 rpm, were never put on LP and have
long been out of print. Frank Driggs, a writer who is extremely

knowledgeable in the area of Kansas City jazz, says of these records, "In the main, they were good, stable swing arrangements. À La Bridges is a standout as a theme; Dig It has some interesting brass figures; and My Dream, the most interesting changes. However, you wouldn't have been able to foresee Dameron's future development from any of these." Some other Leonard titles were never issued in any form. One, Dameron Stomp, is obviously Tadd's, but most likely it too is in the same vein.

This was the time when he met Charlie Parker. He wasn't to meet Gillespie until he returned to New York. After war was declared, Tadd went into war-plant work in Chicago and Lima, Ohio. "There was no music for me," he said.

In 1942 he joined the Jimmie Lunceford organization. He came to New York and worked out of the office of Lunceford's manager, Harold Oxley. Lunceford was usually on the road, and Dameron didn't travel with the band. "Sometimes, they would send for me, and I'd rehearse the band," he said. "A lot of things I did, everybody thought Sy [Oliver] did. So many things. Lunceford didn't record them. That's been the story of my life. The very good arrangements I'd make for the band, nobody recorded. I made I Dream a Lot About You, things for the vocal group. . . .

"Then I quit Lunceford, and I was just writing for different bands—Benny Carter, Teddy Hill. They were at the Savoy."

Then came the meeting with Gillespie and the first piano solo. "Dizzy was playing at the Onyx club with Max Roach, Oscar Pettiford, Don Byas, and George Wallington. I had met him at Minton's with Monk and Kenny Clarke. So one night George had to go somewhere, so Don said, 'Why don't you come down and just chord for us?' and I said, 'I don't take any solos,' and he said, 'Come on, come on, you know the changes to all the tunes.' So I'm sitting there playing, and all of a sudden, Dizzy says, 'You got it.' So I started playing. But I never wanted to play."

In the sixties, he still scoffed at having won a piano poll in 1948, conducted by Leonard Feather on his radio program. He attributed it to the popularity garnered during the long stay at the Roost and the "live" broadcasts every Friday night. "It was the biggest surprise of my life when Leonard called me up," he said, laughing. "Stan Kenton got second."

The type of piano that Dameron played has often been de-

scribed as "arranger's piano." Although not a great soloist, he was
a catalytic "comper," combining his harmonic knowledge with a
solid beat. Tadd said that his rich chording was something that
went back a long way. "I always had that, because I could never
see that comping—you know, the way they used to oom-pah. I
could never get a job in Cleveland except for Freddie Webster's
band. I just never wanted to oom-pah."

In early 1947 he was the pianist with Babs's Three Bips and a
Bop, a vocal-instrumental group, headed by singer Babs Gonzales, that recorded for Blue Note. Most of the group's numbers
consisted of large portions of wordless vocalizing in syllables like
"loop-a-do-blu" and "oopy-doopy-lop-pow." Although he admired
Babs's ideas, the singing was not for him. "All of a sudden it
dawned on me, 'I can't go through life doing this. This is not my
story.'

"I also played for a few singers. I played for Billy Eckstine.
But I said, 'What am I doing?' After I got through playing about
ten or twelve numbers, then he'd say, 'And incidentally, people,
how about a nice hand for . . .' This is not my role."

Dameron was at his best as a solo pianist at slower tempos.
"I've been criticized about playing my bass so strongly while we
have a bass player," he said. It was the absence of a bass in his
brother's band that made him play a heavier style. "I should
really play by myself. I'd like to make a solo album."

Even so, Tadd still minimized his role as a pianist and said that
he didn't like to arrange. "I'm the most misplaced musician in the
business, because I'm a composer. I'm not an arranger or a pianist. They forced me to be an arranger, because nobody would
play my tunes unless I would write them out. I don't like to
arrange music. I like to direct the band, I like to rehearse a band.
I like to supervise a date, to bring out the beautiful things that
are happening in other arrangers. I'd like to see another arranger's idea of my tunes."

Others saw his arranging talent in a far more favorable light.
An anonymous musician told Barry Ulanov: "You never feel held
down by his stuff, because he always writes wide voicings, as
much as four octaves apart. There are always big holes to fit into,
and let me tell you that's no small help after you've been playing
Flying Home and *I Got Rhythm* voiced in thirds."

Dexter Gordon, who played Dameron's arrangements in the

Billy Eckstine band, once said, "Several things always impressed me about his writing. One was that in playing his music, I found that the parts he writes are so melodic in themselves. It's almost as if every part was lead, in that sense. Usually when a cat writes the secondary parts—I mean the harmony parts—according to the writer and how good he is, they vary as to the sound and the interest and so forth. But with Tadd, his parts were always beautiful. A lot of times I'd play the fourth parts, and they were beautiful."

Gordon recalled an arrangement of *Good Bait* into which Dameron wrote one of Charlie Parker's solos for the Eckstine sax section. "My part was a gas—I loved it."

The ability to make a bandsman enjoy his part puts an arranger that much closer to his ultimate objective. Gordon spoke for a great many musicians when he said, "I think Tadd really is the romanticist of the whole period—he's a poet."

Gordon then recounted a meeting with Dameron at Tadd's house in the spring of 1962. "I had a tune—really rather simple, but the way it lays, the only conceivable thing that I could think of it was like a cha-cha. I was trying to pick it out on the piano, showing it to Tadd. Then he started playing it—working on it, polishing it, the changes. And when he got through with it, he made that thing sound so beautiful. He's got a musical green thumb."

Two of Dameron's best melodies were first presented in small-band contexts without the benefit of large-scale arrangements. *Hot House*, written in 1945 specifically for the Gillespie-Parker Guild recording date, is stretched over a chordal framework partly borrowed from Cole Porter's *What Is This Thing Called Love?* Dameron not only provided a new melody, but reworked the chords as part of an integrated composition. And instead of following the usual AABA song pattern, he wrote *Hot House* in an ABCA scheme. By introducing fresh material in the second eight bars, he made the summation in the final eight all the more meaningful.

The other song, *If You Could See Me Now*, inspired by the coda of Dizzy Gillespie's solo on *Groovin' High*, is one of the most beautiful of jazz ballads. Sarah Vaughan's Musicraft recording (often reissued since) is the definitive version, with a poignant trumpet introduction by Freddie Webster. Dameron claimed he also wrote the lyrics to *If You Could See Me Now*. He was responsible for the words that Earl Coleman sang to Parker's *Yardbird Suite*.

In addition to writing for Eckstine, Dameron contributed to the Georgie Auld book from 1944 to 1946, and his writing for Sarah Vaughan grew out of an arrangement he wrote for her to sing on an Auld record date. That arrangement remained dear to him. It was for *A Hundred Years from Today*. "I liked it pretty well for that day and age, and it still sounds good today," Tadd once said.

In the mid-forties, Dameron wrote arrangements on his own compositions for Eckstine's band (*Cool Breeze*) and Gillespie's (*Our Delight*). He remembered it as a generally creative period. "Monk was doing some beautiful things. He and I used to get together and go up to Mary Lou's [Williams] and write. It was then I wrote *Soulphony in Three Hearts*." The latter, an extended composition, was played by Gillespie's band at Carnegie Hall but has never been recorded. Barry Ulanov described it and some other Dameron compositions in this general way: "While hardly experimental, this music is listenable, an effective exploitation of the popular idiom, a less lush, more mature use of David Rose's genre."

This sounds like the "bridge between popular music and the so-called modern music" that Tadd spoke of years later.

In 1947, Dameron won the new-star arranger award in the *Esquire* critics' poll. It was also the year he became affiliated with Monte Kay, a man who has never been given the credit he deserves for his role in promoting modern jazz and whose early story bears telling here. From the early 1940's, Kay had been promoting weekend jam sessions all over New York, from the Village to Fifty-second Street. Originally a collector of Dixieland records, his tastes changed when he heard Roy Eldridge and Ike Quebec and grew progressively more modern as he heard and hired men like Parker and Gillespie. In 1945 he decided to present the two giants of the new music, then working together on Fifty-second Street, in a May concert at Town Hall. Three weeks before the concert, the ticket sale was negligible. At the suggestion of one of the owners of the Three Deuces, Kay took his problem to Symphony Sid, who was then a disc jockey on WHOM, a small local station. "He was playing Louis Jordan records," Kay said, "and some swing records. I made him my partner immediately—he got half of it if he could help sell it. I brought the records up to him [the Guild records Gillespie and Parker had made], and he liked them and started to play them, and we had about thirteen hundred people—almost a full house —three weeks later. It was so good that we did another concert a month after that."

When Dameron met Kay and Sid, Tadd said they told him, "Look, you ought to get a group. With your style of writing and your playing, get six pieces." Dameron worked all over Fifty-second Street—at the Onyx, the Three Deuces, and the Famous Door; he used Charlie Rouse, Ernie Henry, Fats Navarro, Doug Mettome, Kenny Clarke, Art Blakey, Shadow Wilson, Nelson Boyd, and Curly Russell, in various combinations.

Then came the Royal Roost. It was a Broadway chicken restaurant, run by Ralph Watkins, where they had music from time to time. Kay had been in Florida, and when he returned to New York, he went to visit Watkins. The Jimmie Lunceford band was appearing there. "It was after Lunceford had died," said Kay, "but the band sounded good. And the place was empty. I don't think there were fifty people there on a Saturday night."

Kay became involved in an argument with Watkins. "I knew there was an audience for jazz, but they were a little tired of standing up at the bar on Fifty-second Street and nursing a beer through a whole set for a buck or a buck and a half," Kay said.

Watkins decided to let Kay and Sid promote a Tuesday-night session with modernists Charlie Parker, Miles Davis, Dexter Gordon, Fats Navarro, Allen Eager, and Dameron. They drew seven hundred people the first night—the night Dexter Gordon played *Pied Piper* at two in the morning. After five successful Tuesdays, the sessions were held three nights a week, and finally it became a full-time operation. Since Kay was his manager, Dameron became leader of the house band. He had Navarro and Eager and, for a time, Kai Winding. Later, people like Rudy Williams, Wardell Gray, and a young tenor man from Texas, Jimmy Ford, helped fill the bandstand.

All of Dameron's bands from the late forties are well represented on records. The group he had on The Street recorded for Savoy and Blue Note; the Roost sextet, for Blue Note (and air checks were later released on Jazzland); and a ten-piece group, with Navarro, Gordon, Cecil Payne, and Sahib Shihab, which Dameron led at the Roost in January, 1949, for Capitol.

Navarro was a vital factor on all these recordings. The Savoys from June, 1947, include *The Tadd Walk*, based on *Sunday*, and *A Bebop Carroll*, based on *Mean to Me*. The first Blue Note sides, cut in September, 1947, with Navarro, Rouse, and Henry, contain *The Squirrel*, a stop-and-go blues that also showed up as a background part in Tadd's arrangement of *Cool Breeze* for the Eckstine band. He got the idea for the piece as he watched a squirrel in Central Park one day. The second Blue Note session, of September, 1948, was notable for the first recording of *Lady Bird*. Gillespie's band had played it but had not cut it.

One of the Capitol sides, *Casbah,* a Dameron conversion of *Out of Nowhere,* has a girl, Rae Pearl, singing the theme in a wordless coloratura above the ensemble, which includes Afro-Cuban percussion. British writer Jack Cooke described it "as the most musically extravagant three minutes in modern jazz. . . . For all its lavishness, however, *Casbah* is as a whole a definite and logical step beyond the previous Blue Notes, and a significant pointer to the later Prestige sessions. Although on *Casbah* Dameron's concern for beauty became involved with the exotic, both this piece and its companion, *Sid's Delight,* demonstrate Dameron's by now remarkable command of small band orchestration."

The Roost was an unusual success story. It happened at a time when the nightclub business in general was in one of its periodic doldrums. Kay called it a fluke. Even though the crowds had been amazing for the weekly sessions and continued to be large when the three-days-a-week policy was started ("Ninety-cent admission was the gimmick," said Kay), the management was leery when Kay suggested presenting jazz full time. "Friday night about eight-thirty, there were some women passing by who would ordinarily come in for their chicken, and the owners of the place stood there and insisted that everybody be let in free who said they wanted to have dinner, because they didn't want to take a chance on blowing their business. They didn't think anyone would come. We didn't have any advertising—except that Thursday night, Sid said it on the air, and we announced it to the people in the audience. Well, just off the street and from the word of mouth that had been around, we did four hundred or five hundred Friday night, a packed house Saturday night, and we never stopped."

On the official opening night under the new policy, the featured performers were Charlie Ventura, with Jackie Cain and Roy Kral; Billy Eckstine; and Dameron's group. "There was a packed house," Tadd said, "and Monte came up to me and said, 'Make a speech.' I didn't know what to say, but finally I said, 'You lucky people, do you know who you have here tonight?' It went over real big."

Dameron played for thirty-nine weeks at the Roost. What made Kay decide to encourage Dameron as a leader? "Of all the guys," Monte said, "it was easiest to sit down with him and say, 'Let's do this and this and this'; whereas the other men, all that mattered to them was that they got paid and had a chance to play what they wanted to play and to work fairly steady."

At that time, there was some talk that Dameron was a very strict leader. Kay said, "Well, comparatively. . . . He couldn't hold a candle to John Lewis in strictness, but he was able to get a lot out of the guys—to call rehearsals and have them show up and pay attention. And they respected him. They respected him for his writing ability—to take the time to do it. Because every time Fats would blow a solo, he'd 'write' something as good if not better; but to sit down and write it out and call people to rehearse it—no. And Tadd was a little older than the other guys too, so he got their respect that way. And he had their liking— they all liked him."

Tadd often became a mentor to the musicians he was associated with: Sarah Vaughan ("I influenced her to go on her own"), Navarro, Eager, and Clifford Brown. First there was Freddie Webster. "He and I talked about the business of *singing* on your horn," Dameron told Bill Coss. "Breath control was the most important thing if you had the other things. So many people forgot that. I would work with Fats Navarro, Freddie, Sarah and Billy [Eckstine], and tell them to think this way—sound the note, then bring it out, then let it slide back. Another thing so many musicians forget is what happens between the eighth and ninth bar. It's not a place to rest. What you play there is terribly important. It should be. It should make all the difference between the great musician and just someone else."

Navarro is one whose talent Dameron really fostered. "I used to tell him, 'Fats, when you play a solo, your going from your first eight bars into your second eight, that's where you really play—those turnbacks.' That helped him a lot. I used to tell him, 'Look, there's where you can tell whether a man can really blow—when he starts playing that eighth and ninth bar and then when he comes out of the middle into the last eight. Those turnbacks mean so much.' I told Clifford that too. I tell all my soloists that."

When the scene shifted from the Roost to Bop City and Birdland in 1949, Dameron's locale changed too. He went to France with Miles Davis to play at the Paris Jazz Festival and decided to remain overseas. He was based in England for two years, writing for the bands of Ted Heath, Vic Lewis, Geraldo, and some outfits from the Continent. Jack Cooke wrote of this period: "It seems a pity that Dameron's talents were so little used during his stay in England, considering the difference that a writer of his stature and imagination would have made to modern jazz here had he been able to occupy a position similar to that of Benny Carter in the 1930's."

When he returned to the United States in 1951, Dameron joined the small band of Bull Moose Jackson, the vocalist-saxophonist formerly with Lucky Millinder. "It was really my band," said Tadd, "but he fronted it. We had some good people—Benny Golson, Johnny Coles, Philly Joe Jones, and Jymie Merritt." This was strictly a rhythm-and-blues outfit, although the band did play a few of Dameron's jazz arrangements.

Tadd's strong involvement with narcotics stemmed from this period, and this is strange, for although one cannot say that jazz musicians stopped using heroin when the forties ended, there was a definite decline after 1950. The players coming up, such as Clifford Brown, Horace Silver, Art Farmer, Benny Golson, and Gigi Gryce, inherited the music but not the habits of the giants of the forties. Also, several of the players who had been involved with drugs in the forties had successfully dealt with their problem. It was ironic that one who had survived the hectic forties should succumb to the habit at a relatively late date.

After leaving Jackson in 1952, Dameron formed his own nine-piece band in the spring of 1953. It included Golson and Philly Joe Jones and also a young trumpeter from the Philadelphia area whom Dizzy Gillespie and Miles Davis had recommended to Tadd, Clifford Brown. The band recorded for Prestige and spent part of the summer at a club in Atlantic City, New Jersey. Besides playing their own sets, they also backed the rest of the show, for which Dameron had written all the words and music.

When the band dispersed, Dameron went to Cleveland for two years. As far as music is concerned, he said, "I did nothing." Then one night, Dizzy Gillespie, who was playing there, prodded Tadd about coming back to New York. Dameron finally left Cleveland at the behest of Max Roach. Roach and Clifford Brown were passing through town on their way back to New York. "Max said he was so tired that he couldn't drive, and he said, 'Tadd, why don't you come back to New York?'"

So relief driver Dameron found himself back in New York, and in 1956 he resumed his career. For Roach and Brown he contributed *The Scene Is Clean,* a typically lyrical Dameronian theme, which they recorded for Mercury in February, 1956. Less than a month later, he led his own octet through five originals for Prestige. One was *The Scene Is Clean,* issued under the title *Clean Is the Scene.* It was in the album called *Fontainebleau,* so named for one of the pieces, a completely written piece of program music depicting the impressions, both physical and historical, that the site of the famous palace near Paris made on Dameron. The composition is divided into three parts, which melt one into the other without strong lines of demarcation: *Le Forêt (The Forest), Les Cygnes (The Swans),* and *L'Adieu (The Good-bye).* The latter refers to Napoleon's farewell before leaving for Elba in 1814. Max Harrison praised the work thusly: "The thematic cross-references from one section to another help to produce a satisfyingly tight structure, and the interest is sustained by a ready melodic invention. Orchestration is effective, but variety is achieved by diversified themes—and the melodic constructions arising from them—not by instrumental textures." British conductor Sir Thomas Beecham thought enough of *Fontainebleau* to record it. However, the recording was never released, and therefore, like many other Dameron efforts of the past, the music never reached our ears. Typical of this was the work he did for another Thomas—Dorsey—in 1956. "I made some good arrangements for him," said Tadd, "and then he died."

There was one other Dameron LP in 1956. This was *Mating Call,* which originally was to be recorded with a quintet but ended up with John Coltrane as the only horn. His blowing is very forceful, but with one horn there is no chance for the texture of the usual Dameron ensemble to come through, despite the obvious beauty of several of the tunes. *On a Misty Night,* based on *September in the Rain,* is a piquantly beautiful theme, and *Soultrane* is an aptly-named ballad.

The Scene Is Clean referred to the state of Dameron's health and to his narcotics problem—but if it was true at the time, the scene didn't stay clean long. In 1958, the law caught up with Dameron. He was arrested on January 17 and sentenced on February 19. On April 12 he arrived at Lexington. At first, he busied himself with music. He took over as conductor of the twenty-two-piece band and wrote for it as well. There were many good musicians in the orchestra, but the fluctuation of personnel was great, owing to the fact that a large percentage of the inmates are voluntary patients and are free to leave when they choose.

After a time, Dameron left the band and went to work for a family living in the vicinity. Every night he would return to the hospital. The James H. Crawfords were "a wonderful family," Tadd said. "They influenced me a lot." Mr. Crawford, a sanitation engineer, teaches dancing as a sideline, and both his wife and daughter play the piano. Dameron served as their cook. He had learned this skill at the age of 7, and later he had worked at the two restaurants his family owned in Cleveland. In his two and a half years with the Crawfords, he "began to realize that people can be nice." He used the piano extensively and would stay there "until it was time to go in, until I finished writing. They'd be so happy that I'd be writing." On his return to New York, Dameron kept in touch with the Crawfords through the mails with letters and records.

It was a letter from Orrin Keepnews, jazz recording chief at Riverside Records, that gave Tadd further incentive. During the preparation of an album for trumpeter Blue Mitchell, strings, and brass in 1960, it was decided to solicit some arrangements from Dameron. The recordings, taped in December of 1960 and March of 1961, were issued in the album *Smooth As the Wind,* the name of one of two Dameron compositions in the LP. The two originals plus five arrangements of standards marked Tadd's return to jazz. Before this, he claimed, excepting *A Hundred Years from Today,* "I've never had an arrangement on a record that I really liked."

The Mitchell album drew his qualified approval. "I like *But*

Beautiful and *Smooth As the Wind,* but on some other things, the strings played so loud. If I'd have been there . . . because no one can direct my arrangements like I can. But it's a good record." Then he reiterated, "You have to be there."

From late June, 1961, until his death from cancer on March 8, 1965, Dameron was "there"—in New York, that is. A gracious, soft-spoken man, he said of his nonmusical interests, "I like sports, all types of sports, as a spectator. World News. I'm interested in everything. I don't concentrate on anything, but I try to know a bit about everything. I used to read a lot, but now I don't have time."

The lack of time in which to pursue his outside interests was due to his concentration on his life's work, in an effort to make up for lost time. His affiliation with Riverside continued, and because he was "there" to conduct the orchestra on *The Magic Touch* LP, he was able to produce an album with which he was happy from all angles. He redid *Fontainebleau, On a Misty Night, Dial B for Beauty,* and *Our Delight,* and he introduced several sparkling new themes. He also wrote four arrangements for Milt Jackson's *Big Bags* album for Riverside, some numbers with a brass ensemble for a Sonny Stitt Atlantic LP, a few charts for Benny Goodman's 1963 Russian tour, some things for Tony Bennett and Sarah Vaughan, and a ballet for a Mexican dance company. But heart trouble slowed him down, and the fatal cancer brought him to a standstill in his last months. His last public performance was playing some of his compositions at an afternoon tribute arranged for him by Babs Gonzales at the Five Spot on November 8, 1964. (He had been released from the hospital just for the day.)

Tadd named Gil Evans, Gerry Mulligan, and Benny Golson as arrangers whose work he enjoyed in the sixties. (Golson is one of many young writers in the generation that followed Dameron who were influenced by his voicings.) "Dizzy is wonderful— Miles too," he said, "but they don't specialize in arranging.

"I like a lot of things that Bill Holman does—he does some swinging things. I think things should swing. Pretty or not, it's supposed to swing," he said, inverting his statement of 1953. "I think beauty is an international language. If something's pretty and it swings, so much the better."

The arrangers of the forties whom he admired are some of the men who, along with Dameron himself, deserve recognition for their pioneering. His list included John Lewis, Gil Fuller, George Handy, and Ralph Burns. Lewis did some fine arranging for the Gillespie band, including *Two Bass Hit, Stay on It, Minor Walk,* and the extended *Toccata for Trumpet and Orchestra.* The latter, like Dameron's *Soulphony,* was presented at Gillespie's 1947 Carnegie Hall concert but never recorded. (George Russell's *Cubana Be, Cubana Bop,* from the same period, was recorded on Victor.) But Lewis' talent did not fully develop until the fifties when he became musical director of the Modern Jazz Quartet.

Walter "Gil" Fuller was most closely identified with the Gillespie band. The association began with the forming of Dizzy's first orchestra. "He was helping me organize the band in 1945, when we went on that tour," said Gillespie, referring to a touring unit called the Hepsations of 1945. Fuller did not alone compose any of the pieces for Gillespie; they were the result of close collaboration with the trumpeter. "We'd get to a piano and have an idea for an arrangement," explained Dizzy. "I'd sit at the piano and play it, and he'd write it down and score it. He understood what I meant. We were a good team. We turned out a lot of arrangements."

A good example is the volcanic *Things to Come,* which Gillespie did for Musicraft in 1946. It is a big-band adaptation of Dizzy's line *Bebop,* originally done by five pieces. Other collaborations with Gillespie included *One Bass Hit, Manteca,* and *Swedish Suite.* Fuller also teamed with Ray Brown for *Ray's Idea* and *That's Earl, Brother.* On his own, Fuller wrote and arranged *Tropicana* and *The Fuller Bop Man* for a James Moody Blue Note recording date in 1948. A big-band date of his own for Discovery in 1949 again presented *Tropicana,* along with another Fuller original, *The Scene Changes.* Max Harrison has written of Fuller's work for Gillespie: "While possessing a fine sense of the big band style and an acute awareness of the requirements of the large ensemble he appeared to sacrifice fewer of the new innovations and to compromise less with tradition. In spite of this, his arrangements, more complex than Basie's, less subtle of texture than Ellington's, seem in their use of the orchestra as a virtuoso instrument to derive from Sy Oliver's work with Lunceford. Marked differences arise from Fuller's harmonic and melodic vocabulary, but both men used their orchestras as vehicles for dazzling ensemble virtuosity with sharp, almost dramatic contrasts of texture. Yet Fuller's imagination, like Oliver's, was disciplined and he never wrote passages that were eccentric or unbalanced. The work of both arrangers is characterized by clarity of texture and exceptional fullness and depth of sound. If there is a band score that reflects the spirit of Gillespie's solos it is Fuller's *Things to Come.*"

There were many big bands in the forties, and each one had its arrangers. Eckstine, in addition to using Dameron, employed Fuller for a while, but more important to his band were Jerry Valentine and Budd Johnson. Valentine, who had played trombone with Earl Hines, did the same for Eckstine. More importantly, he rescored two of the numbers he had done for Earl, *Second Balcony Jump* and *Jitney Man,* and also did the arrangements of *Blowin' the Blues Away* and *Lonesome Lover Blues.* Sarah Vaughan's first recording, *I'll Wait and Pray,* done with the Eckstine band for DeLuxe, had a Valentine arrangement. Jerry also arranged Eckstine's pop hits *Cottage for Sale* and *Prisoner of Love.* There was nothing terribly avant-garde about Valentine's writing, but he showed awareness of the new idiom through the inclusion of bop figures and some extended harmonies in his generally swing and blues-oriented style.

Budd Johnson not only wrote for Eckstine and Hines but also contributed to the books of Boyd Raeburn, Woody Herman, and Dizzy Gillespie. He also organized the first bop record session— the 1944 Coleman Hawkins Apollo date with Gillespie—and was responsible for bringing many of the modern players into the Hines band when he was musical director. He served for six months in the same capacity for Eckstine when Gillespie left to form his own band. For Eckstine he wrote the arrangements for *Rhythm in a Riff* and *I'm in the Mood for Love* on National and for *Airmail Special,* which was done for a transcription agency. Leonard Feather accurately has called him "probably the most underrated of the catalytic figures who helped bring about the full emergence of bop."

Mention must be made of Mary Lou Williams, who, like Hawkins and Johnson, came from the previous era, but who not only encouraged the modern musicians but participated actively in the movement with such compositions as *Kool, In the Land of Oo-Bla-Dee, Knowledge,* and, for Benny Goodman, *Lonely Moments.*

The Raeburn band, which at one time or another in 1944–1945 had Gillespie, Benny Harris, Oscar Pettiford, Al Cohn, Sonny Berman, and Serge Chaloff in its ranks, recorded Gillespie's *A Night in Tunisia* under the title of its first vocal version, *Interlude*. George Handy, the arranger with the band, was replaced by Dodo Marmarosa on piano but continued to write the group's scores. Handy, who was given to wearing cardigan jackets and beards long before they were in vogue, showed a grasp of the bop idiom with *Diggin' for Diz*, but his works for Raeburn were heavy with modern classical influences. Barry Ulanov wrote of Handy's arrangements of *There's No You* and *Out of This World*: "These were the echoes of Bartok and Debussy and Stravinsky, all rolled into one big holler." Handy's originals, such as *Dalvatore Sally* and *Tonsillectomy*, also showed direct influences from outside jazz. *Dalvatore Sally* is in and out of tempo, and *Stocking Horse*, which he did for Alvino Rey, was described by Ulanov as "most striking in its time changes, as it shuttles between 4/4, 5/4 and other multiples of the quarter note which still permit the rhythm section to retain its basic beat."

The Bloos, recorded in 1946 for Norman Granz, with a thirty-piece orchestra (including strings and bassoons), under Handy's direction, was issued in 1949 as part of *The Jazz Scene* album, a set partly dedicated to the future of jazz. Sections of cascading crescendos right out of Stravinsky are contrasted with introspective Bill Harris trombone and a driving tenor solo by Herbie Steward, backed by no less than three drummers.

Handy's small-group album *Handyland, U.S.A.*, done in the mid-fifties, is devoid of any of his former modern classicisms. It devotes itself to the swinging of charming themes, several of them based on the blues, with echoes of the music of Parker and Gillespie.

In obscurity for close to ten years, Handy showed up in 1965 as a record reviewer for *Down Beat*.

Another arranger who wrote for Raeburn was Ed Finckel, who was also represented in the books of Gene Krupa and Buddy Rich and, as a pianist, on Allen Eager's Savoy sides. His *Boyd Meets Stravinsky* for Raeburn was one of the band's most exciting originals, a "flag-waver," as the up-tempo big-band numbers were called.

The band that drew most interest from Stravinsky himself was not Raeburn's but Woody Herman's, for which he wrote *Ebony Concerto*. What first attracted Stravinsky to Herman was the five-trumpet unison on *Caldonia*, which mirrored the new music of Gillespie. Actually it was the work of one of Herman's trumpeters, Neal Hefti. First it had been his solo on Herman's warhorse *Woodchopper's Ball*, then it became the property of the whole section, and finally, in this set form, it was made part of the arrangement of *Caldonia*. Hefti later wrote boppish originals like *The Good Earth* for Herman and *Mo-Mo* for Georgie Auld, as well as an arrangement on *How High the Moon* for Charlie Ventura's short-lived big band. His later work, in the fifties, was more Basie-oriented and quite appropriately written specifically for that band.

Herman's chief arranger in this period was Ralph Burns. He was a devotee of Stravinsky, Ravel, Duke Ellington, and Strayhorn. Although he had a hand in shaping the many "head" arrangements the band did and in breathing new life into ordinary pop tunes, Burns's chief contributions were *Bijou*—the "rhumba à la jazz" that was a showcase for Bill Harris—and his extended compositions *Summer Sequence* and *Lady McGowan's Dream*. The last part of *Summer Sequence* was eventually extracted and done as *Early Autumn* in a three-minute arrangement featuring Stan Getz. In the early fifties, Burns did an album for Norman Granz called *Free Forms*, with Lee Konitz as soloist. Burns's comments on the back of the album are self-revealing about his music in general: "These are random thoughts, little melodies I found myself humming and have set down for a small chamber orchestra—i.e., string quartet, woodwind quintet, alto sax, French horn and rhythm section. Some of them are jazz tunes, some are not. All are representative of music in toto from Bach and Verdi to Duke Ellington and Charlie Parker."

Although he did some jazz albums in the late fifties, Burns's main area of concentration is now in commercial record dates, films, and TV.

Early Autumn featured the so-called Four Brothers sound—tenor lead with two other tenors and a baritone—first introduced into the Herman band via Jimmy Giuffre's arrangement of *Four Brothers*. This sound grew out of a rehearsal band that arranger Gene Roland had led in New York and one he later led at Pontrelli's in Los Angeles in the mid-forties; the latter group in-

cluded Giuffre, Getz, Zoot Sims, and Herbie Steward. Gene
Roland was also an arranger for Stan Kenton. Getz has said: "The
three tenors and bary idea wasn't new, but Roland was the first to
try it successfully."

The main arranger for Stan Kenton in the mid-forties was Pete
Rugolo. Much was made of his studies with Darius Milhaud and
his classical background, and perhaps this was as it should have
been, for his best work was a nonjazz composition called *Mirage*.
A descriptive piece representing the crossing of the desert to
California, it captures the desolate, dry atmosphere remarkably.
Rugolo's jazz work for Kenton consisted, for the most part, of bor-
rowings from the later Lunceford and of tired, repeated riffs that
added instruments rather than interest as they went. Mike Levin,
reviewing *Concerto to End All Concertos* in *Down Beat* (March
26, 1947), wrote: "Climaxes are built rather than coming of their
own accord. An artificial tension of tempo rather than solo
creativeness is constantly maintained." In all fairness, it must be
said that Rugolo showed much more variety in his writing for his
own bands in the fifties, although there was still the tendency toward screaming brass and other Kentonian effects that have become synonymous with the Hollywood movie-score jazz of Buddy
Bregman and Elmer Bernstein.

One of the first arrangers to make Kenton swing was Shorty
Rogers, who had done things like *Keen and Peachy, More Moon,
That's Right,* and *Keeper of the Flame* for Woody Herman in the
late forties. Later, he succumbed to Hollywood and, as John S.
Wilson put it, "soon spread his talents so thin that much of his
work was reduced to a set of dreary clichés."

Rogers' inspiration came from the late-thirties–early-forties
Basie band and the innovations of Parker and Gillespie. The same
can be said of arrangers such as Johnny Mandel, Al Cohn, and
Tiny Kahn, all of whom were first active in the second half of the
forties.

Johnny Mandel played trombone and wrote for Raeburn. His
arrangement of *Not Really the Blues* for Herman was one of
Woody's best, and *John Had the Number*, a piece the Wood-
choppers used to do, employed the "stops" that Charlie Parker
was so fond of playing. Herman's small group never recorded it,
but Terry Gibbs did it for New Jazz as *Speedway*. Another "take"
of the piece was issued as *Cuddles*. Mandel later played with and

arranged for Elliot Lawrence and, for a while, played bass trumpet with Basie before moving to Hollywood. His writing for the movie *I Want to Live* represents one of the few examples of the intelligent use of jazz for a film score.

Al Cohn, who did much more writing in the fifties, scored *You're Blasé* for Sarah Vaughan's record with Georgie Auld and contributed *The Goof and I* and *Music to Dance To* to Woody Herman's book in the forties. Like Mandel, he wrote for and played with Elliot Lawrence in the early fifties. In the late fifties and early sixties, he was active writing for TV and singers. However, an arrangement like *Lady Chatterley's Mother*, done for the Gerry Mulligan orchestra in 1960, is proof that he is still one of our wittiest, swingingest arrangers.

Mulligan himself, who rose to prominence in the fifties, was actually contributing modern arrangements to the big bands in the late forties—*Disc Jockey Jump* for Gene Krupa in 1947 and *Elevation* (later recorded by Elliot Lawrence) for Red Rodney's group on the Keynote *Bebop* album.

Tiny Kahn, who died short of his thirtieth birthday in 1953, was much respected among colleagues like Mandel and Cohn for his writing as well as his drumming. His *Tiny's Blues* and *Father Knickerbopper* for Chubby Jackson's big band were exemplary swingers, and *Over the Rainbow* for Charlie Barnet "gave indications of the great scope and possibilities that was Kahn the arranger," to quote Burt Korall. Again, like Mandel and Cohn, he played and arranged for Elliot Lawrence.

Mulligan's greatest early achievement was his writing for the Miles Davis nonet of the late forties—his arrangements of *Jeru*, *Venus De Milo*, and *Godchild*. For this band, John Lewis wrote *Rouge* and arranged *Move* and *Budo*.

Two other important arrangers were also involved with Davis —Gil Evans, who had previously written charts on *Anthropology*, *Yardbird Suite*, and *Donna Lee* for Claude Thornhill; and Johnny Carisi, who had played trumpet for Thornhill and others and also arranged for Vincent Lopez and several more jazz-oriented groups. Dizzy Gillespie mentioned Carisi when he spoke to me about Minton's. "He was the only white boy at Minton's. He was right there—every night. Play too! He knew all those crazy tunes of Monk's." For Davis, Evans scored *Boplicity* and *Moondreams*, and Carisi wrote *Israel*. Davis' group and its 1949–1950 records for

Capitol pointed toward the musical environment of the next decade. The arrangers represented were the great force behind that expression.

Tadd Dameron would have been part of that expression had he not gone to Europe or gotten involved with narcotics. If not for his illnesses, he also would have had a lot more to do with the music of the sixties. His kind of writing is a perfect example of how jazz material and techniques can have a positive effect on so-called popular music.

Dameron was not too happy with some of the trends prevalent in jazz today. "I was amazed when I came out," he said, "to hear fellows playing things with no format. I don't know; it just seems they were just blowing—and people are clapping. The people don't know what they're clapping about, but they're supposed to. One fellow gets up and blows, and this other fellow gets up and blows—they blow and they blow. It loses its form.

"And then on top of it, they're trying to play so weird. . . . I don't want to baffle the people. I want the people to understand what I'm doing—at least appreciate it. I want them to walk out and be whistling something I've written."

Recommended Listening

Mr. B. and the Band, SAVOY SJL 2214
The Miles Davis-Tadd Dameron Quintet/Paris International Jazz Festival, COLUMBIA JC 34804
The Arranger's Touch, PRESTIGE P-24049
A Blue Time (with Blue Mitchell), PRESTIGE P-47055

(see also Navarro)

BIBLIOGRAPHY

Adderley, Cannonball: "Record Reviews," *Jazz Review*, October, 1958.
Berton, Ralph: "The Half Note," *Jazz Review*, August, 1959.
Bittan, Dave: "Don't Call Me Bird," *Down Beat*, May 14, 1959.
Clar, Mimi: "Erroll Garner," *Jazz Review*, January, 1959.
Cooke, Jack: "Tadd Dameron—An Introduction," *Jazz Monthly*, March, 1960.
Coss, Bill: "Charlie Parker, 1920–1955," *Metronome Yearbook*, 1956.
———: "Back to Stay: Howard McGhee," *Down Beat*, January 18, 1962.
———: "Tadd's Back," *Down Beat*, February 15, 1962.
———: "Lennie Tristano Speaks Out," *Down Beat*, December 6, 1962.
Crawford, Marc: "The Drummer Most Likely to Succeed," *Down Beat*, March 30, 1961.
Driggs, Frank: "Budd Johnson, Part II," *Jazz Review*, January, 1961.
Edey, Maitland, Jr.: "Dizzy Gillespie: An Interview," *Paris Review*, Vol. 9, No. 35, 1965.
Feather, Leonard: "Blindfold Test: Dizzy Gillespie," *Metronome*, January, 1947.
———: "Be-Bop??!!—Man, We Called It Kloop-Mop!!" *Metronome*, April, 1947.
———: "Blindfold Test: Allen Eager," *Metronome*, January, 1948.
———: "Blindfold Test: A Bird's-Ear View of Music," *Metronome*, August, 1948.
———: *Inside Jazz*, J. J. Robbins, New York, 1949.
———: "Parker Finally Finds Peace," *Down Beat*, April 20, 1955.
———: *The Book of Jazz*, Horizon, New York, 1957.
———: "John 'Dizzy' Gillespie," in *The Jazz Makers*, Nat Shapiro and Nat Hentoff (eds.), Rinehart, New York, 1957.
———: *Jazz*, Trend Books, Los Angeles, 1959.
———: *The New Encyclopedia of Jazz*, Horizon, New York, 1960.
———: "Blindfold Test: Dizzy Gillespie," *Down Beat*, January 18, 1962.
———: "Blindfold Test: Dexter Gordon," *Down Beat*, May 20, 1965.
———. "Yardbird Flies Home," *Metronome*, August, 1947.
Ferrara, Don: "The Trumpet," *Metronome*, June, 1956.
Frost, Harry: "Dizzy and the Heckler," *Down Beat*, October 10, 1963.
Gillespie, Dizzy (with Gene Lees): "The Years with Yard," *Down Beat*, May 25, 1961.
Gitler, Ira: "Modern Jazz Today," in *Just Jazz*, Sinclair Traill and the Hon. Gerald Lascelles (eds.), Peter Davies, London, 1957.
———: "The Colorful World of Zoot Sims," *Down Beat*, April 13, 1961.
———: "The Remarkable J.J. Johnson," *Down Beat*, May 11, 1961.
———: "Saga of a Saxophone Sage," *Down Beat*, May 24, 1962.

Gleason, Ralph J.: "Pettiford Is Sent Home from Korea After Brawl on Plane," *Down Beat*, February 22, 1952.

————: "Pettiford At Fault in Brawl, Drank Too Much: McGhee," *Down Beat*, March 7, 1952.

Hadlock, Richard: "Benny Harris and the Coming of Modern Jazz," *Metronome*, October, 1961.

Hamalainen, Ruth, and Barry Ulanov: "Lennie Tristano," *Metronome*, November, 1946.

Harrison, Max: "Record Reviews," *Jazz Review*, February, 1959; October, 1959; November, 1959; June, 1960; February, 1960.

————: *Kings of Jazz: Charlie Parker*, A. S. Barnes, New York, 1961.

Hentoff, Nat: "Lennie Tristano: Multitaping Doesn't Make Me a Phony," *Down Beat*, May 16, 1956.

————: "An Oscar," *Down Beat*, March 21, 1957.

Hodeir, André: *Jazz: Its Evolution and Essence*, Grove Press, New York, 1956.

Hoefer, George: "Diz Starts Own Disc Firm to Wax What He Pleases," *Down Beat*, June 1, 1951.

————: "Hot Box: Max Roach," *Down Beat*, March 31, 1965.

James, Michael: "Stitt, Parker and the Question of Influence," *Jazz Monthly*, January, 1960.

————: *Kings of Jazz: Dizzy Gillespie*, A. S. Barnes, New York, 1961.

————: "Dexter Gordon—A Critical Study," *Jazz Monthly*, March, 1961.

"Jazz Musicians Challenge Changes and Criticisms," *Metronome*, March, 1958.

Johnson, Brooks: "Forum for Three," *Metronome*, December, 1961.

Johnson, J.J. (with J. Lee Anderson): "The Just Intonation of J.J. Johnson," *Theme*, January, 1957.

Korall, Burt: "Background Music," *Metronome*, March, 1956.

————: "View from the Seine," *Down Beat*, December 5, 1963.

Lees, Gene: "Dizzy Gillespie: Problems of Life on a Pedestal," *Down Beat*, June 23, 1960.

————: "In Walked Ray," *Down Beat*, August 31, 1961.

"Lennie Tristano: Return of the Native," *Down Beat*, October 30, 1958.

Lind, Jack: "Something Rockin' in Denmark," *Down Beat*, September 13, 1962.

Maher, Jack: "The Teaching of Jazz: Inside Tristano-Land," *Metronome*, December, 1955.

Metronome Yearbook 1956, Bill Coss (ed.).

Morgenstern, Dan: "Caught in the Act," *Down Beat*, July 15, 1965.

————: "Framework for Blowing: The Dizzy Gillespie Quintet," *Down Beat*, June 17, 1965.

Morrison, Allan: "Can a Musician Return from the Brink of Insanity," *Ebony*, August, 1953.

Offen, Ron, and George Demos: "Tristano: The Living Myth," *Literary Times*, July–August, 1964.

"Panel Discussion: Musicians Discuss Technique," *Metronome*, February, 1958.

Pease, Sharon: "Bud Powell's Style Has Widespread Influence," *Down Beat*, June 15, 1951.

Pekar, Harvey: "Record Reviews," *Jazz Review*, June, 1960.

————: "Lennie Tristano Has Been One of the Real Originals in Jazz," *Jazz Review*, July, 1960.

Perlongo, Robert A.: "Bud Powell in Paris," *Metronome*, November, 1961.
Reisner, Robert George: *Bird: The Legend of Charlie Parker*, Citadel Press, New York, 1962.
Rostaing, Hubert: "Charlie Parker," *Jazz Hot*, special edition, 1948.
Russell, Ross: "Bebop," in *The Art of Jazz*, Martin Williams (ed.), Oxford University Press, New York, 1959.
———: "The Legendary Joe Albany," *Jazz Review*, April, 1959.
———: "Record Reviews," *Jazz Review*, November, 1960.
Schuller, Gunther: "Sonny Rollins and the Challenge of Thematic Improvisation," *Jazz Review*, November, 1958.
Shapiro, Nat, and Nat Hentoff (eds.): *Hear Me Talkin' to Ya*, Rinehart, New York, 1955.
"The Sheep in the Herman Herd," *Metronome*, December, 1945.
Simon, Bill: "Charlie Christian," in *The Jazz Makers*, Nat Shapiro and Nat Hentoff (eds.), Rinehart, New York, 1957.
Shera, Michael G.: "Fats Navarro, Part II," *Jazz*, May, 1965.
Tynan, John: "Meet Dr. Getz," *Down Beat*, February 20, 1957.
———: "Stan the Man," *Down Beat*, March 20, 1958.
Ulanov, Barry: "George Handy," *Metronome*, May, 1946.
———: "Sonny Berman," *Metronome*, March, 1947.
———: "Miles and Leo," *Metronome*, July, 1947.
———: "Tadd Dameron," *Metronome*, August, 1947.
———: "Fats Navarro," *Metronome*, November, 1947.
Weidemann, Erik: "Ornithologically Speaking," *Jazz Review*, June, 1959.
Willard, Patricia: "Dizzy Gillespie," in *Laughter from the Hip*, Leonard Feather and Jack Tracy (eds.), Horizon, New York, 1963.
Williams, Martin: "Charlie Parker: The Burden of Innovation," *Evergreen Review*, September–October, 1960.
———: "Jazz Composition—What Is It?" *Down Beat*, February 15, 1962.

INDEX

287

Other DA CAPO titles of interest